Basel Abbas//Ruanne Abou-Rahme//Kathy Acker//
Moradewun Adejunmobi//
Algün//Gloria Anzaldúa//
Arendt//José María Argue
Baggs//Paul Baker//Jame
Humberto Beck//Alice Bec
Homi K. Bhabha//Sujata B
Geta Brătescu//Susan Buck-Morss//Judith Butler//Luis
Camnitzer//Barbara Casavecchia//Barbara Cassin//
Theresa Hak Kyung Cha//Gayatri Chakravorty Spivak//
Diana d'Arenberg//Jesse Darling//Gilles Deleuze//
Jacques Derrida//Henry Dreyfuss//Brian Droitcour//
Friedrich Engels//Okwui Enwezor//Jacob Fabricius//
Frantz Fanon//Jean Fisher//Parastou Forouhar//Dana
Friis-Hansen//Jean Genet//Félix Guattari//Stuart Hall//
Omar Robert Hamilton//Michael Hardt//Camille
Henrot//Susan Hiller//bell hooks//IM International
(Tania Bruguera)//Emily Jacir//James Joyce//Helen
Keller//Irena Klepfisz//David Levine//Sarat Maharaj//
Karl Marx//Suzana Milevska//Naeem Mohaiemen//
Stephen Morton//Gerardo Mosquera//Herta Müller//
Antonio Negri//Shirin Neshat//Christian Nyampeta//
Hélio Oiticica//Rick Poynor//S.S. Prawer//Walid Raad//
Alastair Reid//Adrienne Rich//Philip Rizk//Susan
Rosenberg//Martha Rosler//Alix Rule//Naoki Sakai//
Kurt Schwitters//Yinka Shonibare//Sisters of Perpetual
Indulgence//Slavs and Tatars//George Steiner//Hito
Steyerl//Mladen Stilinović//Kate Sutton//Erika Tan//
Jennifer Tee//Stefan Themerson//Trinh T. Minh-ha//
Wu Tsang//Lawrence Venuti//Miyó Vestrini//Dmitry
Vilensky//Danh Võ//Stephen Willats//Wong Bing Hao//
Xu Bing//Katarina Zdjelar

α
'

Translation

Whitechapel Gallery
London
The MIT Press
Cambridge, Massachusetts

Edited by Sophie J. Williamson

TRANSLATION

Documents of Contemporary Art

Co-published by Whitechapel Gallery
and The MIT Press

First published 2019
© 2019 Whitechapel Gallery Ventures Limited
All texts © the authors or the estates of the authors,
unless otherwise stated

ISBN 978-0-85488-267-0 (Whitechapel Gallery)
ISBN 978-0-262-53792-6 (The MIT Press)

A catalogue record for this book is available from
the British Library

Library of Congress Cataloging-in-Publication Data

Names: Williamson, Sophie J., editor.
Title: Translation / Sophie J. Williamson.
Description: Cambridge : The MIT Press, 2019. |
Series: Whitechapel:
   documents of contemporary art | Includes
   bibliographical references and
   index.
Identifiers: LCCN 2019027229 | ISBN
   9780262537926 (paperback)
Subjects: LCSH: Translating and interpreting. |
   Translating and interpreting in literature.
Classification: LCC P306 .T6795 2019 | DDC 418/.02-
   -dc23
LC record available at https://lccn.loc.
   gov/2019027229

Whitechapel Gallery   10 9 8 7 6 5 4 3 2 1
The MIT Press   10 9 8 7 6 5 4 3 2 1

Series Editor: Iwona Blazwick
Commissioning Editor: Anthony Iles
Project Editor: Francesca Vinter
Design by SMITH
Gemma Gerhard, Justine Hucker, Allon Kaye
and Claudia Paladini
Printed and bound in China

Cover, Yinka Shonibare, The British Library, detail
(2014). © Yinka Shonibare CBE. All Rights Reserved,
DACS/Artimage 2019. Courtesy Stephen Friedman
Gallery. Photo: Jonathan Bassett.

Whitechapel Gallery Ventures Limited
77–82 Whitechapel High Street
London, E1 7QX
whitechapelgallery.org

Distributed to the book trade (UK and Europe only)
by Thames & Hudson
181a High Holborn
London, WC1V 7QX
+44 (0) 20 7845 5000
sales@thameshudson.co.uk

The MIT Press
Cambridge, MA 02142
mitpress.mit.edu

Documents of Contemporary Art

In recent decades artists have progressively expanded the boundaries of art as they have sought to engage with an increasingly pluralistic environment. Teaching, curating and understanding of art and visual culture are likewise no longer grounded in traditional aesthetics but centred on significant ideas, topics and themes ranging from the everyday to the uncanny, the psychoanalytical to the political.

The Documents of Contemporary Art series emerges from this context. Each volume focuses on a specific subject or body of writing that has been of key influence in contemporary art internationally. Edited and introduced by a scholar, artist, critic or curator, each of these source books provides access to a plurality of voices and perspectives defining a significant theme or tendency.

For over a century the Whitechapel Gallery has offered a public platform for art and ideas. In the same spirit, each guest editor represents a distinct yet diverse approach – rather than one institutional position or school of thought – and has conceived each volume to address not only a professional audience but all interested readers.

Series Editor: Iwona Blazwick; Commissioning Editor: Anthony Iles; Project Editor: Francesca Vinter; Editorial Advisory Board: Roger Conover, Sean Cubitt, Neil Cummings, Sven Spieker, Gilane Tawadros, Sofia Victorino

WHAT GETS
LOST...
IS NOT WHAT GETS
LOST
IN TRANSLATION,
BUT RATHER WHAT GETS
LOST
IN LANGUAGE ITSELF

Alastair Reid, 'Lo que se pierde/What Gets Lost', 1978

LANGUAGE,
INCONTESTABLY,

REVEALS
THE SPEAKER

(overlapping, superimposed text repeating "LANGUAGE, INCONTESTABLY, REVEALS THE SPEAKER")

REVEALS
THE SPEAKER

James Baldwin, 'If Black English Isn't a Language, Then Tell Me, What Is?', 1979

Sophie J. Williamson
Introduction//Between Languages

The movement of global populations, and subsequently the task of translation, underlies contemporary culture: the intricacies of ancient and modern diaspora; generations of colonisation and the transportation of slaves now superimposed by contemporary economic movement; forced political exiles; widespread refugees and imminent environmental migration on an unprecedented scale. With growing nationalism, much popular discourse pivots on identifying who 'we' are: who is included and where the line of the Other is drawn. Amid a growing global identity crisis, this publication seeks to assert the role of contemporary art in cultural translation, navigation and frictions. By enabling us to see the world from the perspectives of others, artistic agency lies in negotiating the personal and the political. Whilst it might be assumed that a publication on the subject of translation would centre around linguistics, the urgency of the subject in an ever more turbulent, precarious world lies fundamentally in the need to nurture understanding and empathy amongst one another. Non-verbal autistic blogger, Amanda Baggs, in her video *In My Language* portrays a world of deep sensory non-linguistic dialogue with everything surrounding her, a language that would be unfathomable to most of us reading this book. Explaining the precarious position of non-verbal people around the world – considered 'non-persons' Baggs suggests, as they don't speak a standard language – she implores the viewer that justice and human rights will only become possible once 'the many shapes of personhood are recognised'. The imperative role of translation must be seen as much more than transferring one language to another, but its ability to communicate and enable individuals to be *heard*; only then can the speaker ascend from the dehumanising position of Agamben's *bare life*.[1] Throughout human history the opacity of language has divided and alienated; the task of translation is to bridge this violent, troubling chasm.

In the field of translation sensitivity is paid to authorship, intent and where authenticity lies; these questions crumble into insignificance however if we do not first address the inequalities of who has the opportunity to speak and the privilege to be heard. Gayatri Spivak, writing on the vital role of translation in pursuing the larger feminist agenda of achieving women's solidarity, compels us to take responsibility to first learn the mother tongues of others, rather than assuming solidarity as an *a priori* given: '[t]here are countless languages in which women all over the world have grown up learning and have been female or feminist, and still the languages we keep learning the most are the powerful European ones, sometimes the powerful Asian ones, least often the chief African ones.'

The selection of texts in this anthology are far from exhaustive; there are areas of the subject that are barely touched upon that would fill volumes in themselves, most notably perhaps – against a backdrop of terrifying ecological precarity – translation beyond our species. There are also vast regions, cultures and positions that don't appear: numerous incredible artists, writers and thinkers whom there has not been the space to include; and incalculable others that I have not had access to knowledge of in the first place. Whilst the breadth of contributions here is diverse and rich with varying perspectives, they have nevertheless been selected from a canon of accessible cultural texts. If language is a means to express the self, solidarity – feminist or otherwise – cannot therefore be contemplated without suppressed voices first being given the platform to communicate. Throughout this publication this task is taken up from a spectrum of positions: contributors have explored the importance to social identity of employing minor languages in cultural production (Moradewun Adejunmobi); created platforms to disseminate local voices to an international audience (Philip Rizk); connected disparate locales (Omar Robert Hamilton); called for self-referential art histories to be rewritten to seek outward exchange (Suzana Milevska); and circumnavigated Western hegemonic filters by undertaking collective projects of self-translation (Christian Nyampeta).

In the opening chapter, Spivak positions translation as 'the most intimate act of reading'. For Slavs and Tatars, tracing the shape-shifting of a single phoneme *kh*, this manifests in the careful archaeological uncovering of the convergences and divergences in languages, where they are quashed and where they burst forth again in another tongue. For deaf and blind human rights activist, Helen Keller, language is a tenderness that manifests across the whole spectrum of the senses; and for Spivak this intimacy lies in tracing the Other in the self. Moving between languages requires a fundamental understanding of the subtleties of each society and its culture, customs, and sensibilities; the construction of meaning in one, does not seamlessly marry with that of another. Bertrand Russell asserts no one can understand the word 'cheese' unless they have a non-linguistic acquaintance with cheese.[2] Whilst quality of translation might crudely be assumed to be a perfectly transparent transferal (Norman Shapiro), Russell's truism applies not only to individual words and sentences but also to the translator's knowledge of the context from which a text has been borne. In the field of translation studies, the pejorative term *translatese* refers to the awkwardness of unidiomatic translation, such as clunky language or over literal conversion of idioms or syntax: exposing the translator's ineptitude in authentically translating the meaning of the original. In Simon Fujiwara's series

Lactose Intolerance (2015), glasses of milk are each painted according to a selection from the style catalogue of the North Korean state-run art manufacturer from which Fujiwara commissioned them, from nostalgic through to hyperrealist and early Pop.[3] Closed-off from the outside world, the circumstances in which the paintings were made in is as alien to the Western art-going public as a glass of fresh milk is to the unnamed artists who painted them: there is no dairy production in the country. This aesthetic *translatese* instigates a productive disjuncture, registering the geopolitical chasm of interpretation. The works take on a superficial mimicry, a fictitious familiarity of both the art history and the subject matter they imitate. Mimesis is crucial to aesthetic experience, it is hard-wired into human perception to use existing knowledge to interpret new or unfamiliar objects, words or artworks. Consequently it is inevitable that one's experience of cultural specificity creates subjective interpretation when translating from one context to another.

Translation historian and theorist Lawrence Venuti therefore rejects the author's singular genius, instead proposing that a translation is always 'a work in its own right'. In his seminal work, *The Translator's Invisibility*, he proposes the increased visibility of the translator's role and, by extension, the process of translation itself, allowing readers to register and confront the works' foreignness rather than have it concealed from them: translators should resist the temptation to create new works that seem to have been written in their target languages. This is not to endorse a perspective of cultural opacity. As Sarat Maharaj notes, the doctrine of an absolute 'epistemic barrier' between Self and Other underpinned the institutionalised ethnic and cultural separation of Apartheid. For the artists and writers included in this publication, translation implies an understanding about understanding; what it means to know a language and what it means not to know it. As poet and translator, Alastair Reid, writes: '*lo que se pierde* what gets lost […] is not what gets lost in translation, but rather / what gets lost in language itself *lo que se pierde*.'

Throughout human history, the alienating forces of language have been mercilessly deployed by colonisers to quell, divide and ideologically impose – in George Steiner's words, 'zones of silence to other men' and 'razor-edges of division'. Chapter 2 explores linguistic governance as the active agent at the core of the international geopolitical landscape. In 'The Negro and Language', Frantz Fanon examines the internalisation of the racial hierarchy imposed by the loss of cultural heritage and native language, highlighting the importance of natural, unabased expression in the creation of one's identity. He asserts that, 'to speak means to be in a position to use a certain syntax, to grasp the morphology of this or that language, but it means above all to assume a culture, to support the weight of a civilisation'. Mapping the violent erasure of cultural identities in the burning of libraries or the destruction of archives, Susan Buck-Morss suggests that it is blindness to alterity that is the most common form of eradication: excavating the past only for what fits within the linear narrative of the dominant culture. Whether in the United States (bell hooks, James Baldwin, Glenn Ligon), Latin America (Hélio Oiticica, Gerardo Mosquera) or Asia (Theresa Hak Kyung Cha), strategies of aggressive systemic cultural appropriation, expulsion of mother tongues and eradication of histories, utilised throughout world history, has a continued active legacy, embedded in contemporary society, identity politics and cultural practices. Contributors to this chapter explore how language evolves within this repression, be it as a means of survival amongst slaves of disparate origins, contemporary diasporic vernacular that carves its own history into its words or the corruption of visual language by the periphery against hegemonic infiltration. Whilst societies may superficially operate with an authoritative lingua franca, kinship and commonality often remains artificial and precarious. As Adrienne Rich so eloquently puts it, '[t]his is the oppressor's language / yet I need it to talk to you'. The efficiency of linguistic violence remains bubbling under the surface.

Under a neoliberal agenda, art is often tasked with initiating and pollinating 'cross-cultural understanding', with the ultimate goal of procuring a cohesive, multicultural society. But with the rush to understand one another, do we run the risk of razing nuanced individual narrative? As Hannah Arendt points out in her essay 'We Refugees', the often traumatic experience of displacement is not only the loss of leaving behind the familiarity of one's homes and confidence of everyday life, divided from one's family and social network, but the loss of one's language without which 'the naturalness of reactions, the simplicity of gestures, the unaffected expression of feelings' is also lost. In Chapter 3, Theresa Hak Kyung Cha's profound text, *Dictee*, reflects on her Korean mother's displacement in China as a young woman: forbidden to speak Korean, her mother tongue becomes a place of refuge. Others explore the struggle to keep hold of one's language (Irena Klepfisz, Sujata Bhatt), seeking to recreate one's homeland in exile (Shirin Neshat), traversing borders closed to others (Emily Jacir) and the questionable ethics of sovereign statehood (Tania Brugeura). This chapter looks at the contexts in which the mother tongue stops mothering, where displacement throws open questions not only of one's ability to communicate with intimacy and fluency, but where translation between 'home' and an elsewhere becomes inherent to one's being.

However, this space of disjuncture is also a space of potential and reclamation. In the novel *Deep Rivers* (1958), the mystically whizzing rhythm of the *zumbayllu* spinning top is imbued with the ancient spirits of the Andean indigenous people.[4] The book's author, José María Arguedas (1911–1969), though born into a wealthy Peruvian mestizo family, was raised by Quechuan servants. For him, the hegemonic Spanish language – in which he was obliged to write – was incapable of capturing the union of the self, nature and spiritual ancestry so embedded in his Quechuan perspective. Written in Spanish, though shaped by Andean expression and sensibility, and accentuated with Quechuan syntax and vocabulary, he flexes and bends language to depict a spectrum of nuanced experiences and peculiarities nameless or unacquainted to the colonial reader. The lyrical duel and dense symbolism spun through encounters shared between the Quechuan and Spanish characters, captures the cultural movements of convergence and dispersion, unison, tension and conflict. Where language's malleability reaches its limit, Quechua remains in its mother tongue. The poignant void left by the unattainable translatory task reveals not only the mestizos' struggle to navigate the disparity of their divided identity, but the near impossibility of translating this to a non-mestizo reader. Situated in a different era and continent, living through Nicolae Ceaușescu's dictatorial persecution in Romania, Herta Müller's text 'The Space between Languages' reflects a troubled and fragmented relationship to identity. Her complicated relationship to language and linguistic identity as a Banat-Swabian (a German-speaking ethnic minority in Romania) feeds both a fascination in the divergences between words and a distrust of language, playing out this dislocation in her literary collages, meshing together pre-existing elements of commercial language – both German and Romanian – from newspapers, magazines and catalogues. Though writing from vastly different contexts, the uneasy multilingual clashes and metaphors in Arguedas' and Müller's works exemplify the ways that identity is to be found in the messy space between language and culture. In both authors' works the merging of linguistic approaches serves to expose – and to some extent overcome – the disparate cultural perspectives. As a German-speaking Jew living in Prague, Franz Kafka once decried the impossibility of writing in German yet the impossibility of writing otherwise. 'Minor literature' offers a solution, challenging the hegemonic language to accept difference, carving out a cultural space for minor cultures and as a minority citizen, understanding oneself in relation to the dominant Other. Pitted against one another, in the tussle between languages and perspectives lies a cross-pollination, extending the linguistic gene pool of a language, and is the space in which a language has the opportunity to develop, mature and build the nuanced texture of understanding between the self and Other.

This strategy of fractured amalgamation is central to the hybrid identities of a generation of younger artists, where the diasporic experience of earlier generations is further superimposed by international travel and a digital globe at our fingertips. In his essay 'Patriotism and its Futures', sociocultural anthropologist

Arjun Appadurai argues that the formula of hyphenation (i.e. Italian-American, Asian-American, and African-American) has reached saturation, where the 'right-hand side of the hyphen can barely contain the unruliness of the left-hand side'. As cultural formations become ever more protean, surmising cultural identity becomes too slippery to fit within the rhetoric of national identity or the 'delocalised transnationism' of diasporic communities. Even amongst the artistic community represented in this book, it is commonplace to have parents of two different nationalities, been born and raised in a third, and perhaps now live in a fourth. Subsequently, art production equally tangles these multiple reference points: Chinese-British-Indonesian-Dutch artist Jennifer Tee's imaginary meetings between Hilma af Klint, Wassily Kandinsky and Tao magic; Korean-Canadian Zadie Xa's personalised semiotics drawing from Talchum and hip-hop alike; or the cultural symbolism found, by Vietnamese-born Danish, and Berlin-based Danh Võ, in a Bomann refrigerator received from The Immigrant Relief Program. This complex geopolitical landscape of contemporary international experience is what Sarat Maharaj has termed the 'scene of translations', and has long been battleground of negotiation for artists whose practices fall outside of hegemonic spheres. Chapter 4 explores the varying approaches to growing contemporary creolisation and the new liminal 'third space' of hybridity, with its inherent frictions, insecurities and infinite irregularities, where languages supplement and prop up one another (Gloria Anzaldúa) and the new capitalist instrumentalisation that it risks offering up (Dmitry Vilensky). Whilst hybridity presents a space of subversion, clawing at the edges of the nation state, one hopes the end point is not a flattening of cultural specificities into a singular homogenised murk. Other contributors to this chapter review attempts to challenge the authority of hegemonic language by creating new community-specific languages, such as argot (Alice Becker-Ho) or polari (Sisters of Perpetual Indulgence, Paul Baker), and varying approaches at universal communication (Erika Tan, Henry Dreyfuss, Xu Bing). Meanwhile, artists such as Wu Tsang and Jamie Crewe seek to uncover lineages of transfeminine ancestry to reposition and untangle the binary gender narratives constructed and enforced by hegemonic culture. Here, the interrogation of language acts to redeploy previously undermined voices in history, translating and nurturing kinship between eras. Language is malleable and fluid; used, constructed and reconstructed to suit the needs of those who employ it. Beyond the ability to simply reflect the world, here language is shown to shape new personal experiences, constructing new narratives; renewing language fit-for-purpose for future generations, which will in turn become a tool to transform the world.

Language is what binds communities together in collective identity and shapes our concept of the world around us. Subsequently people speaking very different languages also live in very different conceptual spheres: as linguist Benjamin Whorf describes, 'for the Hopi a new sun rises every day' and 'the Navaho-speaking people categorise colours by intensity rather than hue'.[5] In Susan Hiller's blank-image film *The Last Silent Movie*, we hear voice recordings of speakers whose extinct languages have now fallen into irretrievable silence: and consequently extinction of other realities. As many of the artists in this publication exemplify, untranslatable specificity is built into the fabric of not only language but being. Underlying translation therefore is the inherent impossibility of the task. As R.D. Laing asserts: 'I cannot experience your experience. You cannot experience my experience. We are both invisible men. All men are invisible to one another'.[6] Integral to building our sense of identity therefore is an understanding of what we are not and likewise to establish meaning, one has to attend to what cannot be expressed, 'its constitutive outside' (Stuart Hall). This 'insoluble sediment' between languages, as Dmitry Vilensky has termed it, becomes the raw material of production for many artists in this publication; the awkward disjuncture between languages, where the loss of meaning, slippage and misunderstanding throws into focus the limitations of language to transfer one's self without compromise. Acknowledging the limitations of language, Chapter 5 explores the disjuncture where translation fails. For Trinh T. Minh-ha to travel is to practice difference, operating an unsettling inversion of one's identity where the self loses its fixed boundaries: 'I become me via an other'. Parastou Forouhar's loss of her mother tongue emerges instead within in a visual field, where characters shift back and forth between words and ornaments, and in the poetic Persian-ness of her German. In Katarina Zdjelar's work the para-poetic slippages in phrases, accent and pronunciation exposes her otherness and denies her belonging. Kathy Acker, stating that ordinary language lies outside essence, describes the impossibility of articulating the language of the body linguistically, as in itself it constitutes a somatic dialogue.

Though unfortunately not included in the selection of texts, the profound ethical and existential experiences engrained by Teresa Margolles' work have shaped and informed the publication. Margolles seduces her audiences with tantalising sensory treats – *En el aire*'s (2003) shimmering soap bubbles, blissfully floating throughout a gallery space, for example – before plunging them into a reality they have the privilege of otherwise being blind to. Collecting her material from the most dangerous border cities in Mexico, where thousands are violently murdered by the drug cartels each year, the soap is made with water used to wash bodies at a morgue. As the glistening iridescent bubbles burst on our skin, we are repulsed by our own repulsion. Whilst the works of artists such as Margolles, Slavs and Tatars, Pratchaya Phinthong and Emily Jacir illuminate otherwise overlooked geopolitics at play in the abstract, artists in Chapter 6 explore how political relationships emerge through material and contextual transformation. For Kurt Schwitters, working under the shadow of the Nazi regime, the act of positioning two disparate objects together to disrupt the assumed taxonomy of things was a ferocious political act, subverting dictatorial authority, whilst with others the thinking body traversing between language and movement (Trisha Brown) or drawing and writing (Geta Brătecsu) is an existential act, discharging complex energies between body and mind. In his book, *The Radicant*, Nicholas Bourriaud lays out the nomadic nature of the contemporary artist, who travelling globally spatialises time and construct their paths in history as well as geography. Here, Walid Raad, tongue-in-cheek, proclaims the inability of his work on the Lebanese civil war, *The Atlas Group*, to travel to Beirut, resulting in the scaling of each piece perfectly to 1:100th of its original size; and Basel Abbas and Ruanne Abou-Rahme present a dizzying critical reading of the everyday trappings of occupation and territorial borders, mining the histories of the Arab world to radically re-imagine the apocalyptic imagery, reworking it to create ritual and myth for an imaginary parallel unrealised time. The artists in this chapter render assumed cultural narratives as intimately subjective and fragile, translating and transferring details to define personal cultural cosmologies, drawing on the instability and fluidity of cross-cultural and cross-temporal existence.

In his influential text *The Society of the Spectacle*, Guy Debord writes that 'the spectacle is not a collection of images; rather it is a social relationship between people that is mediated by image'.[7] Over the past forty years, each successive generation of artists has been confronted with an ever more frenzied cacophony of material unleashed by the digital world. Meanwhile, economic interdependence between nations has long since been subsumed by an economic oligarchy, described by Hardt and Negri as 'Empire'. In Chapter 7, contributors grapple to carve out creative autonomy in this new world order. Photojournalist, Shahidul Alam and art historian Suzanna Milevska reassert the need for their global counterparts to speak to the world in their own terms, resisting the hegemonic lens; Luis Camnitzer looks at the authoritarian imposition of literacy and the power relations inherent in linguistic order; Alix Rule and David Levine describe a flattening of disparate practices and contexts, articulated in a catch-all 'International Art English' regurgitated for easy worldwide consumption; whilst Ryan Trecartin's scripts of frantic commercial lingo confound delimitation between the corporate and the corporeal to terrifying effect. Grating against the hegemonising communication of global capital vie the democratic voices that online spaces offer, allowing users to become editors, critics and co-collaborators as never before, blurring the distinction between translator and reader, audience and author. In the early 2010s, we watched the construction of social and political reality during the

Arab Spring through an inherently visual politics, where the energised competing image – battling, reversing, erasing and replacing one another online and the doctrines they broadcast – emerged from the streets. Hito Steyerl's often-cited essay 'In Defense of the Poor Image', describes the life of the online image as one of acceleration and deterioration; 'a copy in motion'.[8] The 'poor image' is one which has been 'thrust into digital uncertainty' – somersaulted through successions of uploading, downloading, reformatting, reediting and redistribution. In turn, images are valued not by their quality or content, but by velocity, accessibility and spread. Likewise, translation at speed loses its quality.

As we face a reconfigured global society, in the aftermath of widespread ecological migration and displacement on an unprecedented scale, urgent cultural concern can no longer singly focus on modes of cross-cultural dialogue. Instead we must establish a cultural ecosystem that recognises and allows space to hold the geopolitical, and consequently cultural, clashes and miscommunications implicating our immediate and everyday social climate. To return to Spivak's text, she speaks not only of the limits of language but also of the silences it holds. If Arguedas' Peru can be seen as a microcosm for the cultural disparities that now transpire worldwide, perhaps a similarly fluid, unconfined cultural esperanto, 'a language between languages (Judith Butler), is needed to sing the unpronounceable nuances of contemporary society; one which accepts the fraying edges of where language – and translation – reaches its limits of communicability. Far from being a mode of universal communication or a metalanguage, it is here that hegemonic dominance is shattered, where the 'labour of transaction and translation which belongs to no single site', as Judith Butler proposes 'but is the movement between languages, and has its final destination in this movement itself'. If, as Spivak asserts, translation is the most intimate act of reading, far from this being a translatory defeat, it is these chasms in translation, where meaning remains malleable and unconfined, that the empathetic agency of the receiver is called to action. In the somersaults of language and meaning, constantly transferring from one to another – vital, porous, living – translation is not a linguistic task to be outsourced to learned professionals; it is a human instinct woven into the fabric of our being.

1   Giorgio Agamben, *Homo Sacer: Sovereign Power and Bare Life*, trans. Daniel Heller-Roazen (Stanford: Stanford University Press, 1998).

2   Bertrand Russell, 'Logical Positivism', in *Actas del Primer Congreso Nacional de Filosofía, Mendoza, Argentina*, vol. 2 (March–April 1949) 1219.

3   *Lactose Intolerance* as an artwork so aptly illustrates my idea of visual translatese, yet sadly at the time of writing, no suitable text was found available for inclusion in this publication.

4   José María Arguedas, *Deep Rivers*, trans. Francis Horning Barraclough (Long Grove, IL: Waveland Press, 1978).

5   Susan Hiller quoted in Mark Godfrey, 'The Last Silent Movie', in *Susan Hiller: The Last Silent Movie* (London: Matt's Gallery, 2008) 6.

6   R.D. Laing, *The Politics of Experience and the Bird of Paradise* (Harmondsworth: Penguin, 1967) 16.

7   Guy Debord, *The Society of the Spectacle*, trans. Donald Nicholson-Smith (New York: Zone Books, 2012) 12.

8   Hito Steyerl, 'In Defense of the Poor Image', *e-flux Journal*, no. 10 (November 2009) (www.e-flux.com/journal/10/61362/in-defense-of-the-poor-image/).

I SEE TRANSLATION AS THE ATTEMPT TO PRODUCE A TEXT SO TRANSPARENT THAT IT DOES NOT SEEM TO BE TRANSLATED.

Norman Shapiro, quoted in Lawrence Venuti, *The Translator's Invisibility*, 1995

THE INTIMACY OF TRANSLATION

Gayatri Chakravorty Spivak
The Politics of Translation//1993

The idea for this title comes from the British sociologist Michele Barrett's feeling that the politics of translation takes on a massive life of its own if you see language as the process of meaning-construction.[1] In my view, language may be one of many elements that allow us to make sense of things, of ourselves. I am thinking, of course, of gestures, pauses, but also of chance, of the subindividual force-fields of being which click into place in different situations, swerve from the straight or true line of language-in-thought. Making sense of ourselves is what produces identity. If one feels that the production of identity as self-meaning, not just meaning, is as pluralised as a drop of water under a microscope, one is not always satisfied, outside of the ethicopolitical arena as such, with 'generating' thoughts on one's own. (Assuming identity as origin may be unsatisfactory in the ethicopolitical arena as well, but consideration of that now would take us too far afield.) I have argued [...] that one of the ways of resisting capitalist multiculturalism's invitation to self-identity and compete is to give the name of 'woman' to the unimaginable other. The same sort of impulse is at work here in a rather more tractable form. For one of the ways to get around the confines of one's 'identity' as one produces expository prose is to work at someone else's title, as one works with a language that belongs to many others. This, after all, is one of the seductions of translating. It is a simple miming of the responsibility to the trace of the other in the self.

Responding, therefore, to Barrett with that freeing sense of responsibility, I can agree that it is not bodies of meaning that are transferred in translation. And from the ground of that agreement I want to consider the role played by language for the *agent*, the person who acts, even though intention is not fully present to itself. The task of the feminist translator is to consider language as a clue to the workings of gendered agency. The writer is written by her language, of course. But the writing of the writer writes agency in a way that might be different from that of the British woman/citizen within the history of British feminism, focused on the task of freeing herself from Britain's imperial past, its often racist present, as well as its 'made in Britain' history of male domination.

Translation as Reading
How does the translator attend to the specificity of the language she translates? There is a way in which the rhetorical nature of every language disrupts its logical systematicity. If we emphasise the logical at the expense of these

rhetorical interferences, we remain safe. 'Safety' is the appropriate term here, because we are talking of risks, of violence to the translating medium.

I felt that I was taking those risks when I recently translated some eighteenth-century Bengali poetry. I quote a bit from my 'Translator's Preface':

> I must overcome what I was taught in school: the highest mark for the most accurate collection of synonyms, strung together in the most proximate syntax. I must resist both the solemnity of chaste Victorian poetic prose and the forced simplicity of 'plain English', that have imposed themselves as the norm [...] Translation is the most intimate act of reading. I surrender to the text when I translate. These songs, sung day after day in family chorus before clear memory began, have a peculiar intimacy for me. Reading and surrendering take on new meanings in such a case. The translator earns permission to transgress from the trace of the – other before memory – in the closest places of the self.[2]

Yet language is not everything. It is only a vital clue to where the self loses its boundaries. The ways in which rhetoric or figuration disrupt logic themselves point at the possibility of random contingency, beside language, around language. Such a dissemination cannot be under our control. Yet in translation, where meaning hops into the spacy emptiness between two named historical languages, we get perilously close to it. By juggling the disruptive rhetoricity that breaks the surface in not necessarily connected ways, we feel the selvedges of the language-textile give way, fray into *frayages* or facilitations.[3] Although every act of reading or communication is a bit of this risky fraying which scrambles together somehow, our stake in agency keeps the fraying down to a minimum except in the communication and reading of and in love. (What is the place of 'love' in the ethical? As we saw, Irigaray has struggled with this question.) The task of the translator is to facilitate this love between the original and its shadow, a love that permits fraying, holds the agency of the translator and the demands of her imagined or actual audience at bay. The politics of translation from a non-European woman's text too often suppresses this possibility because the translator cannot engage with, or cares insufficiently for, the rhetoricity of the original.

The simple possibility that something might not be meaningful is contained by the rhetorical system as the always possible menace of a space outside language. This is most eerily staged (and challenged) in the effort to communicate with other possible intelligent beings in space. (Absolute alterity or otherness is thus differed-deferred into another self who resembles us, however minimally, and with whom we can communicate.) But a more homely staging of it occurs across two earthly languages. The experience of contained alterity in an unknown language spoken in a different cultural milieu is uncanny.

Let us now think that, in that other language, rhetoric may be disrupting logic in the matter of the production of an agent, and indicating the founding violence of the silence at work within rhetoric. Logic allows us to jump from word to word by means of clearly indicated connections. Rhetoric must work in the silence between and around words in order to see what works and how much. The jagged relationship between rhetoric and logic, condition and effect of knowing, is a relationship by which a world is made for the agent, so that the agent can act in an ethical way, a political way, a day-to-day way; so that the agent can be alive, in a human way, in the world. Unless one can at least construct a model of this for the other language, there is no real translation.

Unfortunately it is only too easy to produce translations if this task is completely ignored. I myself see no choice between the quick and easy and slapdash way, and translating well and with difficulty. There is no reason why a responsible translation should take more time in the doing. The translator's preparation might take more time, and her love for the text might be a matter of a reading skill that takes patience. But the sheer material production of the text need not be slow.

Without a sense of the rhetoricity of language, a species of neocolonialist construction of the non-Western scene is afoot. No argument for convenience can be persuasive here. That is always the argument, it seems. This is where I travel from Barrett's enabling notion of the question of language in post-structuralism. Post-structuralism has shown some of us a staging of the agent within a three-tiered notion of language (as rhetoric, logic, silence). We must attempt to enter or direct that staging, as one directs a play, as an actor interprets a script. That takes a different kind of effort from taking translation to be a matter of synonym, syntax and local colour.

To be only critical, to defer action until the production of the utopian translator, is impractical. Yet, when I hear Derrida, quite justifiably, point out the difficulties between French and English, even when he agrees to speak in English – 'I must speak in a language that is not my own because that will be more just' – I want to claim the right to the same dignified complaint for a woman's text in Arabic or Vietnamese.[4]

It is more just to give access to the largest number of feminists. Therefore these texts must be made to speak English. It is more just to speak the language of the majority when through hospitality a large number of feminists give the foreign feminist the right to speak, in English. In the case of the third world foreigner, is the law of the majority that of decorum, the equitable law of democracy, or the 'law' of the strongest? We might focus on this confusion. There is nothing necessarily meretricious about the Western feminist gaze. (The 'naturalising' of Jacques Lacan's sketching out of the psychic structure of the gaze in terms of group political behaviour has always seemed to me a bit shaky.) On the other hand, there is nothing essentially noble about the law of the majority either. It is merely the easiest way of being 'democratic' with minorities. In the act of wholesale translation into English there can be a betrayal of the democratic ideal into the law of the strongest. This happens when all the literature of the Third World gets translated into a sort of with-it translatese, so that the literature by a woman in Palestine begins to resemble, in the feel of its prose, something by a man in Taiwan. The rhetoricity of Chinese and Arabic! The cultural politics of high-growth, capitalist Asia-Pacific, and devastated West Asia! Gender difference inscribed and inscribing in these differences!

For the student, this tedious translatese cannot compete with the spectacular stylistic experiments of a Monique Wittig or an Alice Walker.

Let us consider an example where attending to the author's stylistic experiments can produce a different text. Mahasweta Devi's 'Stanadayini' is available in two versions.[5] Devi has expressed approval for the attention to her signature style in the version entitled 'Breast-Giver'. The alternative translation gives the title as 'The Wet-Nurse', and thus neutralises the author's irony in constructing an uncanny word; enough like 'wet-nurse' to make that sense, and enough unlike to shock. It is as if the translator should decide to translate Dylan Thomas' famous title and opening line as 'Do not go gently into that good night'. The theme of treating the breast as organ of labour-power-as-commodity and the breast as metonymic part-object standing in for other-as-object – the way in which the story plays with Marx and Freud on the occasion of the woman's body – is lost even before you enter the story. In the text Mahasweta uses proverbs that are startling even in the Bengali. The translator of 'The Wet-Nurse' leaves them out. She decides not to try to translate these hard bits of earthy wisdom, contrasting with class-specific access to modernity, also represented in the story. In fact, if the two translations are read side by side, the loss of the rhetorical silences of the original can be felt from one to the other.

First, then, the translator must surrender to the text. She must solicit the text to show the limits of its language, because that rhetorical aspect will point at the silence of the absolute fraying of language that the text wards off, in its special manner. Some think this is just an ethereal way of talking about literature or philosophy. But no amount of tough talk can get around the fact that translation is the most intimate act of reading. Unless the translator has earned the right to become the intimate reader, she cannot surrender to the text, cannot respond to the special call of the text. [...]

If you want to make the translated text accessible, try doing it for the person who wrote it. The problem comes clear then, for she is not within the same history of style. What is it that you are making accessible? The accessible level is the level of abstraction where the individual is already formed, where one can speak individual rights. When you hang out and with a language away from your own (*Mitwegsein*) so that you want to use that language by preference, sometimes, when you discuss something complicated, then you are on the way to making a dimension of the text accessible to the reader, with a light and easy touch, to which she does not accede in her everyday. If you are making anything else accessible, through a language quickly learned with an idea that you transfer content, then you are betraying the text and showing rather dubious politics.

How will women's solidarity be measured here? How will their common experience be reckoned if one cannot imagine the traffic in accessibility going both ways? I think that idea should be given a decent burial as ground of knowledge, together with the idea of humanist universality. It is good to think that women have something in common, when one is approaching women with whom a relationship would not otherwise be possible. It is a great first step. But, if your interest is in learning if there is women's solidarity, how about stepping forth from this assumption, appropriate as a means to an end like local or global social work, and trying a second step? Rather than imagining that women automatically have something identifiable in common, why not say, humbly and practically, my first obligation in understanding solidarity is to learn her mother tongue. You will see immediately what the differences are. You will also feel the solidarity every day as you make the attempt to learn the language in which the other woman learned to recognise reality at her mother's knee. This is preparation for the intimacy of cultural translation. If you are going to bludgeon someone else by insisting on your version of solidarity, you have the obligation to try out this experiment and see how far your solidarity goes.

In other words, if you are interested in talking about the other, and/or in making a claim to be the other, it is crucial to learn other languages. This should be distinguished from the learned tradition of language acquisition for academic work. I am talking about the importance of language acquisition for the woman from a hegemonic monolinguist culture who makes everybody's life miserable by insisting on women's solidarity at her price. I am uncomfortable with notions of feminist solidarity which are celebrated when everybody involved is similarly produced. There are countless languages in which women all over the world have grown up and been female or feminist, and yet the languages we keep on learning by rote are the powerful European ones, sometimes the powerful Asian ones, least often the chief African ones. We are quite at home, and helpful, when large migrant populations are doing badly in the dominant countries, our own. The 'other' languages are learned only by anthropologists who must produce knowledge across an epistemic divide. They are generally (though not invariably) not interested in the three-part structure we are discussing.

If we are discussing solidarity as a theoretical position, we must also remember that not all the world's women are literate. There are traditions and situations that remain obscure because we cannot share their linguistic constitution. It is from this angle that I have felt that learning languages might sharpen our own presuppositions about what it means to use the sign 'woman'. If we say that things should be accessible to us, who is this 'us'? What does that sign mean? […]

1   The first part of this essay is based on a conversation with Michèle Barrett in the summer of 1990.

2   Nirode Mazumdar, Sena Rāmaprasāda and Gayatri Chakravorty Spivak, *Song for Kali: A Cycle of Images and Songs* (Calcutta: Seagull Books, 2000).

3   'Facilitation' is the English translation of the Freudian term Bahnung (pathing) which is translated frayage in French. The dictionary meaning is: Term used by Freud at a time when he was putting forward a neurological model of the functioning of the psychical apparatus (1895): the excitation, in passing from one neurone to another, runs into a certain resistance; where its passage results in a permanent reduction in this resistance, there is said to be facilitation; excitation will opt for a facilitated pathway in preference to one where no facilitation has occurred [Jean Laplanche & Jean-Bertrand Pontalis, *The Language of Psychoanalysis* (London: Hogarth Press, 1973) 157].

4   Jacques Derrida, 'The Force of Law: "The Mystical Foundation of Authority"', in 'Deconstruction and the Possibility of Justice', *Cardozo Law Review*, vol. 11, no. 5–6 (July–August 1990) 923.

5   'The Wet-Nurse', in Kali for Women (eds.), *Truth Tales: Stories by Indian Women* (London: The Women's Press, 1987) 1–50 (first published by Kali for Women, Delhi, 1986), and 'Breast-Giver', in Spivak, *In Other Worlds*, 222–240.

Gayatri Chakravorty Spivak, extracts from 'The Politics of Translation', in *Outside in the Teaching Machine* (New York: Routledge, 1993) 179–83, 191–2.

Lawrence Venuti
The Translator's Invisibility//1995

I see translation as the attempt to produce a text so transparent that it does not seem to be translated. A good translation is like a pane of glass. You only notice that it's there when there are little imperfections – scratches, bubbles. Ideally, there shouldn't be any. It should never call attention to itself.
– Norman Shapiro

'Invisibility' is the term I will use to describe the translator's situation and activity in contemporary British and American culture. It refers to at least two mutually determining phenomena: one is an illusionistic effect of discourse, of the translator's own manipulation of the translating language, English in this case; the other is the practice of reading and evaluating translations that has long prevailed in the United Kingdom and the United States, among other cultures, both Anglophone and foreign-language. A translated text, whether prose or poetry, fiction or non-fiction, is judged acceptable by most publishers, reviewers and readers when it reads fluently, when the absence of any linguistic or stylistic peculiarities makes it seem transparent, giving the appearance that it reflects the foreign writer's personality or intention or the essential meaning of the foreign text – the appearance, in other words, that the translation is not in fact a translation, but the 'original'. The illusion of transparency is an effect of fluent translation strategy, of the translator's effort to insure easy readability by adhering to current usage, maintaining continuous syntax, fixing a precise meaning. But readers also play a significant role in insuring that this illusory effect occurs because of the general tendency to read translations mainly for meaning, to reduce the stylistic features of the translation to the foreign text or writer, and to question any language use that might interfere with the seemingly untroubled communication of the foreign writer's intention. What is so remarkable here is the effect of transparency conceals crucial intervention. The more fluent the translation, the more invisible the translator, and, presumably, the more visible the writer or meaning of the foreign text. […]

Translating for 'prose-meaning and interpretation', practising translation as simple communication, rewrites the foreign text according to such English-language values as fluency and the accompanying effect of transparency, but entirely eclipses the translator's domesticating work – even in the eyes of the translator.

The translator's invisibility is also partly determined by the individualistic conception of authorship that continues to prevail in British and American cultures. According to this conception, the author freely expresses his thoughts and feelings in writing, which is thus viewed as an original and transparent self-representation, unmediated by transindividual determinants (linguistic, cultural, social) that might complicate authorial originality. This view of authorship carries two disadvantageous implications for the translator. On the one hand, translation is defined as a second-order representation: only the foreign text can be original, an authentic copy, true to the author's personality or intention, whereas the translation is derivative, fake, potentially a false copy. On the other hand, translation is required to efface its second-order status with the effect of transparency, producing the illusion of authorial presence whereby the translated text can be taken as the original. To point out these implications is not to argue that the translator should be seen as comparable to the foreign author: translations are different in intention and effect from original compositions, and this generic distinction is worth preserving as a means of describing different sorts of writing practices. The point is rather that the precise nature of the translator's authorship remains unformulated, and so the notion of authorial originality continues to stigmatise the translator's work.[...]

The search for alternatives to the domesticating tradition in English-language translation can locate different kinds of foreignising practices, both in the choice of foreign texts and in the invention of translation discourses. A translator can signal the foreignness of the foreign text, not only by using a discursive strategy that deviates from the prevailing discourses (e.g. dense archaism as opposed to transparency dependent on current standard usage), but also by choosing to translate a text that challenges the contemporary canon of foreign literature in the translating language. Foreignising translation is a dissident cultural practice, maintaining a refusal of the dominant by developing affiliations with marginal linguistic and cultural values in the receiving situation, including foreign cultures that have been excluded because of their own resistance to dominant values.[1] On the one hand, foreignising translation enacts an ethnocentric appropriation of the foreign text merely by using a discourse in the translating language, like dissidence. On the other hand, it is precisely this dissident stance that enables foreignising translation to signal the linguistic and cultural difference of the foreign text and perform a work of cultural restoration, admitting the ethnodeviant and potentially revising literary canonsin the translating language.

[...] Nontheless, alternative theories and practices of translation are worth recovering today because they offer translators exemplary modes of cultural resistance, however qualified they must be to serve a different and highly unfavourable scene. The domesticating translation that currently dominates British and American cultures, both elite and popular, can be challenged only by developing a practice that is not just more self-conscious, but more self-critical. Knowledge of the source-language culture, however expert, is insufficient to produce a translation that is both readable and resistant to a reductive domestication. Translators must also possess a commanding knowledge of the translating language and culture, past and present. And they must be able to deploy this knowledge in writing. The selection of a foreign text for translation and the invention of a discursive strategy to translate it should be grounded on a critical assessment of receiving culture, its hierarchies and exclusions, its relations to foreign cultures worldwide. Before a foreign text is chosen or a translation commission is accepted, translators must scrutinise the current situation or the genre or text type, field or discipline in which they are working. Literary translators should be familiar with the canons of foreign literatures in

English as well as the canons of British and American literatures, set against patterns of intercultural exchange and geopolitical relations (for a powerful example of this sort of cultural diagnosis, see Said 1990). Translators working in other disciplines of the human sciences should be familiar with the body of foreign texts that have achieved authority in British and American academic institutions as well as the Anglophone scholarship that is regarded as authoritative, similarly set in a global framework.

The ethnocentric violence of translation is inevitable: in the translation process, foreign languages, texts and cultures will always undergo some degree and form of exclusion, reduction and inscription that reflect the cultural situation in the translating language. Yet the domesticating work on the foreign text can be a foreignising intervention, pitched to question existing cultural hierarchies. [...]

1   My concept of foreignising translation as a 'dissident' cultural practice is indebted to Alan Sinfield's work on political forms of literary criticism [...]. Especially pertinent to the politics of foreignising translation is Sinfield's remark that 'political awareness does not arise out of an essential, individual, self-consciousness of class, race, nation, gender or sexual orientation; but from involvement in *a milieu, a subculture*' [Alan Sinfield, *Faultlines: Cultural Materialism and the Politics of Dissident Reading* (Berkeley and Los Angeles, CA: University of California Press, 1992) 37].

Lawrence Venuti, extracts from *The Translator's Invisibility: A History of Translation* (1995), rev. edn (London and New York: Routledge, 2008) 1–2, 6–7, 148, 309–10.

José María Arguedas
The Struggle for the Style: The Regional and the Universal//2002

[...] [T]here was a perplexing hindrance to the realisation of that burning desire. How to describe those villages, towns, and fields; in what language could I write about their placid and at the same time disquieting life? In Spanish? After having learned, loved and lived it in the sweet and pulsing Quechua language? It was a seemingly insoluble situation.

I wrote the first tale in the most correct and 'literary' Spanish at my command. Later I read the story to some of my writer friends from the capital and they praised it. But I came to detest those pages more and more. No, they were not like that – neither the men, the town, nor the landscape I wished to describe, I should almost say to denounce! Under the spurious language, an apparently contrived world – marrowless and bloodless – was shown; a typically 'literary' world in which the word had consumed the work. While in my memory, deep within, the real theme went on smouldering away untouched. I rewrote the story and finally understood, once and for all, that my Spanish would be inadequate if I kept on using it in a traditional literary fashion. In those days I was reading Vallejo's *Tungsteno* and Güiraldes' *Don Segundo Sombra*. Both books lighted my way.

Could I perhaps be advocating the Indianisation of Spanish? No. But there is a case, a real case, in which the man from those regions, feeling ill at ease with the Spanish he has inherited, sees the need to use it as a raw material that he may modify, taking from and adding to it, until he transforms it into his own means of expression. This possibility, which has already been realised more than once in literature, is a proof of the limitless qualities of Spanish and of the highly evolved languages.

We are not referring, in this case, to the clearly differentiated Spanish spoken by the people in some countries such as Argentina, but to the literary expression of the American countries in which the dominant survival of the native languages has created the complex problem of bilingualism. Each case presents a different problem: in the former it is a matter of linguistic fait accompli, which the writer may or may not take up, make use of, and re-create. In the latter case, he must solve a more serious problem but, in exchange, may count on an advantage especially sought after by the artist: the possibility of, the necessity for a more absolute act of creation.

In contrast to the solution of these particularly critical situations in literary expression, there has always been the problem of universality, the danger of a regionalism that contaminates the work and constrains it. This is the danger that the latest introduction of foreign materials into an already clean and perfect means of expression always implies! But in such cases one is not primarily concerned with universality; instead it is a matter of simply being able to achieve self-realisation. To realise oneself, to translate oneself, to transform a seemingly alien language into a legitimate and diaphanous torrent, to communicate to the almost foreign language the stuff of which our spirit is made; that is the hard, the difficult question. The universality of this rare balance of content and form, a balance achieved after nights of intense labour, is a thing that will come as a function of the human perfection attained in the course of such a strange effort. Do the real features of the human being and of his sojourn exist in the depths of this work? It does not matter if those features are painted with unfamiliar colours – such an outcome could lend greater interest to the picture. Just so the colours are not a mere tangle, the grotesque tracks of the movements of a powerless being, that is what is essential. But if the language, so charged with strange essences, lets one see the depths of the human heart, if it transmits to us the history of his passage over the earth, the universality may be a long time coming but nevertheless it will come, as we all know that man owes his pre-eminence and his dominion to the fact that he is one and unique.

In my personal experience the search for a style, as I have already stated, was long and anguished. And one of those days I began to write, for me, as fluidly and luminously as water slips through millennial channels. I finished the first story in a few days and timorously laid it aside.

I had already written 'Warma Kuyay', the last story in *Agua*. The Spanish was docile and appropriate for the expression of my intimate moments, my own history, my romance. Here was the story of the first love of a highland mestizo, of a mestizo of the most culturally advanced type. Frustrated and impossible love for an Indian girl, with the saddest, most ill-fated ending. I know now that even in that story the Spanish is imbued with the Quechua soul, but its syntax is untouched. The same construction, the Spanish of 'Warma Kuyay', acclimated as it is, was of no use to me in the interpretation of the community's struggles, the epic theme. As soon as my spirit mingled with that of the Quechua-speaking people, the desperate search for a style began. Was it simply a matter of an elemental lack of knowledge of the language? And yet I have no complaints about the style of 'Warma Kuyay'. While I was deeply immersed in the community's home I did not have the same command of Spanish, could not use it as naturally and properly. Many of the essences I felt to be best and most legitimate could not be diluted into Spanish terms of familiar construction. It was necessary to discover subtle ways to disarrange the Spanish in order to make it into the fitting mould, the adequate instrument of expression. And since it was a case of an aesthetic discovery, it was made in an imprecise, dreamlike fashion.

It was made naturally for me, the seeker. Six months later, I turned to the pages of the first story in *Agua*. There was no longer anything to complain about. That was the world! The small village burning beneath the fire of love and of hatred, of the great sun and of the silence; amid the singing of robins that had taken shelter in the bushes; beneath the highest and most avaricious of skies, beautiful but cruel. Would that world be transmitted to others? Would they be able to feel the extreme passions of the humans who dwelt therein? Their great lamentation and the incredible, the transparent joyfulness with which they were wont to sing in moments of calm? It seems they did.

Yawar Fiesta is still within the stylistic limits of *Agua*. For five years I struggled to tear out the Quechua idioms and make literary Spanish into my sole means of expression. I rewrote the first chapters of the novel many times and always came back to the starting point: the laboured, anxiety-laden solution of the bilingual writer.

But some day the two worlds into which these countries descended from

Tahuantinsuyo are divided – the Quechua and the Spanish – will be merged or separated definitively. Until then the bilingual artist's Way of the Cross will continue to exist. With reference to this grave problem of our destiny, I have tentatively cast my vote in favour of Spanish.

What language should the Indians be made to speak in literature? For the bilingual person, for one who first learned to talk in Quechua, it seems impossible to have them suddenly speak Spanish; on the other hand, whoever has not known them throughout childhood, from deep experience, can perhaps conceive of them expressing themselves in Spanish. I solved the problem by creating for them a special Spanish language, which has since been used with horrible exaggeration in the work of others. But the Indians do not speak that Spanish, not with Spanish speakers, and much less among themselves. It is a fiction. The Indians speak in Quechua. All of the southern and central highlands, with the exception of some cities, are completely Quechua-speaking. People from other regions who go to live in the southern towns and villages have to learn Quechua; it is an unavoidable necessity. So it is false and horrendous to present the Indians speaking the Spanish of Quechua servants who have become accustomed to living in the capital. I am just now, after eighteen years of effort, attempting a Spanish translation of the Indians' dialogues. The first solution was to create for them a language based on the Spanish words that have been incorporated into Quechua and on the elementary Spanish that some Indians manage to learn in *their own villages*. The realistic novel, it seemed, had no other road.

Excising the Quechua words is an even longer and more arduous feat than taking out the Quechua turns of phrase. It is a question of not losing one's soul, of not being completely transformed by this long, slow undertaking! But care must be taken and one must be vigilant and work to retain the essence. As long as the source of the work is the world itself, it should glow with whatever fire we succeed in kindling; our use of the other style, for which we are unrepentant despite its strangeness and its native elements, should be infectious.

Was and is this a search for universality through the search for form, for form alone? For form insofar as it means a conclusion, an equilibrium reached through the necessary mixture of elements seeking to constitute themselves into a new structure?

I do not doubt – and may I be pardoned for expressing this conviction – I do not doubt the value of the novels published in this book[1] – their value in relation to the one I am writing at the present time. To have attempted to express oneself with a sense of universality through the steps that lead one to master another language, to have attempted this in mid-leap, that was the reason for the never-ending struggle. I aspired to and sought a universality that would not disfigure, would not diminish the human nature and terrain I attempted to portray, that would not yield one iota to the external and apparent beauty of the words.

I believe that in the novel *Los Rios Profundos*, this process has come to an end. It could only have one ending, the use of Spanish as the legitimate means of expressing the Peruvian world of the Andes: noble whirlwind in which different spirits, as if forged on antipodal stars, struggle, attract, repel, and mingle with one another amid silent snows and lakes, frost and fire.

It is not a matter, then, of a search for form as it is superficially and customarily understood, but rather a problem of the spirit, of the culture, in those countries in which alien currents meet and for centuries do not blend, but instead form narrow zones of confluence, while in the deepest and widest places the main currents flow on, unyielding, incredibly.

And why should the literature that shows us the disturbed and misty features of our people and of our own countenance in such a tormented fashion be called *indigenista*? It is quite evident that it does not deal solely with the Indians. But those who classify literature and art frequently fall into imperfect and misleading conclusions. Nevertheless we should be grateful to them for having obliged us to write this kind of self-analysis, or confession, which we do in the name of all those who must and do suffer deeply from the same drama of literary expression in these regions. [...]

1   [Footnote 4 in source] This essay was to be used as a prologue to the second edition of *Agua* and *Yawar Fiesta*, a project of Editorial Huascarán, Lima, that was not completed.

José María Arguedas, extracts from 'The Struggle for the Style: The Regional and the Universal', in *Yawar Fiesta* (Prospect Heights, IL: Waveland Press, 2002) xvii–xxi.

Miyó Vestrini
On Translation//1985

What is translation? A job, a chance procedure, an act of treason, a robotic task? Confusion. No definition of such a clumsy and impossible undertaking can satisfy either the wary or unwary.

Each generation translates again and again, tirelessly bringing serious or joyful demystification. The text takes it all, is disturbed, is still, rages and always comes back, now full of another text. There is, therefore, no Tower of Babel, but a language of its own, lalangue, thus stuck with its meanings and signifiers. The translator must know their own language, cleanly and severely, approach it like a fugitive prostitute, take its tongue in front of a mirror and, finally, force it to say great poetry from another language.

[…] If we accept that the translation was first and the original came after (read The Old Testament), we must admit that all of civilisation depends on translation. We depend, with bound feet, hands and tongue, on that impossible figure of the translator. Dangerous enemy, if they do evil. The best accomplice, if they do well.

Miyó Vestrini, extracts from 'La Civilization Descansa Sobre La Traduccion', *Criticarte* (December 1985); reprinted as 'Miyó Vestrini On Translation', in *Grenade in Mouth: Some Poems of Miyó Vestrini*, eds. Faride Mereb & Elisa Maggi, trans. Anne Boyer & Cassandra Gillig (Chicago: Kenning Editions, 2019) 14.

Slavs and Tatars
Khhhhhhh//2012

[…] **WANTED: Single Phoneme of Colour Seeks dependable Grapheme for LTR**
If breathing is the stuff of life, then [kh] is borne on an alluring whisper of turbulence. Merely to pronounce it requires constricting the passage of air in the vocal tract. It's difficult to overlook or miss the fricative indulgence of the rasp, the friction at the back of the throat. While the Germans (see *Bach*), Spaniards (see *joder*) and Scots (see *loch*) have an approximation, it is perhaps the Anglo-Saxons who suffer most when trying to pronounce this pesky phoneme, as if it were an affront to the guttural skills of fading empires: 'Khhhhhhhhhhhhhhhh-hhhhhhhhhhhhhh.'

If [kh] were single and dating, it would be draped in red, waving flags: the colour growls at our linguistic loins, while the fabric's frenzied whipping warns all interested parties of baggage, be it phonetic or more fundamental. Even true paramours of transliteration like us must acknowledge the frightening complexity when it comes to introducing a grapheme, the smallest unit in a written language, to this particular phoneme. For starters, it is not clear where [kh] ends and other letters begin. The Pre-Canaanite alphabet does not differentiate between [kh] and [h]. For some – like the Turkic peoples of the former Soviet Union (Kazak, Uzbek, Azeri) – [kh] has been packed into к along with the competitively charming epithets 'K with descender' and 'Cyrillic Qaf'. Yet its pronunciation begs for yet another letter: Latinised as a q and sounding like [gh], as in Qur'an. […]

Less is More Maximalism

A dangerous positivism rumbles beneath our feet, its echo rolling off our tongues. Raised on a diet of globalised givens, we assume that with time's passage, languages only get richer. Foreign words brought by newcomers, neologisms forged by common parlance, multiple meanings aided and abetted by rhetorical devices: among many, many others, these certainly attest to a sensational polyphony of languages. Yet, what of the synthetic powers necessary to say many things with just a few words or a mere sound? True to Slavs and Tatars' maximalist inclinations, we wonder if there is not also a grain of truth to the 'less-is-more' maxim, at least when it comes to language's expressive abilities.

It is fitting perhaps that Velimir Khlebnikov, the grandfather of Russian Futurism, a man who devoted his life to a search for poetics as rich as the universe itself, would be spoiled with epithets: from 'The King of Time' to the 'Columbus of new poetic continents' (according to Vladimir Mayakovsky). One of the vessels that carried Khlebnikov to uncharted linguistic shores was his belief in an inherent correspondence between the sound – or shape – of a letter and its meaning. He called this the 'inner declension' of words, and mined a fertile, if slippery, terrain to include letters, numbers and sounds. Never mind that this stands in stark opposition to what we have learned from Saussurian linguistics: namely, that to study language as a formal system implies that linguistic form itself is arbitrary. For Khlebnikov, nothing could be further from the truth: 'language is just as wise as nature and we are only learning to read it with the growth of science... the wisdom of languages precedes the wisdom of science.' The 'inner declension' in words points to a spatial understanding of the word, one where conflict between letters and their sounds could play out. [Kh], if followed by [l], produces an entirely different meaning to a [kh] followed by [r]. Changing the л [l] of the Russian хлам (*khlam*, junk), into an р [r], operates the equivalent of a sex-change in the otherwise wholesome world of lexicology: junk is sublimated and becomes храм (*khram*, shrine). It is as if letters, like individuals, have an agency, if not a responsibility, vis-à-vis other letters; not a social contract but a collective being towards, dependent on their neighbours. Khlebnikov himself had three sieges: 'the siege of time, of the word, and of the multitudes'. [...]

Khlebnikov was not alone in such linguistic investigations, though. To name just a few, Rudolf Steiner's Anthroposophy assigned colours and movements to the letters of the alphabet; Milca Mayerova choreographed the ABCs in Nezval's *ABECEDA*; and Apollinaire drafted calligrammes as a precursor to concrete poetry. One would be forgiven for wondering if there was something in the water supply of the early twentieth century's alphabet soup. Whether it was his attempts to create linguistic laws that govern time, not space; a desire to unite all Slavonic words to create a Pan-Slavic language; or a utopian interest in re-creating a universal language, Khlebnikov's linguistic experiments shared an affinity with his contemporaries. What distinguished him from his colleagues, though, was his commitment to put these otherwise abstract theories into practice within language itself, and his rigorous – if not obsessive – attempt to recreate a new language, one that would do justice to the original metaphysical mission of words, sounds, and letters. […]

Language, as our primary hermeneutic tool, has blood on its hands, or rather, tongues. We tend to see words exclusively as a means of expression, forgetting their ability to hide as much as they reveal. Our taste for the transparent predates Twitter revolutions and Wiki incontinence, dating back at least to the Enlightenment. We certainly do not believe that which we do not see, and trust even less that which we do not understand. In this tension between the exoteric and the esoteric, the outer meaning of the Torah and the תודיסח (chassidut) or inner meaning – what Sufis call the ظاهر (zahir) and the باطن (batin) – Khlebnikov saw a similar dynamic between the everyday (бытовое) word and the pure or self-sufficient (чистое) word. The everyday usage of a word inevitably conceals other meanings, debasing its higher calling. […]

Divide Alphabets and Conquer Common Language

In the beginning of the last century, it wasn't only down to philosophers, artists and writers to experiment with language. While the likes of Steiner, Khlebnikov, Apollinaire and Kurt Schwitters (to name just a few) were breaking up words only to put them back together, Vladimir Lenin was advocating his own linguistic face-lift. Called 'The Revolution of the East', Lenin wished to Latinise the various languages of Soviet Muslims in an effort to modernise and also, essentially, to cut them off from their Arabic script – and thus their ties to Islam. In 1929, the Muslim subjects of the nascent USSR were asked to begin reading from left to right in a new script, and to burn any extant documents and books bearing the Arabic script. A mere ten years later, Stalin suspected Soviet Muslims of swaying too close to the West and identified the Latin alphabet as the culprit. In an about-face that would be amusing if it were not so tragic, Soviet Muslims were asked to begin afresh: this time, keeping the left to right but using the Cyrillic alphabet instead. To thwart any potential for organised resistance amongst Soviet Muslims, as well as to quash a (partially German-financed) threat of Pan-Turkism, the Turkic languages were each latinised and cyrillicised slightly differently, with variations in the transcription of certain letters. To take an example close to our hearts, the gutturally hefty ق (qof) became a variation of the Cyrillic for g, ғ, in Azeri and Kazakh but in nearby Uzbek, қ. The ج [dz] as pronounced in the English 'joke' became ч in Azeri but a traditional Russian Cyrillic ж in Uzbek.

It is in towns that languages decay, by becoming worn out, like the things and institutions they designate. Nomads, who live to some extent outside time, conserve their language better; it is the only treasure they can carry around with them in their pastoral existence; the nomad is a jealous guardian of his linguistic heritage.
–Titus Burckhardt (aka Ibrahim Izz al-Din)

Today, we need not only intellectual acrobatics but also metaphysical ones: Substitution requires us to cultivate the agility, coordination, and balance necessary to tell one tale through another, to adopt the innermost thoughts, experiences, beliefs and sensations of others as our own, in an effort to challenge the very notion of distance as the shortest length between two points. To understand contemporary Iran, we turned to Poland and Solidarność (Friendship of Nations: Polish Shi'ite Showbiz); to grasp the nature of political agency in the twenty-first century, we studied Muharram and the 1300-year-old Shi'ite ritual of perpetual protest (Reverse Joy); to demystify Islam, we adopted similar tactics employed once upon a time vis-a-vis Communism (Not Moscow Not Rome, Secession); and it is through mysticism that we now intend to address modernity (Beyonsense, MoMA). When we first set the backs of our throats on [kh], it was fricative at first sight, or rather, rasp.

Coaches, athletes and sports enthusiasts alike tell us there's no 'me' in 'team'. Despite their expertise in the field, linguists themselves don't seem to enjoy the plethora of catchy slogans – or the hefty yelling of pep-rallies, for that matter. After all, there are certainly many me's in phoneme, lexeme and morpheme. Notwithstanding the occupational hazards of those devoted to the tongue – misunderstandings, the untranslatability of language, Babel's broken record – language is 'not a place of closure and retreat; rather, it constitutes the always finite anthropological commitment to the world'. Through the seemingly micro-perspective of a single letter, Khhhhhhh allows us to reconsider the sacred potential of language and the siege of history by the very vowels and consonants rolling off our tongues and scraping the back of our collective throats.

To better translate the noise of the present, we press ourselves close to individual letters, before pulling back to see a numinous pact, a language of strength, between them. [...]

From our tent-like tea salon for Friendship of Nations: Polish Shi'ite Showbiz at the 10th Sharjah Biennial and the flying carpet meets floating rahlé of Prayway at the New Museum to the syncretic shrine of fruits in Not Moscow Not Mecca at Vienna's Secession, our practice has engaged, often unwittingly, a notion of hospitality both linguistically and physically generous. Whether it's serving tea to escape the sweltering sun or offering merely a place to sit in the otherwise unforgiving spaces of museums, hospitality allows us to forge a pluralism that is not just spoken and critically articulated but also breathed, lived and considered. To do so, it is imperative to embrace that which we do not understand, with which we might disagree, especially in an increasingly polarised world.

Slavs and Tatars, extracts from *Khhhhhhh* (Brno/Milan: Moravian Gallery/Mousse Publishing, 2012) 7–14, 22–4, 36–50 [footnotes omitted].

Walter Benjamin
The Task of the Translator//1921

[...] Translatability is an essential quality of certain works, which is not to say that it is essential for the works themselves that they be translated; it means, rather, that a specific significance inherent in the original manifests itself in its translatability. It is evident that no translation, however good it may be, can have any significance as regards the original. Nonetheless, it does stand in the closest relationship to the original by virtue of the original's translatability; in fact, this connection is all the closer since it is no longer of importance to the original. We may call this connection a natural one, or, more specifically, a vital one. Just as the manifestations of life are intimately connected with the phenomenon of life without being of importance to it, a translation issues from the original - not so much from its life as from its afterlife. For a translation comes later than the original, and since the important works of world literature never find their chosen translators at the time of their origin, their translation marks their stage of continued life. [...]

The history of the great works of art tells us about their descent from prior models, their realisation in the age of the artist, and what in principle should be their eternal afterlife in succeeding generations. Where this last manifests itself, it is called fame. Translations that are more than transmissions of subject matter come into being when a work, in the course of its survival, has reached the age of its fame. Contrary, therefore, to the claims of bad translators, such translations do not so much serve the works as owe their existence to it. In them the life of the originals attains its latest, continually renewed, and most complete unfolding.

As the unfolding of a special and high form of life, this process is governed by a special high purposiveness. The relationship between life and purposiveness, seemingly obvious yet almost beyond the grasp of the intellect, reveals itself only if the ultimate purpose toward which all the individual purposivenesses of life tends is sought not in its own sphere but in a higher one. All purposeful manifestations of life, including their very purposiveness, in the final analysis have their end not in life but in the expression of its nature, in the representation of its significance. Translation thus ultimately serves the purpose of expressing the innermost relationship of languages to one another. It cannot possibly reveal or establish this hidden relationship itself; but it can represent it by realising it in embryonic or intensive form. This representing of something signified through an attempt at establishing it in embryo is of so singular a nature that it is rarely met with in the sphere of nonlinguistic life. In its analogies and symbols, it can draw on other ways of suggesting meaning than intensive – that is, anticipative, intimating – realisation. As for the posited innermost kinship of languages, it is marked by a peculiar convergence. This special kinship holds because languages are not strangers to one another, but are, a priori and apart from all historical relationships, interrelated in what they want to express. [...]

Walter Benjamin, extracts from 'The Task of the Translator' (1921), in *Walter Benjamin Selected Writings Vol.1, 1913-1926*, eds. Marcus Bullock & Michael W. Jennings, trans. Harry Zohn (Cambridge MA: The Belknap Press of Harvard University Press, 2004) 254, 255.

Stuart Hall
Representation//1997

[...] There are broadly speaking three approaches to explaining how representation of meaning through language works. We may call these the reflective, the intentional and the constructionist or constructivist approaches. You might think of each as an attempt to answer the questions, 'where do meanings come from?' and 'how can we tell the "true" meaning of a word or image?'

In the reflective approach, meaning is thought to lie in the object, person, idea or event in the real world, and language functions like a mirror, to reflect the true meaning as it already exists in the world. As the poet Gertrude Stein once said, 'A rose is a rose is a rose'. In the fourth century BC, the Greeks used the notion of mimesis to explain how language, even drawing and painting, mirrored or imitated Nature; they thought of Homer's great poem, *The Iliad*, as 'imitating' a heroic series of events. So the theory which says that language works by simply reflecting or imitating the truth that is already there and fixed in the world, is sometimes called 'mimetic'.

Of course there is a certain obvious truth to mimetic theories of representation and language. As we've pointed out, visual signs do bear some relationship to the shape and texture of the objects which they represent. But, as was also pointed out earlier, a two-dimensional visual image of a rose is a sign – it should not be confused with the real plant with thorns and blooms growing in the garden. Remember also that there are many words, sounds and images which we fully well understand but which are entirely fictional or fantasy and refer to worlds which are wholly imaginary – including, many people now think, most of *The Iliad*! Of course, I can use the word 'rose' to refer to real, actual plants growing in a garden, as we have said before. But this is because I know the code which links the concept with a particular word or image. I cannot think or speak or draw with an actual rose. And if someone says to me that there is no such word as 'rose' for a plant in her culture, the actual plant in the garden cannot resolve the failure of communication between us. Within the conventions of the different language codes we are using, we are both right – and for us to understand each other, one of us must learn the code linking the flower with the word for it in the other's culture.

The second approach to meaning in representation argues the opposite case. It holds that it is the speaker, the author, who imposes his or her unique meaning on the world through language. Words mean what the author intends they should mean. This is the intentional approach. Again, there is some point to this argument since we all, as individuals, do use language to convey or communicate things which are special or unique to us, to our way of seeing the world. However, as a general theory of representation through language, the intentional approach is also flawed. We cannot be the sole or unique source of meanings in language, since that would mean that we could express ourselves in entirely private languages. But the essence of language is communication and that, in turn, depends on shared linguistic conventions and shared codes. Language can never be wholly a private game. Our private intended meanings, however personal to us, have to enter into the rules, codes and conventions of language to be shared and understood. Language is a social system through and through. This means that our private thoughts have to negotiate with all the other meanings for words or images which have been stored in language which our use of the language system will inevitably trigger into action.

The third approach recognises this public, social character of language. It acknowledges that neither things in themselves nor the individual users of language can fix meaning in language. Things don't mean: we construct meaning, using representational systems – concepts and signs. Hence it is called the constructivist or constructionist approach to meaning in language. According to this approach, we must not confuse the material world, where things and people exist, and the symbolic practices and processes through which representation, meaning and language operate. Constructivists do not deny the existence of the material world. However, it is not the material world which conveys meaning: it is the language system or whatever system we are using to represent our concepts. It is social actors who use the conceptual systems of their culture and the linguistic and other representational systems to construct meaning, to make the world meaningful and to communicate about that world meaningfully to others. [...]

Stuart Hall, extract from *Representation: Cultural Representations and Signifying Practices* (London/ Thousand Oaks/New Delhi: SAGE Publications, 1997) 24–5.

Philip Rizk
Translating Dissent: Voices from and with the Egyptian Revolution //2016

[...] One way I would sum up what Mosireen and Intifadat Intifadat are about is translation. We came together to try to translate the spirit of the revolt; in a sense, we sought to translate the street through images, in the hope of breeding anger, in the hope of forcing the audience to face the reality of the brutality of the regime, in the hope of instigating revolt. This goes for most of the collectives' work, but if I speak particularly of my own involvement, one of the important intentions was to dislodge the middle-class milieu of activists, of whom the collectives were a part, from the position of the main protagonists of revolt. As you well know, the narrative of 25 January that has gained the most traction amongst elites both in and outside Egypt is that the revolt was flamed by an Internet-savvy middle-class milieu; this narrative would later clearly reveal itself to be part of the strategy of the counter-revolution's undermining of the revolution. Intifadat Intifadat, which was already active during the first eighteen days of the revolution, was exactly about this: the interlocutors of the revolt had to be those who carried it through, not those who were already made to represent it. After all, as Max Weber wrote years ago, representation is a structure of domination. Here, the act of translating the positions and opinions of an underclass was of the essence, in order to counter a much more dominant account of who the protagonists of this revolt were. I remember around March or April of 2011 filming a march protesting a draft law that sought to ban protest, a law that of course was implemented at the end of 2013 and is the reason why so many are behind bars today. After the march, we gathered in Tahrir Square and I was filming a working-class man who was enraged about the scope of the law. As he referenced the revolution's key motivation, عيش، حرية، عدالة اجتماعية / 3eish, 7lureyya, 3adala igtema3eyya ('bread, freedom, social justice'), a very shrill voice of a woman off-frame cut him off, yelling, 'No, no, this is a revolution for كرامة انسانية [/karama insaneyya (human dignity)]'. The man stopped speaking immediately out of respect. I turned to find a clearly middle-class woman in her late 30s trying to convince me to stop filming because this man didn't know what he was talking about. This was a very direct experience of what was happening on a much wider scale in competition over the narrative of the revolution.

I often think of the main protagonists of protest though a trope of 'the street', which of course is a very subjective, abstract category that remains constantly in flux. Without a consistent, clear position, the majority of protagonists of revolt are difficult to represent, to categorise, to generalise in the manner that is the very essence of metanarratives like those of the mainstream press or authorities. The protagonists of 'the street' are the unseen actors with enough wrath, and often with not enough to lose, to risk their lives in an attempt to oppose a regime of coloniality with full force. Most of us who make up Mosireen, on the other hand, are the privileged few; speaking multiple languages, with more rights in a society with few to speak of. Most of us were politicised before 2011, thus we were amongst this crowd of wrath but always set apart in a vital sense. Of course the chroniclers of metanarratives are unlikely to put it in just such terms, and here clearly one of the difficulties, one of the dangers of the position we have chosen for ourselves, emerges. We place ourselves in a position of the translator, a position we cannot fully escape. Through a structure that is collective and for the most part nameless, we attempt to subvert some of the potential violence that this act of image-making and dissemination entails, but we cannot escape it completely. [...]

Philip Rizk, extract from Mona Baker, 'Interview with Philip Rizk', in *Translating Dissent: Voices from and with the Egyptian Revolution*, ed. Mona Baker (Abingdon and New York: Routledge, 2016) 227–8.

Christian Nyampeta
How to Translate Ourselves//2017–19

'*How*' suggests a manner, *a way* of being, thinking and doing, a *manner, manual,* a way of handling, a way of holding, of holding oneself, of and/or against being held. 'How' can be a rule, a law, a policy. 'How' can be a *quest,* a *search,* a questioning; it is a *philosophising.*

The French term for 'How' is *Comment.* This meaning is *sedimented* in English: 'to comment,' 'commentary,' 'to command,' 'commando,' but also 'common'.

In Kinyarwanda, 'How' is '*uko*', and this is the same term which gives meaning to '*ubwoko*', race, ethnicity, type, character: '*Ubwo*' – truth and '*ko*' – *that-which.*

'*To*' indicates a movement: this can be *a break,* a waywardness, a destination, *transgression,* a renunciation, a reduction, but also an *excess.* 'To' is a vector, and even when it points to a stasis, it is an orientation, it points the way, purposefully or otherwise. 'To' is a rhythm. It can indicate a declension and an ascension, for instance *un*- of unlearning, or *de*- of decolonial, and in our case *desedimentation.*

Living Commons Collective is an experimental publishing imprint by philosopher Denise Ferreira da Silva and theorist Rashné Limki. It is 'set amid and apart from neoliberal practices wherein sterilisation of thought is lucrative business and from autonomist practices that have ceded themselves a peculiar racial valence,' and its output is 'a reflection of the inherent counter-disciplinarity of thinking'; and it traces 'the political as constituted across the various modes of the creative and the material, that is, the ideational, the emotional, and the spiritual.'

The meaning of translation was related to the *removal* of a saint's body or *relics to a new place.* Because theology presupposes demons, then there is a demonological imperative in the practice of translation. Otherwise, what compels the movement and the relocation of the bones of the saint? What does a relic signify and what does it translates?

The colonising West considered the colonised subjects as *non-human* on the account of their supposed absence of textual writing; of 'philosophy;' and of religion. Also, the discourse of globality still regards a specific Western faculty of intellection, of logic, or the concept, as the marker of what is 'human,' of what is 'holy' of what can be a relic, of what can be translated.

This is why *translation as desedimentation* is useful: a de-sanctifying practice, which attends to the care of knowledges that are bereaved from separation, and to those who are endogenous to a world that rejects them by virtue of them into problems, into demons.

Despite their inner contradictions, the work of 'modern' African philosophers such as Abbé Alexis Kagame's *La Philosophie bantu-rwandaise de l'être* (1956) were works of translations: from oral writing to textual writing, and from supposedly 'non-philosophy' to 'philosophy.' Reading these writers today involves thinking through the limit of the translatability of being: such reading is not only a matter of cultural, disciplinary or linguistic translations, but it involves instead a task of geographic and temporal *desedimentation*.

From Maniragaba Balibutsa, these are some of the tasks of the *translator*:

1. Strive to establish the characteristics and the attributes proper to the communities and the localities at hand, and explain these to the newly, defined public in comprehensible terms.
   What is 'being' in our other languages?
2. Develop a critical attitude towards expressions of contestable meaning.
   What does 'that' lead to?
3. Establish the point at which the starting point of one's own philosophy lies.
   What right does suffering give us?
6. Study and promote the new ideas, practices and critique of reality, for example, through analysing the meaning of relevant concepts in one's own languages.
   How to 'name' our reality?
8. Study and enlighten for ourselves the goals for which our governments exist.
   Where are 'we'?
9. Study and clarify the different conceptions of beauty and its supposed opposites.
   Who defines our feelings?

Works referenced

Saidiya Hartman, Intimate Trespass: Hapticality, Waywardness, and the Practice of Entanglement – A Study Day with Saidiya Hartman.

Nahum Dimitri Chandler, *Toward An African Future – Of the Limit of the World* (London: Living Commons, 2013).

Sylvia Wynter, 'Africa, the West and the Analogy of Culture: The Cinematic Text after Man', in ed. Jane Givanni, *Symbolic Narratives/African Cinema: Audiences, Theory and the Moving Image* (London: British Film Institute, 2000).

Alexis Kagame, *La Philosophie bantu-rwandaise de l'être* (Brussels: Academie Royale des sciences coloniales, 1956).

Maniragaba Balibutsa, *Les Perspectives de la pensée philosophique bantu-rwandaise après Alexis Kagame* (Butare: Editions Université Nationale du Rwanda, 1985).

Christian Nyampeta, an edited version (2019) of 'How to Translate Ourselves', a text originally written for the exhibition 'Words after the World' at Camden Arts Centre (2017–18).

Jesse Darling
A Letter to the Translator//2018

This text was written on the occassion of the 2017 Sharjah Biennale for translation into Arabic by a translator. It was subsequently reproduced online with a rollover translation automated from Google Translate.

A preface: I first addressed this to a man, and now I write to a machine. Behind the machine is a wo/man, or wo/men, human people. Some body supplied an integer, furrowed an alley, steered the craft down a given route. But after that, the open sea: the random principle, waves of mazy data, fractal tongues washing froth. The semiotician Ferdinand de Saussure seemed so sure that the signifier and the signified – the word and its work, in so many words – are just two things adrift, latched together by a net that is not fixed, linguistic, determined. It all depends, said the semiotician, on the work the words are put to. A net/work. In this regard, it seems appropriate (for this text has been sifted so fine, and so many times) to cast out the net beyond the vagaries of subjectivity and culture, ultimately arbitrary, full of meaningless sounds. And when the machine returns the garbled form – Dada architectures, open claims, hanging signifiers – who's to say this is not also correct somehow, perhaps even corrective; as though there could ever be a definitive version (in translation or otherwise)! Ludwig Wittgenstein thought of theology as grammar, and grammar as a meaning-production system within 'shared human behavior.' The difference between the wo/man and the machine is that the latter needs no theology since it works with the dogged logic of any god or greater force; without any will or agenda, the machine has nothing to lose or gain. This is the principle of chaos, analogous as far as anyone really knows to the 'will' of God: terrifyingly meaningless, mainly banal, occasionally poetic. At the accidental stroke of a tongue (divine eloquence, the void speaking back), we (the living) are struck [as though] dumb.
– JD, Berlin, 2018

Dear Translator,
You and I grew up speaking different languages. We may never meet, yet here you hold my words in your hands, beneath your fingers, mouse and keyboard. I hand them all to you in perfect trust, for I have no choice. The words between us are like the map of a city with which we both are familiar and in which we both walk as foreigners. Translator, if I revert to the slang of my hometown, will you meet me in the square there as a child? The language in which I write runs across

the page left to right; the language in which you write is its mirror, right to left. If you glance into the mirror, do you see yourself? Or is this perhaps an imposition, the way that bodies eclipse each other in the street, on the news, in the eye of a gun, down the barrel of a viewfinder? [...]

As you and I both know, there is no such thing as translation; a text must be rebuilt from the ground up. What I said, or meant to say, eroded by your own will and words. This is how it must and ought to be. In between there is something unspeakable, or unspoken. [...]

Writing, in my experience, is equated to a stacking up of claims, like a budget report. According to convention, these claims should be grounded in a certain linear history – similar claims made by others in the past, or observations grounded in vernacular experience, quantifiable according to one's subject parameters. At the end of it the conclusion is slapped down hard with a resounding thud of punctuation, like a grand total at the foot of the bill. According to the ministrations of those in the history business – whose observations are grounded in mud and rubble and the dust of bones – the history of writing is a history of invoicing, and the earliest written documents are all records of goods and services owed or delivered. The English word invoice sounds as though it is derived from vox (Latin), or vois (French); a sound produced in the body, a form of agency by which one's presence is expressed and understood – as though to speak is to signify. And history, after all, is in part a story of who speaks and who signifies; which is to say it is a story of who does not speak and who does not signify. No modernity without its other, a long shadow cast by the rectilinear stack of bones. But invoice is in fact derived from the French *envoyer*, from the Latin *inviāre*, derived from *via*: path, road. The only way out is through. The Arabic word فاتورة is derived from a word meaning 'that which has been made': an object or an action. Carved in stone; thud of a tablet set down like a promise. When all is said and done. If it has been said, it may as well be done. The debt is a promise; the story is a currency. We can only hope that this may become an exchange.

Translator, in the spirit of debts and exchanges, I would like to ask you to collude with me. Inevitably, you have already done so; no one writes alone in a foreign tongue, and by now there are two of us here, each with their own idea of where this is going. Let's say that somewhere in this text you have placed a few words of your own. Hiding in plain sight, nobody will ever know. Translator, what I wanted to tell you has become obscure. Since we've never met, why should I presume? But I think I wanted to tell you – very urgently – that the story is slippery, that nothing is written in stone. Though you already know that, better than anyone.

Wishing you a debt to the future, and here's to both (to all) our tongues.

Yours entirely,

JD Oxford, 2017

Jesse Darling, extracts from 'A Letter to the Translator' (2018) (https://accessions.org/article4/a-letter-to-the-translator/).

Helen Keller
The World I Live In//1910

[...] My hand is to me what your hearing and sight together are to you. In large measure we travel the same highways, read the same books, speak the same language, yet our experiences are different. All my comings and goings turn on the hand as on a pivot. It is the hand that binds me to the world of men and women. The hand is my feeler with which I reach through isolation and darkness and seize every pleasure, every activity that my fingers encounter. With the dropping of a little word from another's hand into mine, a slight flutter of the fingers, began the intelligence, the joy, the fullness of my life. Like Job, I feel as if a hand had made me, fashioned me together round about and molded my very soul.

In all my experiences and thoughts I am conscious of a hand. Whatever moves me, whatever thrills me, is as a hand that touches me in the dark, and that touch is my reality. You might as well say that a sight which makes you glad, or a blow which brings the stinging tears to your eyes, is unreal as to say that those impressions are unreal which I have accumulated by means of touch.

The delicate tremble of a butterfly's wings in my hand, the soft petals of violets curling in the cool folds of their leaves or lifting sweetly out of the meadow-grass, the clear, firm outline of face and limb, the smooth arch of a horse's neck and the velvety touch of his nose – all these, and a thousand resultant combinations, which take shape in my mind, constitute my world.

Ideas make the world we live in, and impressions furnish ideas. My world is built of touch-sensations, devoid of physical colour and sound; but without colour and sound it breathes and throbs with life. Every object is associated in my mind with tactual qualities which, combined in countless ways, give me a sense of power, of beauty, or of incongruity: for with my hands I can feel the comic as well as the beautiful in the outward appearance of things. Remember that you, dependent on your sight, do not realise how many things are tangible. All palpable things are mobile or rigid, solid or liquid, big or small, warm or cold, and these qualities are variously modified. The coolness of a water-lily rounding into bloom is different from the coolness of an evening wind in summer, and different again from the coolness of the rain that soaks into the hearts of growing things and gives them life and body.

[…] Some months ago, in a newspaper which announced the publication of the *Matilda Ziegler Magazine for the Blind*, appeared the following paragraph:

> Many poems and stories must be omitted because they deal with sight. Allusion to moonbeams, rainbows, starlight, clouds, and beautiful scenery may not be printed, because they serve to emphasise the blind man's sense of his affliction.

That is to say, I may not talk about beautiful mansions and gardens because I am poor. I may not read about Paris and the West Indies because I cannot visit them in their territorial reality. I may not dream of heaven because it is possible that I may never go there. Yet a venturesome spirit impels me to use words of sight and sound whose meaning I can guess only from analogy and fancy. This hazardous game is half the delight, the frolic, of daily life. I glow as I read of splendors which the eye alone can survey. Allusions to moonbeams and clouds do not emphasise the sense of my affliction: they carry my soul beyond affliction's narrow actuality.

Critics delight to tell us what we cannot do. They assume that blindness and deafness sever us completely from the things which the seeing and the hearing enjoy, and hence they assert we have no moral right to talk about beauty, the skies, mountains, the song of birds, and colours. They declare that the very sensations we have from the sense of touch are 'vicarious', as though our friends felt the sun for us! They deny a priori what they have not seen and I have felt. Some brave doubters have gone so far even as to deny my existence. In order, therefore, that I may know that I exist, I resort to Descartes' method: 'I think, therefore I am.' Thus I am metaphysically established, and I throw upon the doubters the burden of proving my non-existence. When we consider how little has been found out about the mind, is it not amazing that any one should presume to define what one can know or cannot know? I admit that there are innumerable marvels in the visible universe unguessed by me. Likewise, O confident critic, there are a myriad sensations perceived by me of which you do not dream.

Necessity gives to the eye a precious power of seeing, and in the same way it gives a precious power of feeling to the whole body. Sometimes it seems as if the very substance of my flesh were so many eyes looking out at will upon a world new created every day. The silence and darkness which are said to shut me in, open my door most hospitably to countless sensations that distract, inform, admonish, and amuse. With my three trusty guides, touch, smell, and taste, I make many excursions into the borderland of experience which is in sight of the city of Light. Nature accommodates itself to every man's necessity. If the eye is maimed, so that it does not see the beauteous face of day, the touch becomes more poignant and discriminating. Nature proceeds through practice to strengthen and augment the remaining senses. For this reason the blind often hear with greater ease and distinctness than other people. The sense of smell becomes almost a new faculty to penetrate the tangle and vagueness of things. Thus, according to an immutable law, the senses assist and reinforce one another. It is not for me to say whether we see best with the hand or the eye. I only know that the world I see with my fingers is alive, ruddy, and satisfying. Touch brings the blind many sweet certainties which our more fortunate fellows miss, because their sense of touch is uncultivated. When they look at things, they put their hands in their pockets. No doubt that is one reason why their knowledge is often so vague, inaccurate, and useless. It is probable, too, that our knowledge of phenomena beyond the reach of the hand is equally imperfect. But, at all events, we behold them through a golden mist of fantasy.

There is nothing, however, misty or uncertain about what we can touch. Through the sense of touch I know the faces of friends, the illimitable variety of straight and curved lines, all surfaces, the exuberance of the soil, the delicate shapes of flowers, the noble forms of trees, and the range of mighty winds. [...]

Helen Keller, extracts from *The World I Live In* (New York: The Century Co., 1910) 5–8, 38–43.

Amanda Baggs
In My Language//2007

The previous part of this video was in my native language. Many people have assumed that when I talked about this being my language that means that each part of the video must have a particular symbolic message within it designed for the human mind to interpret. But my language is not about designing words or even visual symbols for people to interpret. It is about being in a constant conversation with every aspect of my environment. Reacting physically to all parts of my surroundings. In this part of the video the water doesn't symbolise anything. I am just interacting with the water as the water interacts with me. Far from being purposeless, the way that I move is an ongoing response to what is around me. Ironically, the way that I move when responding to everything around me is described as 'being in a world of my own' whereas if I interact with a much more limited set of responses and only react to a much more limited part of my surroundings people claim that I am 'opening up to true interaction with the world'. They judge my existence, awareness and personhood on which of a tiny and limited part of the world I appear to be reacting to. The way I naturally think and respond to things looks and feels so different from standard concepts or even visualisation that some people do not consider it thought at all, but it is a way of thinking in its own right. However the thinking of people like me is only taken seriously if we learn your language, no matter how we previously thought or interacted. As you heard I can sing along to what is around me. It is only when I type something in your language that you refer to me as having communication.

I smell things.
I listen to things.
I feel things.
I taste things.
I look at things.

It is not enough to look and listen and taste and smell and feel, I have to do those to the right things such as look at books and fail to do them to the wrong things or else people doubt that I am a thinking being and since their definition of thought defines their definition of personhood so ridiculously much they doubt that I am a real person as well. I would like to honestly know how many people if you met me on the street would believe I wrote this. I find it very interesting by the way that failure to learn your language is seen as a deficit but failure to learn my language is seen as so natural that people like me are officially described as mysterious and puzzling rather than anyone admitting that it is themselves who are confused not autistic people or other cognitively disabled people who are inherently confusing. We are even viewed as non-communicative if we don't speak the standard language but other people are not considered non-communicative if they are so oblivious to our own languages as to believe they don't exist. In the end I want you to know that this has not been intended as a voyeuristic freak show where you get to look at the bizarre workings of the autistic mind. It is meant as a strong statement on the existence and value of many different kinds of thinking and interaction in a world where how close you can appear to a specific one of them determines whether you are seen as a real person or an adult or an intelligent person. And in a world in which those determine whether you have any rights there are people being tortured, people dying because they are considered non-persons because their kind of thought is so unusual as to not be considered thought at all. Only when the many shapes of personhood are recognised will justice and human rights be possible.

Amanda Baggs, 'In My Language', transcription from video (first published online 14 January 2007) (www.youtube.com/watch?v=JnylM1hI2jc).

Like desire, **language disrupts,** refuses to be contained within boundaries.

bell hooks, 'Teaching New Worlds/New Words', 1994

DECOLONISING LANGUAGE

Frantz Fanon
The Negro and Language//1952

I ascribe a basic importance to the phenomenon of language. That is why I find it necessary to begin with this subject, which should provide us with one of the elements in the coloured man's comprehension of the dimension of *the other*. For it is implicit that to speak is to exist absolutely for the other.

The black man has two dimensions. One with his fellows, the other with the white man. A Negro behaves differently with a white man and with another Negro. That this self-division is a direct result of colonialist subjugation is beyond question.... No one would dream of doubting that its major artery is fed from the heart of those various theories that have tried to prove that the Negro is a stage in the slow evolution of monkey into man. Here is objective evidence that expresses reality.

But when one has taken cognisance of this situation, when one has understood it, one considers the job completed. How can one then be deaf to that voice rolling down the stages of history: 'What matters is not to know the world but to change it.'[1]

This matters appallingly in our lifetime.

To speak means to be in a position to use a certain syntax, to grasp the morphology of this or that language, but it means above all to assume a culture, to support the weight of a civilisation. Since the situation is not one-way only, the statement of it should reflect the fact. Here the reader is asked to concede certain points that, however unacceptable they may seem in the beginning, will find the measure of their validity in the facts. The problem that we confront in this chapter is this: the Negro of the Antilles will be proportionately whiter – that is, he will come closer to being a real human being – in direct ratio to his mastery of the French language. I am not unaware that this is one of man's attitudes face to face with Being. A man who has a language consequently possesses the world expressed and implied by that language. What we are getting at becomes plain: mastery of language affords remarkable power. Paul Valéry knew this, for he called language 'the god gone astray in the flesh.'[2]

[...] I want to show why the Negro of the Antilles, whoever he is, has always to face the problem of language. Furthermore, I will broaden the field of this description and through the Negro of the Antilles include every colonised man.

Every colonised people – in other words, every people in whose soul an inferiority complex has been created by the death and burial of its local cultural originality – finds itself face to face with the language of the civilising nation; that is, with the culture of the mother country. The colonised is elevated above his jungle status in proportion to his adoption of the mother country's cultural standards. He becomes whiter as he renounces his blackness, his jungle. In the French colonial army, and particularly in the Senegalese regiments, the black officers serve first of all as interpreters. They are used to convey the master's orders to their fellows, and they too enjoy a certain position of honour.

[...] In any group of young men in the Antilles, the one who expresses himself well, who has mastered the language, is inordinately feared; keep an eye on that one, he is almost white. In France one says, 'He talks like a book.' In Martinique, 'He talks like a white man.'

1   [Ed. note: Evidently paraphrasing Karl Marx, Thesis 11 of the 'Theses on Feuerbach': 'philosophers
      have only *interpreted* the world, in various ways; the point is to *change* it.' Karl Marx, 'Theses on
      Feuerbach', in *The German Ideology,* ed. C.J. Arthur (London: Lawrence & Wishart, 1982) 121–123, 123.]
2   [Footnote 1 in source] Paul Valéry, *Charmes* (Paris: Gallimard, 1952).

Frantz Fanon, extracts from 'The Negro and Language' (1952), in *Black Skin White Masks* (London: Pluto Press, 2008) 8–9, 11.

James Baldwin
If Black English Isn't a Language, Then Tell Me, What Is?//1979

The argument concerning the use, or the status, or the reality, of black English is rooted in American history and has absolutely nothing to do with the question the argument supposes itself to be posing. The argument has nothing to do with language itself but with the role of language. Language, incontestably, reveals the speaker. Language, also, far more dubiously, is meant to define the other – and, in this case, the other is refusing to be defined by a language that has never been able to recognise him.

People evolve a language in order to describe and thus control their circumstances, or in order not to be submerged by a reality that they cannot articulate. (And, if they cannot articulate it, they *are* submerged.) A Frenchman living in Paris speaks a subtly and crucially different language from that of the man living in Marseilles; neither sounds very much like a man living in Quebec; and they would all have great difficulty in apprehending what the man from Guadeloupe, or Martinique, is saying, to say nothing of the man from Senegal –

although the 'common' language of all these areas is French. But each has paid, and is paying, a different price for this 'common' language, in which, as it turns out, they are not saying, and cannot be saying, the same things: They each have very different realities to articulate, or control.

What joins all languages, and all men, is the necessity to confront life, in order, not inconceivably, to outwit death: The price for this is the acceptance, and achievement, of one's temporal identity. So that, for example, though it is not taught in the schools (and this has the potential of becoming a political issue) the south of France still clings to its ancient and musical Provençal, which resists being described as a 'dialect'. And much of the tension in the Basque countries, and in Wales, is due to the Basque and Welsh determination not to allow their languages to be destroyed. This determination also feeds the flames in Ireland for [one of] many indignities the Irish have been forced to undergo at English hands is the English contempt for their language.

It goes without saying, then, that language is also a political instrument, means, and proof of power. It is the most vivid and crucial key to identify: It reveals the private identity, and connects one with, or divorces one from, the larger, public, or communal identity. There have been, and are, times, and places, when to speak a certain language could be dangerous, even fatal. Or, one may speak the same language, but in such a way that one's antecedents are revealed, or (one hopes) hidden. This is true in France, and is absolutely true in England: The range (and reign) of accents on that damp little island make England coherent for the English and totally incomprehensible for everyone else. To open your mouth in England is (if I may use black English) to 'put your business in the street': You have confessed your parents, your youth, your school, your salary, your self-esteem, and, alas, your future. [...]

Black English is the creation of the black diaspora. Blacks came to the United States chained to each other, but from different tribes: neither could speak the other's language. If two black people, at that bitter hour of the world's history, had been able to speak to each other, the institution of chattel slavery could never have lasted as long as it did. Subsequently, the slave was given, under the eye, and the gun, of his master, Congo Square, and the Bible – or in other words, and under these conditions, the slave began the formation of the black church, and it is within this unprecedented tabernacle that black English began to be formed. This was not, merely, as in the European example, the adoption of a foreign tongue, but an alchemy that transformed ancient elements into a new language: *a language comes into existence by means of brutal necessity, and the rules of the language are dictated by what the language must convey.*

There was a moment, in time, and in this place, when my brother, or my mother, or my father, or my sister, had to convey to me, for example, the danger in which I was standing from the white man standing just behind me, and to convey this with a speed, and in a language, that the white man could not possibly understand, and that, indeed, he cannot understand, until today. He cannot afford to understand it. This understanding would reveal to him too much about himself, and smash that mirror before which he has been frozen for so long.

Now, if this passion, this skill, this (to quote Toni Morrison) 'sheer intelligence', this incredible music, the mighty achievement of having brought a people utterly unknown to, or despised by 'history' – to have brought this people to their present, troubled, troubling, and unassailable and unanswerable place – if this absolutely unprecedented journey does not indicate that black English is a language, I am curious to know what definition of language is to be trusted.

A people at the centre of the Western world, and in the midst of so hostile a population, has not endured and transcended by means of what is patronisingly called a 'dialect'. We, the blacks, are in trouble, certainly, but we are not doomed, and we are not inarticulate because we are not compelled to defend a morality that we know to be a lie. [...]

James Baldwin, extracts from 'If Black English Isn't a Language, Then Tell Me, What Is?' (1979), *The Black Scholar: Journal of Black Studies and Research*, vol. 27, no. 1 (1997) 5–6.

Adrienne Rich
The Burning of Paper Instead of Children//1971

[...] this is the oppressor's language
yet I need it to talk to you [...]

Adrienne Rich, extract from 'The Burning of Paper Instead of Children' (1971), from *The Will to Change: Poems 1968-1970* (New York: W.W. Norton, 1971) 304.

bell hooks
Teaching New Worlds/New Words//1994

Like desire, language disrupts, refuses to be contained within boundaries. It speaks itself against our will, in words and thoughts that intrude, even violate the most private spaces of mind and body.

[...] Standard English is not the speech of exile. It is the language of conquest and domination; in the United States, it is the mask which hides the loss of so many tongues, all those sounds of diverse, native communities we will never hear, the speech of the Gullah, Yiddish, and so many other unremembered tongues.

Reflecting on Adrienne Rich's words, I know that it is not the English language that hurts me, but what the oppressors do with it, how they shape it to become a territory that limits and defines, how they make it a weapon that can shame, humiliate, colonise. [...]

An unbroken connection exists between the broken English of the displaced, enslaved African and the diverse black vernacular speech black folks use today. In both cases, the rupture of standard English enabled and enables rebellion and resistance. By transforming the oppressor's language, making a culture of resistance, black people created an intimate speech that could say far more than was permissible within the boundaries of standard English. [...]

In contemporary black popular culture, rap music has become one of the spaces where black vernacular speech is used in a manner that invites dominant mainstream culture to listen – to hear –and, to some extent, be transformed. However, one of the risks of this attempt at cultural translation is that it will trivialise black vernacular speech. When young white kids imitate this speech in ways that suggest it is the speech of those who are stupid or who are only interested in entertaining or being funny, then the subversive power of this speech is undermined. In academic circles, both in the sphere of teaching and that of writing, there has been little effort made to utilise black vernacular – or, for that matter, any language other than standard English. When I asked an ethnically diverse group of students in a course I was teaching on black women writers why we only heard standard English spoken in the classroom, they were momentarily rendered speechless. Though many of them were individuals for whom standard English was a second or third language, it had simply never occurred to them that it was possible to say something in another language, in another way. No wonder, then, that we continue to think, 'This is the oppressor's language yet I need it to talk to you.' [...]

Recent discussions of diversity and multiculturalism tend to downplay or ignore the question of language. Critical feminist writings focused on issues of difference and voice have made important theoretical interventions, calling for a recognition of the primacy of voices that are often silenced, censored or marginalised. This call for the acknowledgement and celebration of diverse voices, and consequently of diverse language and speech, necessarily disrupts the primacy of standard English. When advocates of feminism first spoke about the desire for diverse participation in women's movement, there was no discussion of language. It was simply assumed that standard English would remain the primary vehicle for the transmission of feminist thought. Now that the audience for feminist writing and speaking has become more diverse, it is evident that we must change conventional ways of thinking about language, creating spaces where diverse voices can speak in words other than English or in broken, vernacular speech. This means that at a lecture or even in a written work there will be fragments of speech that may or may not be accessible to every individual. Shifting how we think about language and how we use it necessarily alters how we know what we know. [...] I suggest that we may learn from spaces of silence as well as spaces of speech, that in the patient act of listening to another tongue we may subvert that culture of capitalist frenzy and consumption that demands all desire must be satisfied immediately, or we may disrupt that cultural imperialism that suggests one is worthy of being heard only if one speaks in standard English... .

To recognise that we touch one another in language seems particularly difficult in a society that would have us believe that there is no dignity in the experience of passion, that to feel deeply is to be inferior, for within the dualism of Western metaphysical thought, ideas are always more important than language. To heal the splitting of mind and body, we marginalised and oppressed people attempt to recover ourselves and our experiences in language. We seek to make a place for intimacy. Unable to find such a place in standard English, we create the ruptured, broken, unruly speech of the vernacular. When I need to say words that do more than simply mirror or address the dominant reality, I speak black vernacular. There, in that location, we make English do what we want it to do. We take the oppressor's language and turn it against itself. We make our words a counter-hegemonic speech, liberating ourselves in language.

bell hooks, extracts from 'Teaching New Worlds/New Words', in *Teaching to Transgress: Education as the Practice of Freedom* (New York: Routledge, 1994) 167, 168–70, 171, 173–4, 175.

Okwui Enwezor
Text, Subtext, Intertext: Painting, Language and Signifying in the Work of Glenn Ligon//2011

[...] It is important to situate [Ligon] in the context of artistic practices of the 1980s that were rife with politically charged language, such as the work of Richard Prince, Felix Gonzalez-Torres, Barbara Kruger, David Wojnarowicz and others. But while the minimalist and textual effects in the work of such artists largely operated by structuring conjunctions between object-text and image-sign relations through the use of photography and text, in painting Ligon's work opened up the semantic rules of identity and linguistic construction by virtue of its syntactical disposition towards subject-object relations based on the appropriation of language, sign, text and speech as material for his painting practice. In this way, his work can be understood on more discursive levels in the context of the conceptual and post-conceptual practices of African American artists such as Adrian Piper, Howardena Pindell, Lorna Simpson, Carrie Mae Weems and Jean-Michel Basquiat who, like him, were dealing with issues of identity construction in relation to race and gender, and employed text and figuration in their work throughout the 1980s and 1990s as the means to foreground those issues. Ligon's own artistic position, which was formally austere as well as conceptual and reflexive, operated in the discursive gap and intertextual relations conducted between his engagement with literary texts (specifically African American literature) and his reception of a post-structuralist theory of language. At its centre was the investigation of how social norms, through language, engage with structures of identity and identification, as well as modes of disidentification. [...]

The impact of the civil rights movement so completely transformed the American sociopolitical landscape that it would be a matter of extreme intellectual blindness not to notice the shifting historical differences in the linguistic emphases placed on African American identity as the ground of self-definition moved from one racial category to the next: from coloured to negro, black, Afro American and African American. The transformations in naming and the vitality of colour as a social trope measuring the evolution of the 'racial self' in African American identity thus appear in the textual content of Ligon's work and in that of many other African American artists as a matter of self-reflexive historical reckoning. The shifts and changes, slippages and elisions in structures of identity and identification insofar as blackness is concerned adumbrate the nature of race in artistic and literary representations that Ligon seriously takes up in his paintings. The oscillation between legibility and illegibility that forms a prominent feature of the stenciled texts on his canvases not only demonstrably imprints the futility of imaging blackness as a sign of universality, but also assumes it as part of the dialectic of the retinal condition of painting, one posed as an exchange between visuality and opacity, visibility and invisibility, presence and absence. In so doing, Ligon's painting brings to its mottled, coagulated surfaces the very issues involved in looking and seeing, reading and comprehending black formal language and its relationship to universality. In the majoritarian culture of whiteness, in which race becomes a barometer of value, for obvious reasons blackness becomes a value against which the primacy of whiteness as a literal and metaphorical universal sign of aesthetic value is defined and measured.[…] Instead, the work of Ligon and a number of his contemporaries recognise *blackness* as a trope of racialised communication, within whose iterative rendering both a formal relationship to art could be limned as well as a conceptual language for painting constituted. In the broken textural narratives that Ligon employs in his paintings (to powerful retinal and somatic effect), there is a kind of catechesis on the deformations of race and the defamiliarisation of racial identity in literary, linguistic and artistic production. If race is the language around which American social distinctions have been made decisive, blackness is the barbed word that constantly tears at the flesh of that language, which sets its teeth chattering in an endless flow of textualisation and narrativisation. At first glance, it would seem that Ligon's interrogation of the racialised construct of blackness is an *idée fixe*: otherness as social pathology. One reads his artistic inquiry into otherness as an unfolding discourse on the surface of the canvas or panel, worked out in smudgy, sticky, painted black text on white canvas ground. Yet in his use of transposition, citation, the written reference and the sententious, Ligon puzzles over the way that language not only shapes literary narratives but also projects social selves and cultural identity across the landscape of the American literary and artistic imagination.[1] Over the last twenty-five years, Ligon has produced a prodigious body of work across all media (painting, drawing, print, photography, sculpture and video) that deals formally and hermeneutically with the structure of language. However, in his linguistic appropriations, language is not fetishistically deployed only regarding how race is read or even visualised, but also regarding how it is perceived grammatically in writing as words on a page or as spoken word (as with the jarring word *nigger* that constantly recurs in Richard Pryor's comedy routines). In this sense, Ligon's work tends to reflect on the intertextual nature of the African American text within American literary discourse not as distinct but entangled historical traditions. Furthermore, what unites them rests on the adjudication of the status of the black subject, both as a literary figure and social subject. Beginning in 1988, Ligon's work involved the sustained use of stenciled text – usually a phrase, broken into a short focused sentence, a cluster of sentences, an excerpt transcribed from recorded spoken word – hand painted onto paper or onto primed canvas or panel. On one level, this body of work concerned the relationships, citations and references established between the sources of the texts (essays, novels, protest signs, art criticism, plays or invented narratives) and the formal parameters of their production and reception (in painting and print). At another level, the paintings encouraged an intertextual engagement: between text and image, reading and looking; between writing and language, literature and narrative, speaking and hearing, race and American identity. [...]

1   [Footnote 5 in source] Toni Morrison's influential book *Playing in the Dark: Whiteness and the Literary Imagination* (New York: W.W. Norton, 1992) is a powerful analysis of the way blackness is often constructed in American letters in the shadow of whiteness.

Okwui Enwezor, extracts from 'Text, Subtext, Intertext: Painting, Language, and Signifying in the Work of Glenn Ligon', in *Glenn Ligon America*, ed. Scott Rothkopf (New York: Whitney Museum of American Art, 2011) 51–8.

Susan Buck-Morss
The Gift of the Past//2011

[...] The production of knowledge without a patron has been described as apocalyptic in its historical implications.[1] In times of struggle between the guardians of power and the guardians of truth, historical evidence becomes a prophetic weapon. If the rulers claim the role of the restrainer (*katechon*) who holds apocalyptic disorder at bay, the prophets protest against the given order in the name of human happiness, social justice, or God's will.

History writing is the place of this struggle between the need to preserve the present order and the desire to preserve truth. But here is the irony. If the preserved past is entrusted with the task of bearing witness to truth, if the producers of meaning treat the artefacts of the transient, material world with a reverent care close to worship, then how is this painstaking effort to be reconciled with the fact that the past is never given to us whole?

Ephemeral Archives
That which survives in the archives does so by chance. Disappearance is the rule. Annihilation is the fate of whole cities, obliterating far more of the human record

than is preserved. Wars and disasters of nature are indifferent destroyers. Human intention is at work as well. Heresy, degeneracy, blasphemy, treason, disbelief – these are just some of the threats to orthodoxy that call for destruction of the historical record.

Texts and images are both vulnerable to attack. Precisely which objects are available from the past, whose written and visual sources are saved, is astoundingly arbitrary. Only a confirmed believer can be sanguine about their providential arrangement. Great libraries disappear. More than half a million manuscripts, both secular and religious, were produced, collected, and later lost at each of these imperial centres:

Library of Alexandria, founded in Ptolemaic Egypt, 3rd century BCE, disappeared by 5th century CE.

House of Wisdom in Baghdad under the Abbasid Caliphate, 9th–13th centuries.

Library of Córdoba under the Andalusian Umayyads, 9th–10th centuries.

House of Wisdom in Fustat (now Cairo) under the Fatimid Caliphate, 11th–12th centuries.

Europe was late to assemble a major collection (the Vatican Library held only 1,160 volumes when formally established in 1475), but intentional destruction was common. Two cases connected with religious and imperial expansion resulted in irretrievable loss:

The public burning of thousands of Arabic/Andalusian manuscripts by the Spanish Inquisition, Granada, 1499.

The obliteration of Maya sacred books by the Spanish bishop of colonial Yucatán, 1562, along with 5,000 'diabolical' cult images.

Wikipedia lists eighty-seven historical instances of book burning. But the act itself is not the issue. Historical contexts and consequences change. There is no direct continuity between past and present in these instances, at least not for the point being made.

We are concerned with the political connection between knowledge and power that leads to the partial and arbitrary silencing of the past, and here secular modernity has added something new.

If earlier, false belief was under attack, now the enemy takes on ethnic and racial tones. Modern states establish libraries and archives as guardians of the imagined national community, those who claim rights to the land by birth (*natio*). Patriotism appropriates the aura of religion. It purifies present acts of violence against perceived enemies, whose own past is first defiled, and then destroyed. Ethnic archives are obliterated. National libraries come under fire. Recent casualties include:

The Irish National Archives, containing one thousand years of historical documentation, destroyed in the civil war, 1922.

The Catalonian library founded by Pompeu Fabra, destroyed by Franco's troops, 1939.

The Judaica Collection at Birobidzhan, capital of the Soviet Jewish autonomous national zone, established as a socialist alternative to Zionism, destroyed in the anti-Semitic climate of Stalin's last years.

The Załuski Library, Warsaw, founded in the 18th century as one of Europe's first public libraries, destroyed in the burning of the city as punishment for Warsaw's anti-Nazi uprising, 1944.

The Jaffna Public Library in Tamil-dominated northern Sri Lanka, 97,000 volumes, including rare palm-leaf volumes, destroyed by Sinhalese paramilitary, 1981. Statues of Tamil cultural and religious figures were destroyed or defaced.

Bosnia's National and University Library in Sarajevo, shelled and burned by Bosnian Serb gunners in 1992. The library held 1.5 million volumes, including more than 155,000 rare books and manuscripts. The National Museum and Library of Iraq in central Baghdad, destroyed in the U.S. invasion of Iraq, 2003. Statues and other ancient artefacts were looted or destroyed.

There is a less violent, more common form of erasure. It is the practice of preserving only 'our' past that provides a continuous, linear trajectory for imagining 'our' future.

Archaeologists dig quickly through layers of history to find what is of interest to present power. Attention to mythic origins – the stuff of national legend that shores up the dominance of those who rule – dismisses the recent past as refuse. Its ground is a mere construction site for future growth. In the process, material evidence of crimes against living human beings is destroyed. Their records, declared of no value, disappear, and with them the possibility of imagining any community at all.

Excavating the earth in search of the cultural heritage of a particular people while bulldozing the counter-evidence poisons present consciousness by shrouding it in myth. One finds only what has already been determined to be there. 'For it is an irretrievable image of the past which threatens to disappear in any present that does not recognize itself as intended in that image.'[2] But go deeper into the historical evidence, below the level of official legend, and it becomes clear that 'our' past is not, and never has been, our own. Objects survive through trading hands. Books move and thrive in diaspora; scholarship flourishes through cosmopolitan exchange. Texts and artefacts follow the lines of pilgrimages, troops, and trade.

Empires monopolise knowledge through linguistic appropriation, supporting the Great Translation Movements that have marked the rise of their power. Ptolemy's astronomy, Galen's medicine, Plato and Aristotle's philosophy – all of these human achievements owe their survival to a series of imperial languages. This heritage of ancient Greece, lauded by Europe as its own, passed from Greek into Persian translations (under the Sassanids), into Arabic (under the Abbasids), and ultimately into Latin (in Toledo and Sicily), as the precondition for the European Renaissance. When vernaculars of Europe replaced Latin as the languages of power, translations became a strategy of intra-European imperial competition.

The last Great Translation Movement after Europe's decline is into English (the language of this text).

We face an uncomfortable fact: without empires, no cultural heritage. Without diasporas, no national past. […]

Benjamin speaks of 'smashing' the continuum of history. This process entails violence. He uses 'militant terminology' and 'terrorist metaphors' in order to blast apart the dominant historical narrative.[3]

The past ricochets off the present and scatters into enemy territory.

Historical fragments are the remains of an explosion.

Blasted free of official memory, the fragments of history are preserved in images. They retain the nearness of original experience, and with it, ambiguity. Their meaning is released only in a constellation with the present.

They harbour a warning. The gift of the past is a Trojan horse. One thinks one knows whence it comes and to whom it belongs. But the gift is to others, those the so-called rightful heirs are presently destroying.

There is nothing in human history that is foreign to us.

1   Jonathan Z. Smith, *Map Is Not Territory: Studies in the History of Religions* (Leiden: E. J. Brill, 1978) 81.

2   Walter Benjamin, 'On the Concept of History', in *Walter Benjamin: Selected Writings. Vol. 4, 1938–1940*, ed. Michael W Jennings, trans. Edmund Jephcott & Howard Eiland (Cambridge, MA: Harvard University Press, 2003) 389–400, 391.

3   Otto Karl Werckmeister, *Icons of the Left: Benjamin and Eisenstein, Picasso and Kafka after the Fall of Communism* (Chicago: University of Chicago Press, 1999) 24.

Susan Buck-Morss, extracts from 'The Gift of the Past', in *Emily Jacir & Susan Buck-Morss (dOCUMENTA (13): 100 Notizen – 100 Gedanken)* (Ostfildern: Hatje Cantz, 2011) 36–40, 42–3.

Hélio Oiticica
Tropicália//1968

Tropicália was born from the idea and conceptualisation of the 'New Objectivity', which I initiated in 1966. Completed in the beginning of '67, it was exhibited (as an environmental project) in April of '67. With the 'Theory of a New Objectivity', I wanted to establish and define a state of Brazilian avant-garde art, as distinguished from the major movements of world art (op and pop), and aiming at characterising a Brazilian state of art, or its related manifestations [...] In reality in order to arrive at an understanding of a what I want with 'New Objectivity' and *Tropicália*, it is indispensable to know and understand the meaning of *Parangolé* (something actually much more quickly understood by London critic Guy Brett when he wrote in *The Times of London* that the *Parangolé* is 'something never seen before', which may 'strongly influence European and American art', etc.). Yet *Tropicália* is where, from my point of view, the idea becomes completely objectified. The main *Penetrable*, which comprises this environmental project, was my most important experience with images, a sort of experimental image field. For this I created a tropical environment, as it were, with plants, parrots, sand, pebbles (in an interview with Mario Barata of *Jornal do Comércio*, May 21, 1967, I describe an experience which I consider important: it seemed to me, while walking about the environs and set of *Tropicália*, that I was going through the gullies and over the curves of the *morro*, which were organic, like the fantastic architecture of the slums; another life experience: I had the sensation of 'treading the earth' once again). Entering the main *Penetrable*, undergoing several tactile-sensorial experiences available to the participant who, through them, creates their imagistic meaning, one arrives at the end of the labyrinth, in the dark, where a TV set is permanently switched on: it is the image which then devours the participant, because it is more active than his sensorial activity. Actually, this *Penetrable* gave me the powerful sensation of being devoured (I described this in a personal letter to Guy Brett in July of 1967) – it is, in my opinion, the most anthropophagic work in Brazilian art. The problem of the image is posed here objectively – but, since it is universal, I also propose this problem in a context that is typically national, tropical and Brazilian. Ever since I invented the term *Tropicália* (a designation I made myself, long before others took it up and made it fashionable), I wanted to accentuate this new language with Brazilian elements, down to its smallest details, in an extremely ambitious attempt to create a language that would be ours, characteristic of us, that would stand up to the images of international pop and op, in which a good many of our artists were submerged. One could see this even in the 'New Objectivity' exhibition. I asked myself: why use the 'stars and stripes' elements of pop art, or dots and images from Lichtenstein and Warhol (serial repetition of figures, etc. – or, like the orthodox *paulistas*, 'op' illusionism (which, as a matter of fact, could have roots here, much more so than pop art, whose imagery is completely inadmissible among us). In reality, the exhibition 'New Objectivity' was almost entirely immersed in this 'pop' language, hybrid for us, despite the talent and strength of the artists involved. For this reason, I believe that *Tropicália,* which encompasses this entire series of propositions, came to contribute strongly to the objectification of a total 'Brazilian' image, resulting in the downfall of the universalist myth of Brazilian culture, which was a product of the European and North American mind, and based on an Aryanism which is inadmissible here. In reality, with *Tropicália* I wanted to create the 'myth' of miscegenation – we are Blacks, Indians, Whites, everything at the same time – our culture has nothing to do with the European, despite being, to this day, subjugated to it: only the Black and the Indian did not capitulate to it. Whoever is not aware of this is out. For the creation of a true Brazilian culture, distinctive and strong, expressive at least, this accursed European and American influence will have to be absorbed, anthropophagically, by the Black and Indian of our land, who are, in reality, the only significant ones, since most products of Brazilian art are hybrids, intellectualised to the extreme, empty of any meaning of their own. And now, what do we see? Bourgeois, sub-intellectuals, cretins of every kind, preaching 'Tropicalism', *Tropicália* (it's become fashionable!) – in short, transforming into an object of consumption something that they cannot quite identify. It is completely clear! Those who made 'stars and stripes' are now making their parrots and banana trees, etc., or are interested in slums, samba schools, outlaw anti-heroes ('Cara de Cavalo' has become à la mode), etc. Very well, but do not forget that there are elements here that his bourgeois voracity will never be able to consume: the direct life experience (*vivência*) element, which goes beyond the question of the image. Those who speak of 'Tropicalism' just pick up the image for consumption, ultra superficially, but the existential life experience escapes them, because they do not have it. Their culture is still universalistic, desperately in search of folklore, or, most of the time, not even that. I then came to the idea that for me is the main and fundamental consequence of my experiences with my previous formulations of *Parangolé,* 'New Objectivity' and *Tropicália*: this is the Supra-sensorial, which I presented at the Brasilia symposium organised by Frederico Morais in August of 1967. This formulation objectifies certain elements which are extremely difficult to absorb, almost impossible to consume, which, I hope, will set the record straight: it is the definitive overthrow of universality culture among us, of that intellectuality which predominates over creativity – it is the proposition of maximum individual liberty as the only way to defeat this structure of alienated domination and cultural consumption. [...]

Hélio Oiticica, extract from 'Tropicália' (1968), *Folha de São Paolo* (8 January 1984); reprinted in *Tropicália: A Revolution in Brazilian Culture 1967–1972*, ed. Carlos Basualdo (São Paolo: Cosac Naify, 2005) 239–41.

Gerardo Mosquera
Against Latin American Art//2010

[...] The Brazilian modernists created the metaphor of 'anthropophagy' in order to legitimate their critical, selective and metabolising appropriation of European artistic tendencies. This notion has been used extensively to characterise the paradoxical anti-colonial resistance of Latin American culture through its inclination to copy (only the Japanese beat us in this), as well as to allude to its relationship with the hegemonic West. The syncretic character of Latin American culture facilitates this operation, since the hegemonic cultural elements that are embraced are not completely alien, given Latin America's problematic relationship with the West and its centres. This relationship is founded on identity as well as difference, due to the specifics of the region's early colonial history, based on European settlement, the presence of important native populations that were subdued, massive slavery of Africans, creolisation and mixture. However, the metaphor goes beyond Latin America to point out a procedure characteristic of subaltern and postcolonial art in general.

Oswald de Andrade coined the term anthropophagy in 1928, not as a theoretical notion but as a provocative poetic manifesto.[1] Its emphasis in the subaltern subject's aggressiveness by means of appropriating dominant culture is extraordinary, as well as its bold negation of a conservative, lethargic idea of identity. Andrade even dared to affirm: 'It only interests me what is not mine', reversing the fundamentalist politics of authenticity.[2]

Contrary to Homi K. Bhabha's notion of 'mimicry', which outlines how colonialism imposes on the subordinate subjects an alien mask from which they negotiate their resistance amid ambivalence, anthropophagy supposes an attack: to voluntarily swallow the dominant culture to one's own benefit. We have to be aware that Latin American modernism built the notion already from a post-colonial situation. It also corresponded with the early international inclination in Brazilian culture, conditioned by the modernising impulse launched by a cultivated and cosmopolitan bourgeoisie.

Starting from its poetic beginning, the metaphor of anthropophagy has been developed further by Latin American critics as a key notion for the continent's cultural dynamics. On the one hand, it describes a tendency of Latin American culture since the initial days of European colonisation; on the other, it proposes a strategy for action. It has not only survived the pugnacious modernism of its origins: it has been impelled by post-structuralist and postmodern ideas regarding appropriation, resignifying and the validation of the copy, as we can see in the work of most influential critics and scholars during the 1980s and 1990s. The concept was even the subject of the memorable 24th São Paulo Biennial, curated by Paulo Herkenhoff in 1998.

An emphasis on the resistance and affirmation of subaltern subjects is also present in the term 'transculturation', coined by Fernando Ortiz in 1948 to point out the bilateral exchange implicit in any acculturation.[3] Although the active role of the recipient of external elements – who selects, adapts and renews them – had been indicated time ago by anthropology, the new term proposed by Ortiz introduced an ideological element. It emphasised the energy of the subaltern cultures even under extreme conditions, as in the case of the African slaves in Brazil, Cuba and Haiti. The term established a cultural reaffirmation of the dominated at the level of the word itself, as well as a cultural strategy.

In reality, all cultures are hybrid both in anthropologic and – as Bhabha has pointed out – linguistic-Lacanian terms, due to the lack of unity of their signs.[4] All cultures always feed from each other, and cultural appropriation is not a passive phenomenon. The receivers always remodel the elements they appropriate according to their own cultural patterns, thus these appropriations are often not 'correct'.[5] Receivers are usually interested in the productivity of the element seized toward their own ends, not the reproduction of its use in its original context. Such 'incorrections' are usually situated at the base of the cultural efficacy of appropriation, and frequently constitute a process of originality, understood as a new creation of meaning. [...]

Paradoxically, the appropriation paradigms, which are based on the incorporation of differences, underline the polar opposition between hegemonic and subordinate cultures. These days a dialogic relationship seems more plausible, in which the imposed language and culture are experienced as 'own/ alien', as Mikhail Bakhtin stated it in his discussion of literary polyglossia. Hegemonic cultural elements are not only imposed but are also assumed, reverting the schema of power through the apprehending of the instruments of domination, while ambivalently mutating the appropriating subject toward what it appropriates, together with its meanings and discourses.[6] In this way, for example, the syncretism in the Caribbean and Brazil of African deities with Catholic saints and virgins, practised by forcibly Christianised slaves, was not only a strategy to disguise the former behind the latter: it implied the installation of all of them at once in an inclusive, multilayered system.

The old Brazilian paradigm of anthropophagy and the cultural strategies of transculturation, appropriation and syncretism are increasingly being replaced by a new perspective that we could call the paradigm of 'from here'. Rather than appropriating and critically re-functionalising the imposed international culture, transforming it in their own behalf, the artists are actively making that metaculture firsthand, unfettered, from their own imagery and perspectives. They are doing so without manifestos or conscious agendas, just by creating fresh work, by introducing new issues and meanings derived from their diverse experiences, and by infiltrating their differences in broader, somewhat more truly globalised art circuits. This epistemological transformation at the heart of the artistic discourse consists in changing from an operation of creative incorporation to another of direct international construction from a variety of subjects, experiences and cultures.

In general, the work of many artists – rather than naming, describing, analysing, expressing or building contexts – is made from their personal, historical, cultural and social contexts in international terms. The context thus ceases to be a 'closed' locus, related to a reductive concept, in order to project itself as a space from which international culture is built naturally. This culture is not articulated in the manner of a mosaic of explicit differences engaging in a dialogue within a framework that gathers and projects them, but as a specific mode of recreating a set of codifications hegemonically established in the form of global metaculture. In other words, cultural globalisation tends to configure an international code multilaterally, not a multifaceted structure of differentiated cells. That codification acts as an 'English' that allows communication and that is forced, knocked about, and reinvented by a diversity of new subjects that gain access to international networks undergoing outright expansion. In a near sense, Charles Esche has mentioned a combination of sameness and non-self-conscious singularity in art today.[7] Many artists work, as Gilles Deleuze and Félix Guattari claimed regarding 'minor literature'/ 'finding his own point of underdevelopment, his own patois, his own third world, his own desert', within the 'major' language.[8]

Difference is increasingly constructed through specific plural modes of creating artistic texts within a set of international idioms and practices that are transformed in the process, and not by means of representing cultural or historical elements characteristic of particular contexts – it lies in action more than in representation. This inclination opens a different perspective that opposes the cliche of 'universal' art in the centres, derivative expressions in the peripheries, and the multiple, 'authentic' realm of 'otherness' in traditional culture. Obviously, the centre-periphery polarity has been strongly confronted in these porous times of migrations, communications, transcultural chemistries and re-articulations of power. [...]

Although art benefits from the rise of artists from all over the world who circulate internationally and exercise influence, on the other hand it is simplified, since artists have to express themselves in a *lingua franca* that has been hegemonically constructed and established. In addition, all *lingua franca,* before being a language of 'all' is a language of 'somebody', whose power has allowed them to impose it. This makes possible intercontextual communication, but at the same time it indirectly consolidates established structures, while the authority of the histories, values, poetics, methodologies and codes that constituted the language are incorporated. The active, diversified construction and re-invention of contemporary art and its international language by a multitude of subjects who operate from their different contexts, cultures, experiences, subjectivities and agendas, as pointed out above, supposes not only an appropriation of that language, but its transformation from divergences in the convergence. Hence, art language pluralises within itself, although it has been broadly instituted by mainstream orientations. This is crucial, because to control language and representation also entails the power to control meaning.[9] Of course, this dynamic takes place inside a porous strain between renovation and establishment, where the hegemonic structures show their weight. [...]

1   [Footnote 2 in source] Oswald de Andrade, 'Manifesto Antropofago', *Revista de Antropofagia*, year 1, no. 1 (São Paulo, May 1928).

2   [3] Oswald de Andrade, 'Manifesto Antropofego'.

3   [4] Fernando Ortiz, *Contrapunteo Cubano del Tabacoyei Azúcar*, Havana, 1940 (English edition New York: Alfred Knopf, 1947).

4   [5] Homi K. Bhabha , 'Guttural Diversity and Cultural Differences' (1988), in *The Post-Colonial Studies Reader,* eds. Bill Ashcroft, Gareth Griffiths and Helen Tiffin (London and New York: Routledge, 1997) 207–9.

5   [6] R.H. Lowie, *An Introduction to Cultural Anthropology,* New York, 1940; Boris Bernstein, 'Algunas consideraciones en relación con el problems "arte y etnos"', *Criterios,* Havana, no. 5-12 (January 1983–December 1984) 267.

6   [19] Mikhail M. Bakhtin, 'De la prehistoria de la palabra de la novela', *Problemas literariosy estéticos* (Havana: Editorial Arte y Literatura, 1986) 490-91. On all these issues see: Gerardo Mosquera, 'Global Islands', in *Créolité and Creolization, Documenta 11_Platform3,* eds. Okwui Enwezor, Carlos Basualdo, Ute Meta Bauer, Susanne Ghez, Sarat Maharaj, Mark Nash and Octavio Zaya (Ostfildern-Ruit: Hatje Cantz & Museum Fridericianum, 2003) 87-92; Ticio Escobar, *El mito del arte y el mito del pueblo* (Asuncion: Museo del Barro, 1987) 76.

7   [20] Charles Esche, 'Making Sameness', in Arjan van Helmond & Stani Michiels, *Jakarta Megalopolis, Horizontal and Vertical Observations* (Amsterdam, 2007) 27.

8   [21] Gilles Deleuze & Félix Guattari, 'What is a Minor Literature?', in *Out There. Marginalization and Contemporary Cultures,* eds. Russell Ferguson, Martha Gever, Trinh T. Minh-ha and Cornel West (New York/Cambridge, MA: The New Museum of Contemporary Art/MIT Press, 1990) 61.

9   [23] Jean Fisher & Gerardo Mosquera, 'Introduction', in *Over Here. International Perspectives on Art and Culture* (New York/Cambridge, MA: The New Museum of Contemporary Art/MIT Press, 1990) 5.

Gerardo Mosquera, extracts from 'Against Latin American Art', in *Contemporary Art in Latin America,* eds. Phoebe Adler, Tom Howells and Nikolaos Kotsopoulos (London: Black Dog, 2010) 12–14, 16–17.

Jean Fisher
Thinking Otherwise//2013

The survival of any self-organising system depends upon its ability to keep itself open to the flow of energy and matter through it.
– Gregory Cajete

If European anthropocentrism and subjectivism present a thoughtless mis-seeing of the world's 'undivided wholeness', leading to our alienation from it, then it behoves us to ask if Others have and can contribute to other ways of thinking and seeing – if only we could relinquish our arrogance and pay attention. Do the traditional *filiations* to the 'inanimate' and 'animate' of non-European indigenous peoples like the Kogi bespeak an entirely different way of thinking human-animal-ecoworld relations unimaginable to conventional Western metaphysics and knowledge systems?

There is now a vast literature on Native American worldviews, alas, more familiar to New Age fantasists than to philosophers. As Deloria explains: 'In the Native American worldview each entity was bound together in a system of reciprocal relationships which western ecologists only recently have come to call the web of life'. Indigenous thinking was all-inclusive weaving: reciprocity, respect and gratitude in the form of gifts received and given included the inanimate as well as the animate in a sustainable ecosystem. Deloria's 'big picture' of life, which included 'both real and non-physical things' like visions, meant that the Indian was not bound by the measurable, rationalist expectation of cause-and-effect, but, as Gregory Cajete, a professor in Native American Studies, says, by participating in the processes of chaos and creativity, which aligns indigenous thought to quantum/chaos theory. Daniel Wildcat – holding a similar position as Cajete – likewise notes, 'indigenous worldviews… do not relate and connect through simple cause-and-effect mechanisms. Instead they are understood through language and culture built on ancient observations of correspondences and juxtapositions of phenomenal events and situations. This prompts the tantalising question whether, like the Kogi's, the Northern American peoples' synthesis of ecological observation with contemplation and generational wisdom opened onto an 'implicate order' largely inaccessible to Western instrumental logic.

American Indian Thought is one of the first anthologies to address the specificity of Indian philosophy, and in Brian Yazzie Burkhart's essay we are given clear distinctions between Western and Indian epistemological thought processes, which I shall only crudely sum up through his challenge to Cartesian individualism: 'We are, therefore I am.' 'We' here is inclusive and non-hierarchical. As Steve Pavlik, who specialises in Native American Studies, says elsewhere:

> There was no separate or special creation that gave man dominion over other life, and the other animals and plants with which man coexisted with on the Earth were not created merely for his use or pleasure. All entities were equal to each other. Every individual entity – even those deemed as 'non-living' in terms of western thought – such as rivers, rocks, mountains and the sky, possessed its own individual life, spirit and soul, and purpose. Consequently every entity possessed its own inherent right to exist apart from the desires and needs of human beings.

That Western scholars and scientists have recently turned their attention to indigenous knowledge is little cause for celebration. In the first place, Deloria cautions us about how much knowledge was lost with cultural genocide, how much of the old wisdom has had to be reconstituted through discontinuities in generational oral transmission and, ironically, through the written and interpretative accounts of white ethnographers. And Pavlik, too, questions the extent to which Indian communities have retained indigenous thinking in the face of overwhelming external pressures.

More troubling is what philosopher of science Laurie Anne Whitt calls the 'biocolonialism' of indigenous knowledge, especially in the domains of spirituality, agriculture and medicine: the commodification, privatisation and commercialisation of the natural world and genetic life forms, including the USA's efforts to impose its Human Genome Diversity Project on indigenous peoples, despite the lack of clarity on the future 'applications' of this material. Needless to say, agricultural and pharmaceutical corporations do not offer indigenous peoples intellectual property rights on knowledge nurtured and developed over millennia.

However, despite annihilation and acculturation, enough indigenous knowledge survives to indicate that it presents ecospherical 'cosmopolitan' models of coexistence. Global interdependency now demands cooperation in economic and sociopolitical relations that include the biosphere; but this surely demands re-empowering the local, which is the place where we experience our lifeworld? While urbanist postcolonial studies have seldom attended to ecology, they have led to a re-examination of cosmopolitanism as the antithesis of neoliberal capitalist globalisation and ethno-nationalism. Revised thoughts on cosmopolitanism do not mean 'élite lifestyle choices', or 'globalism without attachments', but refer back to the Stoical view by which I introduced this text. Cultural theorist Kwame Anthony Appiah called cosmopolitanism an 'adventure and ideal', defining it as 'respect for difference with a respect for actual human beings'; meaning, a universalising of shared human values, needs and security, but not a homogenisation of ways of life. In sociologist Ulrich Beck's terms, cosmopolitanism is a practice that strives towards enabling everyone to make a contribution to world culture in their own language and symbols. These positions do not, however, take account of animal or indigenous lifeworlds. In contrast to neoliberal 'globalit' as well as most views on cosmopolitanism, we might attend to the scholarship of indigenous philosophers and understand how the indigenous maps the world through a cosmological all-inclusive perspective, following a contrapuntal spatiotemporality based on the dynamics of continuity and change, a trans-gressive and transformative rather than a now discredited pro-gressive (linear) modernity. [...]

Jean Fisher, extract from 'Thinking Otherwise: Cosmopolitanism Indigeneity and the Commons', in *Yes Naturally: How Art Saves the World* (Rotterdam: nai010 uitgevers, 2013) [footnotes omitted].

Moradewun Adejunmobi
Performance and Language Diversity in a Globalising World//2013

The events that precipitated a turning away from writing in English to writing in Gĩkũyũ for the Kenyan author, Ngũgĩ wa Thiong'o, are well known to most scholars of African literature and African performance. According to Ngũgĩ, the first steps were taken during his involvement in the writing and production of a play in a village called Kamĩrĩĩthũ on the outskirts of Nairobi in 1976. It seemed only natural that a play by and for residents of this village, comprising mainly peasants and some factory workers, should be in a local language. The experience and the events that followed had a transformative effect on Ngũgĩ, and from then on, he was to do virtually all his creative writing in Gĩkũyũ. Ngũgĩ himself acknowledges as much in his book, *Decolonising the Mind*, where he stated: 'It was Kamĩrĩĩthũ which forced me to turn to Gĩkũyũ, and hence into what for me amounted to an epistemological break with my past, particularly in the area of theatre.'[1]

And yet, what is often overlooked in the many commentaries that have since followed on Ngũgĩ's decision is the role of performance, and in this case, drama, on Ngũgĩ's transformative experience with his mother tongue. Most readers of *Decolonising the Mind* have rightly drawn conclusions for African creative writing rather than for African performance from the positions taken in this book. This is hardly surprising since the thrust of Ngũgĩ's argument in *Decolonising the Mind* serves to foreground the practice of schooling, the written text and literacy. *Decolonising the Mind* does indeed offer a polemic about the role of African languages in the contemporary world, but it is a polemic articulated specifically in relation to writing.

[...] On the larger question of preserving language diversity, and ensuring a public role for African languages among other marginalised languages in the contemporary world, it is the performed text working in tandem with the written text, rather than the written text by itself that will make a difference. Effective language diversity prevails where a variety of languages spoken within a community have a public role and presence. The more marginalised a language is with respect to the functions of government and bureaucracy in any community, the more likely it is that texts in the language become part of the public sphere mainly through performance. And in speaking of performance here, what I have in mind is verbal performance of speech forms that would correspond to texts as defined by Karin Barber rather than everyday speech acts that are not necessarily recognised as texts within the community where they occur.[2]

The concern with the place of indigenous languages in a globalising and often postcolonial world that we see in Ngũgĩ's work is part of a large and growing movement to protect the world's biocultural diversity, attracting the support of scholar/activists around the world. [...]

Language, Writing and Performance

I would contend that the main challenge facing marginalised languages around the world today is that of ensuring their continued contribution to the formation of a local public sphere. It is not enough, therefore, to ensure that languages are written if the written language has a minimal role in the formation of a local public sphere. Where the written vernacular becomes a major player in the local public sphere – as is happening, for example, with newspapers and news channels in the dominant indigenous languages in India – there is a greater likelihood that such languages will continue to be widely used.[3] By contrast, languages that no longer fulfil a public role in any community are likely to give way to languages that continue, or begin, to play critical roles in the public sphere. In situations where particular languages are marginalised in the bureaucratic order, it becomes ever more important for such languages to be deployed in the constitution of a public sphere. The production of written, and especially bureaucratic, texts in the threatened language is certainly one way of ensuring continued public relevance for the language. But where the language occupies a relatively minor position in the bureaucratic order, it will often be the oralised and performed text that endows the language with a continuing public presence. Significantly, audio visual technologies now make it possible to disseminate these oralised texts widely, especially where the context of broadcasting and dissemination is not solely commercial.

Working with interested parties in Kamĩrĩĩthũ in 1976-77, Ngũgĩ ended up writing a play in the Gĩkũyũ language, titled *Ngaahika Ndeenda*. However, it was the entire process of producing and performing this play, using members of the village community, that made this text a subject of public discourse. The written text was important, not so much as an end in itself, but to the extent that it set the stage for performance and public engagement with the text. The written text then became a record that one could refer to in explaining the significance of the performance. The Moi government's decision in 1977 to prevent further circulation of *Ngaahika Ndeenda* by withdrawing the licence for public gathering in the Kamĩrĩĩthũ Community Centre, and by prohibiting further public 'rehearsals' on the Nairobi University campus in 1982 seemed to have been prompted more by the performance of a text with a supposedly subversive message than by the written text alone.[4] Ngũgĩ's first novel in Gĩkũyũ, *Caitaani Mũtharabainĩ*, written while he was in prison, in 1977 underwent a similar process of oralisation. Ngũgĩ himself recounts how the novel was read aloud, not only within families for the benefit of illiterate family members, but also in bars where bar patrons were apparently willing to buy drinks for a willing reader.[5]

Writing is no doubt important for creating a certain kind of permanent record of texts in a given language, even and especially where a threatened language 'dies' off because there are fewer and fewer living speakers of the language. But the production of such written texts will not necessarily ensure the survival of the language if that language does not become a major and continuing contributor to the formation of public discourse in the society where it is spoken. If the movement of support for language diversity in the contemporary world aims to keep languages alive, and not simply to record their existence for posterity as they continue to disappear, then more attention has to be given to the possibility of using performance to position those languages in the public sphere. In various locations and at certain points in world history, as suggested by both Benedict Andersen and Jürgen Habermas, the entity of the public, and public discourse itself, has been shaped and largely constituted by written texts. But in an age experiencing space-time compression, and where newer audio-visual technologies make it possible to convene larger publics contemporaneously than is possible through writing, performance will surely play a more significant role in generating publics. Certainly among the Yoruba, and in many contemporary locations in and beyond Africa, performance remains the predominant means by which a public is constituted and public discourse is generated.

Furthermore, and as I have argued here, it is such performances that may ultimately ensure a continued public presence for many marginalised and threatened languages. Even where novels represent a diversity of speech types or a plurality of languages, as suggested by Bakhtin,[6] the written text will still not generate as significant a consciousness of belonging to a collective audience as the performed text, especially where electronically mediated forms of performance are available at reasonable cost. In other words, the novel will do less for the constitution of a public than performance where performances are accessible and widely distributed. It is important to underline here that these general observations apply particularly to performances associated with popular culture or with the political sphere and thus with dynamic and contemporary forms of a language, rather than with the conservation of traditional formulations performed in order to preserve a people's heritage. When Maffi refers to a 'right to orality',[7] for example, her concerns appear to bear mostly on the preservation of cultural heritage through traditional means of transmission. While I think it is critical to preserve heritage in this way, among others, I am focused more on keeping endangered languages as a dynamic part of an evolving and contemporary public sphere. [...]

1   Ngũgĩ wa Thiong'o, *Decolonising the Mind: The Politics of Writing in African Literature* (Portsmouth: Heinemann, 1986) 44.

2   Karin Barber, *The Anthropology of Texts, Persons and Publics: Oral and Written Culture in Africa and Beyond* (Cambridge: Cambridge University Press, 2007) 1–14.

3   [Footnote 22 in source] For further information on the growth of newspapers and news channels in Indigenous Indian languages, see Taberez Ahmed Neyazi, 'Cultural Imperialism or Vernacular Modernity Hindi Newspapers In A Globalising India', *Media, Culture & Society,* vol. 32, no. 6 (2010) 907–24.

4   [23] See Ngũgĩ, *Decolonizing the Mind*, 58–9, for an account of the Moi government's response to these performances.

5   [24] *Decolonizing the Mind,* op. cit., 83.

6   [25] Mikhail Bakhtin, *The Dialogic Imagination*, trans. Caryl Emerson & Michael Holquist (Austin, TX: University of Texas Press, 1981) 262.

7   [26] Maffi, 'Language, Knowledge and Indigenous Heritage Rights', 424.

Moradewun Adejunmobi, extracts from 'Performance and Language Diversity in a Globalising World', in *Performance, Politics and Activism,* eds. Peter Lichtenfels & John Rouse (Basingstoke and New York: Palgrave Macmillan, 2013) 17–18, 23–5.

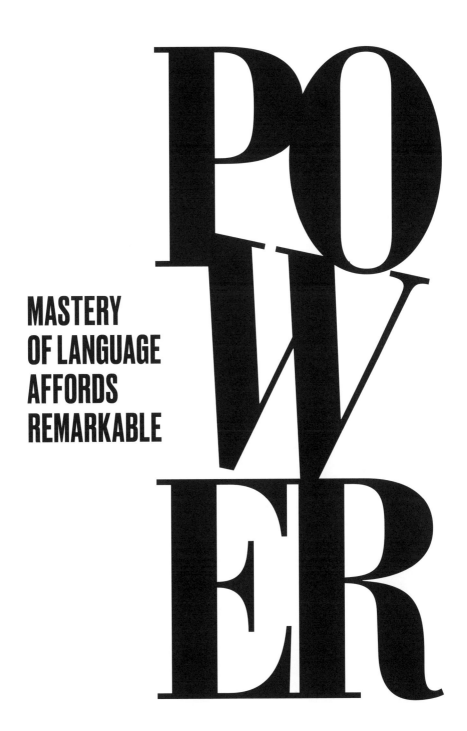

POWER

MASTERY
OF LANGUAGE
AFFORDS
REMARKABLE

Frantz Fanon, 'The Negro and Language', 1952

We lost
our home, which means
the familiarity of daily life.

We lost
our occupation, which means
the confidence that we are of
some use in this world.

We lost
our language, which means
the naturalness of reactions,
the simplicity of gestures, the
unaffected expression of feelings.

Hannah Arendt, 'We Refugees', 1943

DISPLACEMENT AND DIASPORA

Theresa Hak Kyung Cha
Dictee//2001

[...] Mother, you are eighteen years old. You were born in Yong Jung, Manchuria and this is where you now live. You are not Chinese. You are Korean. But your family moved here to escape the Japanese occupation. China is large. Larger than large. You tell me that the hearts of the people are measured by the size of the land. As large and as silent. You live in a village where the other Koreans live. Same as you. Refugees. Immigrants. Exiles. Farther away from the land that is not your own. Not your own any longer.

You did not want to see. You cannot see anymore. What they do. To the land and to the people. As long as the land is not your own. Until it will be again. Your father left and your mother left as the others. You suffer the knowledge of having to leave. Of having left. But your MAH-UHM, spirit has not left. Never shall have and never shall will. Not now. Not even now. It is burned into your ever-present memory. Memory less. Because it is not in the past. It cannot be. Not in the least of all pasts. It burns. Fire alight enflame.

Mother, you are a child still. At eighteen. More of a child since you are always ill. They have sheltered you from life. Still, you speak the tongue the mandatory language like the others. It is not your own. Even if it is not you know you must. You are Bi-lingual. You are Tri-lingual. The tongue that is forbidden is your own mother tongue. You speak in the dark. In the secret. The one that is yours. Your own. You speak very softly, you speak in a whisper. In the dark, in secret. Mother tongue is your refuge. It is being home. Being who you are. Truly. To speak makes you sad. Yearning. To utter each word is a privilege you risk by death. Not only for you but for all. All of you who are one, who by law tongue tied forbidden of tongue. You carry at centre the mark of the red above and the mark of blue below, heaven and earth, tai-geuk; t'ai-chi. It is the mark. The mark of belonging. Mark of cause. Mark of retrieval. By birth. By death. By blood.

[...] You write. You write you speak voices hidden masked you plant words to the moon you send word through the wind. Through the passing of seasons. By sky and by water the words are given birth given discretion. From one mouth to another, from one reading to the next the words are realised in their full meaning. The wind. The dawn or dusk the day earth and travelling birds south bound birds are mouth pieces wear the ghost veil for the seed of message. Correspondence. To scatter the words.

Theresa Hak Kyung Cha, extracts from *Dictee* (Berkeley: University of California Press, 2001) 45–6, 48.

Hannah Arendt
We Refugees//1943

[...] [W]e don't like to be called 'refugees'. We ourselves call each other 'newcomers' or 'immigrants'. [...]

Yes, we were 'immigrants' or 'newcomers' who had left our country because, one fine day, it no longer suited us to stay, or for purely economic reasons. We wanted to rebuild our lives, that was all. In order to rebuild one's life one has to be strong and an optimist. So we are very optimistic.

Our optimism, indeed, is admirable, even if we say so ourselves. The story of our struggle has finally become known. We lost our home, which means the familiarity of daily life. We lost our occupation, which means the confidence that we are of some use in this world. We lost our language, which means the naturalness of reactions, the simplicity of gestures, the unaffected expression of feelings. We left our relatives in the Polish ghettos and our best friends have been killed in concentration camps, and that means the rupture of our private lives.

Nevertheless, as soon as we were saved – and most of us had to be saved several times – we started our new lives and tried to follow as closely as possible all the good advice our saviours passed on to us. We were told to forget; and we forgot quicker than anybody ever could imagine. In a friendly way we were reminded that the new country would become a new home; and after four weeks in France or six weeks in America, we pretended to be Frenchmen or Americans. The more optimistic among us would even add that their whole former life had been passed in a kind of unconscious exile and only their new country now taught them what a home really looks like. It is true we sometimes raise objections when we are told to forget about our former work; and our former ideals are usually hard to throw over if our social standard is at stake. With the language, however, we find no difficulties: after a single year optimists are convinced they speak English as well as their mother tongue; and after two years they swear solemnly that they speak English better than any other language – their German is a language they hardly remember.

In order to forget more efficiently we rather avoid any allusion to concentration or internment camps we experienced in nearly all European countries – it might be interpreted as pessimism or lack of confidence in the new homeland. Besides, how often have we been told that nobody likes to listen to all that; hell is no longer a religious belief or a fantasy, but something as real as houses and stones and trees. Apparently nobody wants to know that contemporary history has created a new kind of human beings – the kind that are put in concentration camps by their foes and in internment camps by their friends.

Even among ourselves we don't speak about this past. Instead, we have found our own way of mastering an uncertain future. Since everybody plans and wishes and hopes, so do we. Apart from these general human attitudes, however, we try to clear up the future more scientifically. After so much bad luck we want a course as sure as a gun. Therefore, we leave the earth with all its uncertainties behind and we cast our eyes up to the sky. [...]

Our identity is changed so frequently that nobody can find out who we actually are. [...]

A man who wants to lose his self discovers, indeed, the possibilities of human existence, which are infinite, as infinite as is creation. But the recovering of a new personality is as difficult – and as hopeless – as a new creation of the world. Whatever we do, whatever we pretend to be, we reveal nothing but our insane desire to be changed, not to be Jews. All our activities are directed to attain this aim: we don't want to be refugees, since we don't want to be Jews; we pretend to be English-speaking people, since German-speaking immigrants of recent years are marked as Jews; we don't call ourselves stateless, since the majority of stateless people in the world are Jews; we are willing to become loyal Hottentots, only to hide the fact that we are Jews. We don't succeed and we can't succeed; under the cover of our 'optimism' you can easily detect the hopeless sadness of assimilationists.

With us from Germany the word 'assimilation' received a 'deep' philosophical meaning. You can hardly realise how serious we were about it. Assimilation did not mean the necessary adjustment to the country where we happened to be born and to the people whose language we happened to speak. We adjust in principle to everything and everybody. This attitude became quite clear to me once by the words of one of my compatriots who, apparently, knew how to express his feelings. Having just arrived in France, he founded one of these societies of adjustment in which German Jews asserted to each other that they were already Frenchmen. In his first speech he said: 'We have been good Germans in Germany and therefore we shall be good Frenchmen in France.' The public applauded enthusiastically and nobody laughed; we were happy to have learnt how to prove our loyalty. [...]

Hannah Arendt, extracts from 'We Refugees' (1943), in *Altogether Elsewhere: Writers on Exile*, ed. Marc Robinson (London: Faber & Faber, 1994) 110–13, 116–19. Available at www.documenta14.de/en/south/35_we_refugees

Irena Klepfisz
We Have Forgotten Speech//1986

And our tongues have become
dry   the wilderness has
dried out our tongues   and
we have forgotten speech.

Irena Klepfisz, from 'Di Rayze aheym/The Journey Home', in *The Tribe of Dina: A Jewish Women's Anthology*, eds. Melanie Kaye-Kantrowitz & Irena Klepfisz (Montpelier, VT: Sinister Wisdom Books, 1986) 49. Reprinted by permission of the author.

Shirin Neshat
Art in Exile//2010

The story I wanted to share with you today is my challenge as an Iranian artist, as an Iranian woman artist, as an Iranian woman artist living in exile. Well, it has its pluses and minuses. On the dark side, politics doesn't seem to escape people like me. Every Iranian artist, in one form or another, is political. Politics have defined our lives. If you're living in Iran, you're facing censorship, harassment, arrest, torture – at times, execution. If you're living outside like me, you're faced with life in exile – the pain of the longing and the separation from your loved ones and your family. Therefore, we don't find the moral, emotional, psychological and political space to distance ourselves from the reality of social responsibility.

Oddly enough, an artist such as myself finds herself also in the position of being the voice, the speaker of my people, even if I have, indeed, no access to my own country. Also, people like myself, we're fighting two battles on different grounds. We're being critical of the West, the perception of the West about our identity – about the image that is constructed about us, about our women, about our politics, about our religion. We are there to take pride and insist on respect. And at the same time, we're fighting another battle. That is our regime, our government – our atrocious government, [that] has done every crime in order to stay in power. Our artists are at risk. We are in a position of danger. We pose a threat to the order of the government.

But ironically, this situation has empowered all of us, because we are considered, as artists, central to the cultural, political, social discourse in Iran. We are there to inspire, to provoke, to mobilise, to bring hope to our people. We are the reporters of our people, and are communicators to the outside world. Art is our weapon. Culture is a form of resistance. I envy sometimes the artists of the West for their freedom of expression. For the fact that they can distance themselves from the question of politics. From the fact that they are only serving one audience, mainly the Western culture. But also, I worry about the West, because often in this country, in this Western world that we have, culture risks being a form of entertainment. Our people depend on our artists, and culture is beyond communication.

My journey as an artist started from a very, very personal place. I did not start to make social commentary about my country. The first one that you see in front of you is actually when I first returned to Iran after being separated for a good twelve years. It was after the Islamic Revolution of 1979. While I was absent [...] the Islamic Revolution had descended on Iran and had entirely transformed the country from Persian to the Islamic culture. I came mainly to be reunited with my family and to reconnect in a way that I found my place in the society. But instead, I found a country that was totally ideological and that I didn't recognise anymore. More so, I became very interested, as I was facing my own personal dilemmas and questions, I became immersed in the study of the Islamic Revolution – how, indeed, it had incredibly transformed the lives of Iranian women. I found the subject of Iranian women immensely interesting, in the way the women of Iran, historically, seemed to embody the political transformation. So in a way, by studying a woman, you can read the structure and the ideology of the country.

So I made a group of work that at once faced my own personal questions in life, and yet it brought my work into a larger discourse – the subject of martyrdom, the question of those who willingly stand in that intersection of love of God, faith, but [also] violence and crime and cruelty. For me, this became incredibly important. And yet, I had an unusual position toward this. I was an outsider who had come back to Iran to find my place, but I was not in a position to be critical of the government or the ideology of the Islamic Revolution. This changed slowly as I found my voice and I discovered things that I didn't know I would discover. So my art became slightly more critical. My knife became a little sharper. And I fell into a life in exile. I am a nomadic artist. I work in Morocco, in Turkey, in Mexico. I go everywhere to make believe it's Iran.

Now I am making films. Last year, I finished a film called *Women Without Men*. *Women Without Men* returns to history, but another part of our Iranian history. It goes to 1953 when American CIA exercised a coup and removed a democratically elected leader, Dr. Mossadegh. The book is written by an Iranian woman,

Shahrnush Parsipur. It's a magical realist novel. This book is banned, and she spent five years in prison. My obsession with this book, and the reason I made this into a film, is because it at once was addressing the question of being a female – traditionally, historically in Iran – and the question of four women who are all looking for an idea of change, freedom and democracy – while the country of Iran, equally, as if another character, also struggled for an idea of freedom and democracy and independence from the foreign interventions.

I made this film because I felt it's important for it to speak to the Westerners about our history as a country. That all of you seem to remember Iran after the Islamic Revolution. That Iran was once a secular society, and we had democracy, and this democracy was stolen from us by the American government, by the British government. This film also speaks to the Iranian people in asking them to return to their history and look at themselves before they were so Islamicised – in the way we looked, in the way we played music, in the way we had intellectual life. And most of all, in the way that we fought for democracy. […]

This film tried to find a balance between telling a political story, but also a feminine story. Being a visual artist, indeed, I am foremost interested to make art – to make art that transcends politics, religion, the question of feminism, and become an important, timeless, universal work of art. The challenge I have is how to do that. How to tell a political story but an allegorical story. How to move you with your emotions, but also make your mind work. These are some of the images and the characters of the film. Now comes the green movement – the summer of 2009, as my film is released – the uprising begins in the streets of Tehran.

What is unbelievably ironic is the period that we tried to depict in the film, the cry for democracy and social justice, repeats itself now again in Tehran. The green movement significantly inspired the world. It brought a lot of attention to all those Iranians who stand for basic human rights and struggle for democracy. What was most significant for me was, once again, the presence of the women. They're absolutely inspirational for me. If in the Islamic Revolution, the images of the woman portrayed were submissive and didn't have a voice, now we saw a new idea of feminism in the streets of Tehran – women who were educated, forward thinking, non-traditional, sexually open, fearless and seriously feminist. These women and those young men united Iranians across the world, inside and outside.

I then discovered why I take so much inspiration from Iranian women. That, under all circumstances, they have pushed the boundary. They have confronted the authority. They have broken every rule in the smallest and the biggest way. And once again, they proved themselves. I stand here to say that Iranian women have found a new voice, and their voice is giving me my voice. And it's a great honour to be an Iranian woman and an Iranian artist, even if I have to operate in the West only for now.

Stephen Morton
The Palestinian State of Emergency and the Art Practice of Emily Jacir//2013

[...] Jacir's photographic series *Where We Come From* (2003) was assembled through a collaborative process. For this project, Jacir asked several Palestinians living within or outside Israel and the occupied Palestinian territories the following question: 'If I could do anything for you, anywhere in Palestine, what would it be?' Among the responses Jacir received were requests to visit a grave in Jerusalem, to go to Haifa to play football with the first Palestinian child you meet in the street, and to visit someone's mother in Haifa. In this photographic series, produced between 2001 and 2003 the textual and photographic documentation of the artist's journeys across the various zones of the occupied West Bank and Gaza to perform particular requests for individual Palestinian residents was made possible in part by Jacir's American passport, which allowed her to travel relatively freely across the Occupied Palestinian territories, and by her intimate connections with Palestinian residents and family relations in the West Bank, who are denied that mobility. As Diane Enns has argued, the military occupation of Palestine has systematically destroyed 'all semblance of normal life through a complicated and extensive web of enforcements from passes, identity numbers, permits, routine interrogations, road blocks that require leaving home in the night to get to work, to surveillance and political assassinations'.[1] The conditions of life under the military occupation may recall Frantz Fanon's account of the compartmentalised world of the European colony in which the borders of the colonial world are policed by violence and the population are severely restricted in terms of their mobility and access to resources.[2] Indeed, Achille Mbembe has argued that Fanon's spatial reading of colonial occupation can help us to understand the Israeli military's regulation of air space, tunnels, bridges, as well as the use of bulldozing in infrastructural warfare in Gaza and the West Bank.[3]

It is against the backdrop of such spatial practices that Jacir's artwork needs to be understood. As in 'Memorial', Jacir in *Where We Come From* produces a political space that interrogates the territorial boundaries of Israel and the diffuse and dynamic geographical tactics of the military occupation. For it is both

Jacir's American citizenship and her relationship to Palestine as a member of the Palestinian diaspora that allows her to question the conflation of bodies and territory in the Occupied Palestinian Territories, and to compose another place from which to speak. [...]

Jacir's walks through the Occupied Palestinian Territories do not of course radically alter the political constituency of Palestine as it is currently defined under Israeli law, but they do ask questions which identify deterritorialising lines within the complex political assemblage of the Occupied Palestinian Territories. As Edward W. Said puts it in an essay on this installation, Jacir's compositions slip through the nets of bureaucracies and non-negotiable borders, time and space, in search not of grandiose dreams or clotted fantasies but rather of humdrum objects and simple gestures like visits, hugs, watering a tree, eating a meal – the kinds of things that maybe all Palestinians will be able to do someday, when they can trace their way home, peacefully and without restriction.[4]

Moreover, by representing the spaces from which the absent Palestinian subjects of the photograph are excluded, Jacir foregrounds the gap between a bounded concept of political representation that excludes Palestinians from the rights and freedoms afforded to the (Israeli) citizen and an unbounded concept of aesthetic representation that interrogates the foundations of such an exclusionary concept.[5] In so doing, Jacir uses the medium of the photograph to transform the grounds of what the Israeli art historian Ariella Azoulay has called an emergency claim. For Azoulay, emergency claims are 'produced on a daily basis in the face of disasters' and 'exist within a discursive framework within which the ruling power is [...] a powerful player'.[6]

In the context of Israel-Palestine, Azoulay argues that 'In most cases, the Palestinian is denied a direct addressing position, being instead effectively interwoven into the body of the dominant narrative that attempts to justify the occupation or into the terms of the leftist Zionist narrative that is opposed to the occupation, but views it merely as a temporary aberration that Israel has to eliminate.'[7] Against this incorporation of the Palestinian body into Israel's narratives of emergency, Jacir's photographs perform a subtle emergency claim that questions the territorialising lines underpinning the distinction between citizen and refugee in the political space of Israel/Palestine. [...]

1   [Footnote 15] Diane Enns, 'Bare Life and the Occupied Body', *Theory and Event*, vol. 7, no. 3 (2004) (http://muse.jhu.edu/journals/theory_and_event/v007/7.3enns.html).

2   [16] Frantz Fanon, *The Wretched of the Earth*, trans. Richard Philcox (New York: Grove Press, 2004).

3   [17] Achille Mbembe, 'Necropolitics', *Public Culture,* 15.1 (2003) 27–9.

4   [24] Edward W. Said, 'Emily Jacir - Where We Come From', *Emily Jacir Belongings: Arbeiten/ Works 1998-2003*, eds. Stella Rollig & Genoveva Rückert (Vienna: Folio Books, 2004) 49.

5   [25] For more on the relationship between photography and the exclusionary concept of citizenship, see Ariella Azoulay, *The Civil Contract of Photography*, trans. Rela Mazali & Ruvik Danieli (New York: Zone Books, 2008).

6   [26] Ibid., 198.

7   [27] Ibid., 200.

Stephen Morton, extracts from 'The Palestinian State of Emergency and the Art Practice of Emily Jacir', in *Performance, Politics and Activism*, eds. Peter Lichtenfels & John Rouse (Basingstoke and New York: Palgrave Macmillan, 2013) 171–2, 173–4.

IM International/Tania Bruguera
International Migrant Manifesto//2011

We have been called many names. Illegals. Aliens. Guest workers. Border crossers. Undesirables. Exiles. Criminals. Non-citizens. Terrorists. Thieves. Foreigners. Invaders. Undocumented.

Our voices converge on these principles:

1. We know that international connectivity is the reality that migrants have helped create, it is the place where we all reside. We understand that the quality of life of a person in a country is contingent on migrants' work. We identify as part of the engine of change.
2. We are all tied to more than one country. The multilaterally shaped phenomenon of migration cannot be solved unilaterally, or else it generates a vulnerable reality for migrants. Implementing universal rights is essential. The right to be included belongs to everyone.
3. We have the right to move and the right not to be forced to move. We demand the same privileges as corporations and the international elite, as they have the freedom to travel and to establish themselves wherever they choose. We are all worthy of opportunity and the chance to progress. We all have the right to a better life.
4. We believe that the only law deserving of our respect is an unprejudiced law, one that protects everyone, everywhere. No exclusions. No exceptions. We condemn the criminalisation of migrant lives.
5. We affirm that being a migrant does not mean belonging to a specific social class

nor carrying a particular legal status. To be a migrant means to be an explorer; it means movement, this is our shared condition. Solidarity is our wealth.

6. We acknowledge that individual people with inalienable rights are the true barometer of civilisation. We identify with the victories of the abolition of slavery, the civil rights movement, the advancement of women's rights and the rising achievements of the LGBTQ community. It is our urgent responsibility and our historical duty to make the rights of migrants the next triumph in the quest for human dignity. It is inevitable that the poor treatment of migrants today will be our dishonour tomorrow.

7. We assert the value of the human experience and the intellectual capacity that migrants bring with them as greatly as any labour they provide. We call for the respect of the cultural, social, technical and political knowledge that migrants command.

8. We are convinced that the functionality of international borders should be re-imagined in the service of humanity.

9. We understand the need to revive the concept of the commons, of the earth as a space that everyone has the right to access and enjoy.

10. We witness how fear creates boundaries, how boundaries create hate and how hate only serves the oppressors. We understand that migrants and non-migrants are interconnected. When the rights of migrants are denied the rights of citizens are at risk.

Dignity has no nationality.

IM International, 'International Migrant Manifesto' (2011). This document was created in collaboration with immigration academics, activists, politicians and community members at a convening at the IM International headquarters in Corona, Queens on 4–5 November, 2011 (http://immigrant-movement. us/wp-content/uploads/2011/12/IM-International-Migrant-Manifesto2.pdf).

Paolo Bartoloni
Travelling Languages//2008

[...] What is language like in philosophical and literary exile? We would be mistaken to think that the language of solitude, the language of those who take flight into their singularity, equates with the idea of language, with pure language. It is rather a language that attempts a return to pure language (home) by retracing the footsteps of its departure from home. It does not matter which trajectories it follows on its return journey. Indeed, these routes might be different from those taken in the past, and yet memories of departure, of leaving, will invariably inform the return. This is a strange journey which changes everything and yet simultaneously preserves everything.

The journey I am writing about now must be understood as the sum of the journey forward, from pure language to language. and the journey backward, from language to pure language, and must be seen as the result of a lengthy process of relation, of exchanges, and of borrowing. The most obvious relations are those between pure language and language and among pure language, language, and the product generated by this relation, that is, potential language. A language that travels is always made of many languages since a language that really travels is always an open language, porous, inclusive, and willing to disappear into another language, from within which its very own singularity will resurface more fully. This is the case of translation, but also of the philosophical and literary language of exile. This travelling, as well as the process of translation, can be understood better if one keeps in mind Heidegger's understanding of translation as not so much a substitution of a word for another word (a replacement), as a transferral of a word, and a language into another language. Transferring – from the Latin *transferre* – means to take something from one place to another place. This has commonly been thought of as a mere act of substitution, in the process of which one language disappears to give place to another language (the latter replacing the former, literally annulling the former). Transferring, in contrast, is a process that brings about the simultaneous coexistence of two languages. One language enters another, is transferred into it, and, in doing so, replenishes both itself and the host language. What is less clear though, is why this process of fusion – some might term it confusion – ought to be replenishing and empowering. Would not the superimposition of two languages ultimately result in unintelligibility?

One thinks immediately of certain poetic experimentations of the avant-garde movements, in which different texts are superimposed on one another, and where a potentially readable text (written in a familiar language) is rendered illegible by scrawl (a potentially readable text written in a foreign, strange idiom). I am thinking here of the visual poetry of the 1970s, especially of Vincenzo Accame's 'Nuova scrittura' (c.1975). Today we are apt to treat these poetic experimentations as significant yet ephemeral provocations. We interpret them as necessary challenges mounted against the cultural establishment in order to open up new avenues, new ways of thinking and writing, alternative poetic modes. They are all this and perhaps no more, clever specimens of protest against a whole society and its canons. And yet – perhaps in spite of themselves – they also make us think of something else, of the clarity that might arise from opacity or, even more simply of an ontological condition which is inextricably linked with potentiality.

They are clearly jumbled-up texts, gratuitous games apparently intent on acts of pure vandalism and sabotage against the known (usual) language upon which mindless and undecipherable scribbles (a potential foreign tongue) are inscribed. Though they might appear to be innocent tricks, or perverse exercises, or even useless maps, they may also more perfidiously be conceived to disorient, distract, and frustrate the reader who is looking for points of orientation. What they principally lack is precision, order, clarity, identity; all of those categories so essential to our sense of security and comfort. These texts are certainly not closed or finished. They are suspended instead in an uncertain, ambiguous space which demands a resolution, an act of faith and courage, a productive leap that will turn them once and for all into clear, precise, and orderly texts.

Disorder and chaos are here the products of a conscious collage of two potentially clear and orderly idioms, and unintelligibility is the result of a peculiar combination of the intelligible. It is the superimposition of sayability that gives rise to the potential and to its very power to restore orientation and familiarity, but also to further suspend sayability in the zone of waiting and oblivion. The scribble can be removed, erased from the face of the familiar, but the familiar can also be removed to focus more clearly on the unknown. We must be mindful of the fact that the act of superimposition does not only occlude what is already known, it also precludes the full and unimpeded visibility of the unknown. The scribble defaces what lies underneath it (making it unreadable) but, by the same token, the writing underneath alters the perception of the scribble. The act of superimposition, because of its very nature of uncategorical and non-normative inclusion, introduces another language that speaks the unspeakable and that communicates the very negativity of language. It is not that translation and exile leave us without language, or identity, or clarity, or orientation. Rather, they leave us with a further language that can say what the other two cannot, that can expose and communicate their limitations.

In contrast to the poetic experiments of twentieth-century avant-garde movements, the relational language of exile and translation is the result of an uncategorical and non-normative process of combination. It might begin with the conscious desire to suspend or even to blur an existing textuality by writing on it a foreign language (mere scribble, or nonsensical sentences), and yet it ends up not as a programmatic manifesto or spectacular gesture of non-conformity and defiance but as a murmur of self-reflective disorientation, ambivalence, and uncertainty through which intense shaft of lights might appear from time to time. This language is uncategorical because it has no premeditated purpose apart from that of moving deep inside the relation that sustains it. The results of such non-normative movement vary greatly and can never be predicted, either polemically or programmatically. It is because of this that exile might be conceived of as the very stuff of productivity and the very core of thinking.

The exile (the translator among them) is first of all one who transfers. The task of transferring is not that of substituting one language with another language, one culture with another culture or one identity with another identity, but that of transferring one language into another language, one culture into another culture, and one identity into another identity. There is no sense in replacing because nothing can be replaced. Everything will remain, yet will be changed in its relation with the other. But how is it possible to write over a given language and subjectivity, a given identity, with a language that is not yet known? Is it enough to scribble at will and to cover the known with seemingly inane signs? Here the difference between the translator and the exile begins to emerge more vividly. While the translator moves from the foreign to the known, the exile moves from the known to the foreign. They engage with exactly opposite transferal vectors. Yet the process is similar, they both expose, open, break, and reduce to rubble what appeared to be complete and finished, and from the rubble they start rebuilding something which will nonetheless never again be complete. Translators inscribe their language on another language. In doing so, they make language 'catch fire' at the instant in which language exposes its limitations but also its great power as absolute guardian of the non-linguistic. In the process of exile, by contrast, it is language that gradually undoes itself by softening its norms, those great pretensions of grandeur and omnipotence, as it abandons the clamours of the familiar. Language's securities gradually dissipate in the presence of the unknown.

Paolo Bartoloni, extract from *On the Cultures of Exile, Translation and Writing* (West Lafayette, IN: Purdue University Press, 2008) 87–90.

Barby Asante
For Ama. For Aba. For Charlotte and Adjoa//2017

[...] 'Freedom is a constant struggle'
– Angela Yvonne Davis

We will declare ours too!

Independence

Autonomy over our bodies, our words, our histories

Our traces elevated to objects of ritual remembering

An archaeology of black memory, a memory practice, Sankofa

I speak in the tongues of my mother and my grandmother and my grandmothers before her

Although I do not know the words

My very being is the evidence of those languages

It is in these words I will speak

It is in these words that I will create

It is in these words that I will question

I question Diaspora as an ideal or narrative

As the distance between becomes more apparent as we get to 2nd, 3rd & 4th generations removed from 'motherlands'

So how do I map myself, my family, the people that left and arrived and continue to arrive, even though they make borders, make check points and build walls

The process of making

Is enacting my presence

The hard navigation of presences, absences, visibility, invisibility

Navigating/ finding routes, ROOTS

Arranging traces of memory from archives that will never be constituted

Entering spaces without invitation

Or spaces that have a antagonistic or conditional invitations

Time limited invitations

Invitations by special arrangement

Presence as a performance of a certain kind of sociability

That explains a connection, but keeps you outside, always arriving, never settled

The need becomes urgent

Utterances become words, sounds, whispers, shouts

The need to collect, assemble, activate the stories the narratives

Undo the knowledges, what is known

To make something visible

Drawing new maps from old.

Barby Asante, 'For Ama. For Aba. For Charlotte and Adjoa' (2017). Extract from a performance text for Dolph Projects, London (http://www.dolphprojects.com/2017/Barby%20Asante/index.html).

Yinka Shonibare
Yoruba: in Bed with Derrida//1997

At home [in Lagos] you would wear ... *ankara* [African-print cloth] so you change from school uniform to a more kind of relaxed 'African' type of clothing. My father would actually come back from work and get rid of the suits and [put on] *agbada* [the Yoruba wide-sleeved gown]... So I came to England to the boarding school, and subsequently to go to an art college. When I was at the art college, I remember, I was doing a series of works about... I think must have been about perestroika, which was a new kind of development in the Soviet Union at that time. And one of my tutors came up to me and said that 'Ooh it's all alright you're doing stuff about the Soviet Union, but it's not really you though, is it?' And I thought 'what is me? I'm a citizen of the world and I watch the news.' So I made work about those things, but anyhow so I thought, 'Okay, you want ethnic, I'll give you ethnic'... I kind of threw out all my canvases and I went to the Brixton Market, looking around as you do. And I started to think about the origins of *ankara*, African [wax print] fabric. And actually the fact is... that they originally come from Indonesia, and [were] then industrially produced in Manchester and also in Holland... so what to do: I decided that I wanted to challenge the idea of authenticity in arts... so the fabrics are for me a metaphor for something which is multicultural and essentially hybrid like my own identity... . Although I speak Yoruba very well, I think in English sometimes and it's rather strange, you know. You move from one way of thinking. Then you think in Yoruba; sometimes you think in English and you dream in English sometimes. It's that kind of existence that in a way my work tries to talk about... my work is actually not about the representation of politics but the politics of representation.

Yinka Shonibare, extract from 'Yoruba: in Bed with Derrida', a talk given at the conference 'Yoruba: Diasporas and Indentities', SOAS, University of London (November, 1997); reprinted in *Yinka Shonibare: Double Dutch* (Rotterdam/Vienna: NAi Publishers/Museum Boijmans Van Beuningen/ Kunsthalle Wien, 2004).

Sujata Bhatt
Search for My Tongue//1988

You ask me what I mean
by saying I have lost my tongue.
I ask you, what would you do
if you had two tongues in your mouth,
and lost the first one, the mother tongue,
and could not really know the other,
the foreign tongue.
You could not use them both together
even if you thought that way.
And if you lived in a place you had to
speak a foreign tongue,
your mother tongue would rot,
rot and die in your mouth
until you had to spit it out.
I thought I spit it out
but overnight while I dream,

munay hutoo kay aakhee jeebh aakhee bhasha
મને હતુ કે આખી જીભ આખી ભાષા મે થા
may thoonky nakhi chay
થૂકી નાખી છે
parantoo rattray svupnama mari bhasha pachi aavay chay
પરંતુ રાતે સૂવપ્નમાં મારી ભાષા પાછી આવે છે
foolnee jaim mari bhasha nmari jeebh
ફૂલની જેમ મારી ભાષા મારી જીભ
modhama kheelay chay
મોઢા મા ખીલે છે
fullnee jaim mari bhasha mari jeebh
ફૂલ ની જેમ મારી ભાષા મારી જેવી
modhama pakay chay
મોઢાં મા પાકે છે

it grows back, a stump of a shoot
grows longer, grows moist, grows strong veins,
it ties the other tongue in knots,

the bud opens, the bud opens in my mouth,
it pushes the other tongue aside.
Everytime I think I've forgotten,
I think I've lost the mother tongue,
it blossoms out of my mouth.

Sujata Bhatt, 'Search for My Tongue', in *Brunizem* (Manchester: Carcanet, 1988); reprinted in *Point No Point: Selected Poems* (Manchester: Carcanet, 2012) 32.

Herta Müller
The Space between Languages//2012

[...] Translation is an art in its own right. I wouldn't dare to translate, although I am fluent in Romanian. For translation doesn't mean just replacing, i.e., finding a familiar word in your own language to substitute for a word in a foreign language. The word has to match, which is much more difficult. A translator has to recreate the sound of the original. The art of translation is looking at words in order to see how those words see the world. Translation requires an inner urgency that will make that which is different as close to the original as possible. Finding this eye-to-eye contact is extremely difficult. It is a great art.

I learnt Romanian quite late in life, when I left my small village for the city at the age of fifteen to go to high school. However, it wasn't until some years later that Romanian became second nature. I was at university and working in a machine factory where I had to translate manuals for newly imported machines from German into Romanian without any idea of how they worked. I did it mechanically, word by word. But I also had to speak Romanian all day long because no one around me spoke any German.

Every time the same object moved from one language into another, a transformation occurred. It made me realise that your mother tongue comes to you without any effort on your part. It is a dowry that comes into your possession without you noticing. It is then judged by another language that has been added later and that comes from somewhere else. Your mother tongue feels as direct and unconditional as your own skin, and it is just as vulnerable if held in low esteem, treated with contempt, or even banned by others. Having grown up in a village speaking a dialect and learning standard German at high school, I found it difficult to find my bearings in the official Romanian spoken in the capital. For the first two years in the city it was easier for me to locate the right street in an unfamiliar part of town than the right word in the national language. Romanian was like pocket money. No sooner would I be tempted by something in a shop window than I would discover I was short of the money needed to buy it. There were so many words I did not know, and those that I did would not come as quickly as they were needed. Today, however, I know that this kind of inching along in another language, the hesitancy that forced me below my intellectual level, also gave me time to marvel at how objects were transformed by the Romanian language. I know that I am fortunate to have experienced this. A swallow suddenly appeared in a different light in Romanian, where it is called *rindunica*, 'sitting-in-a-row'. The bird's name suggests how swallows perch on a wire, close together in a row. I used to see them in my village every summer, before I knew the Romanian word. I was amazed that a swallow could have such a lovely name. I became more and more aware that the Romanian language had words that were more sensuous, more in tune with my perception, than my mother tongue. I would not now want to live without this string of transformations, in speech or in writing. There is not a single Romanian sentence in any of my books. But Romanian is always with me when I write because it has grown into my way of seeing the world.

It is from the space between languages that images emerge. Each sentence is a way of looking at things, crafted by its speakers in a very particular way. Each language sees the world differently, inventing its entire vocabulary from its own perspective and weaving it into the web of its grammar in its own way. Each language has different eyes sitting inside its words.

Another reason why I can't translate is my mistrust of language. When my best friend came to say goodbye the day before I went into exile – we embraced thinking we would never see each other again because I would never be allowed to return to Romania and she would never be able to leave the country – we couldn't bear to let go of each other. She walked out of the door three times and returned each time. Only after the third time did she leave me, walking straight down the street. I could see her pale jacket getting smaller and smaller and, in a strange way, brighter and brighter the more distant it became. I don't know if it was the winter sunshine of that February day, or the tears making my eyes glisten, or perhaps her jacket was made of some shiny fabric, but one thing I know for sure: as I watched her walk away her back glittered like a silver spoon. In this way, intuitively, I was able to put our parting into words. And that is also the best description of that moment. But what does a silver spoon have to do with a jacket? Nothing at all. Nor does it have anything to do with parting. Yet as a poetic image the spoon and the jacket need one another.

That is why I am mistrustful of language. I know from my own experience that to be accurate, language must always usurp something that doesn't belong to it. I keep asking myself what makes verbal images such thieves, why the most apt comparison appropriates qualities that don't belong to it. To get closer to reality we need to catch the imagination unawares. Only when one perception plunders another, when an object snatches material that belongs to another and starts to exploit it – only when things that in reality are mutually exclusive become plausible in a sentence can the sentence hold its own against reality.

I am happy when I succeed in doing that.

Herta Müller, extract from 'The Space between Languages', trans. Julia Sherwood, a speech given in Prague to honour Radka Denemarková (April, 2012). This translation was first published by Asymptote, an award-winning online journal of translation, and can be read alongside translations in ten other languages. Available at www.asymptotejournal.com/nonfiction/herta-muller-the-space-between-languages/

Danh Võ
Mother Tongue//2012

My father will write this letter repeatedly until he dies.

I like the idea that calligraphy can become an act of pure labour.

Traces of the Latin alphabet were found in an Egyptian copper mine that dates back approximately 4000 years. This discovery indicated that at the time, workers who were not able to decipher hieroglyphs invented a new phonetic writing form that was easy to read and use.

In the seventeenth century, Vietnamese was phonetically transcribed by Portuguese missionaries for evangelical purposes. During the French occupation in the early twentieth century, Vietnamese in Latin script became the official language. Since the system was phonetically transcribed and therefore easier for peasants to learn, the phonetic text was also propagated by the Vietnamese National Socialists; they saw it as a tool to combat illiteracy. Today, Vietnamese speakers have universally accepted this writing system, and only scholars have knowledge of the older, Chinese-influenced characters.

My father barely learned to speak, let alone write, Danish. All Western languages are alien to him.

Among the many things arranged on the desk where he transcribes the letter, there is a small Danish flag and an image of Pope John Paul II.

The postcards illustrated in this book depict paintings of the executions of missionaries trained by the Société des Missions Etrangères de Paris, an institution that continues to educate aspiring evangelicals and enlist them in missions abroad. Most French missionaries in the nineteenth century were sent to Asia, 200 years after the Portuguese set foot in the region. The seminary ordered these paintings from converted Vietnamese artisans.

The French missionary killings may have served as an excuse for France to colonise Vietnam in the mid nineteenth century. But the French also supported the English in The Second Opium War against China, for which they needed Vietnam's northern port. Fifty years later, the killings of Christians during the Boxer Rebellion would be used in a similarly political manner. I have many images of the Boxer Rebellion in mind, too.

I am baptised and was given my first communion and later something else, which I don't know the English term for and decided not to look it up.

In 1954, at the Geneva Convention, it was decided that Vietnam would be divided in two; Hồ Chí Minh ruled the Communist North, and the South was ruled by Ngô Đình Diệm, a Catholic Vietnamese supported by the US government. The division was supposed to be temporary but the proposed elections were cancelled by the US once it became obvious that a free election would result in a united Vietnam headed by Hồ Chí Minh.

I have seen film footage of old, wooden Tokyo burned to the ground.

At the first meetings in Potsdam after the Second World War, the US was against the former imperial powers regaining their colonies. The fact that Hồ Chí Minh partly copied his declaration of independence from America's is lost in our collective memory.

Could Diệm have unified Vietnam? It was during his regime that the international news circulated images of protesting monks burning themselves to death. In 1963, a coup d'état supported by the US ended with Diêm's body penetrated by bullets then stabbed repeatedly with a knife.

There is a portrait of Diệm hanging somewhere in my father's flat. He still believes that Diệm, had he lived, would have made things better.

My family has not always been Catholic. I am the second generation of Catholics. My father secretly converted from Confucianism to Catholicism as a protest against Diệm's assassination. Today, he is still a devout Catholic.

Over the past thirty years, I became familiar with my father's handwriting from all the signs and menus that he handwrote for the various small food stalls he owned in Denmark. I like that writing calligraphy can become no different from making a burger. I like the idea that calligraphy can become an act of pure labour.

I confess my brain was gang raped by Jean-Pierre Dardenne and his brother Luc's films. Rosetta and her phallic drive to secure a job (and therefore a place in society), is burned into my mind.

Lower-class immigrants have greater difficulty assimilating into society. My father barely learned to speak, let alone write, Danish. All Western languages are alien to him. When he writes these letters, he recognises the alphabet, but understands none of its contents.

I prefer to keep the price of the letter relatively inexpensive to ensure that my father will get to work a lot. People buy the letter and my father will post it to the new owner.

I think of it as the return of an amputated alphabet.

I think of it as the return of a set of useful sounds back to mere image, like hieroglyphs to the worker, in the copper mine approximately 4000 years ago.

My father will write this letter repeatedly until he dies. [...]

Danh Vō, extract from 'Mother Tongue', from *Phung Vō: 2 Février, 1861* (Bregenz/Cologne: Kunsthause Bregenz/Buchhandlung Walther König, 2012) 232–4.

Emily Jacir
Stazione//2009

Stazione is an intervention that will be situated on each of the *vaporetti* stops along the line #1. It will begin at the Lido stop, weave through the Grand Canal, and end at Piazzale Roma. I propose to translate the names of each *vaporetto* station along this route into Arabic and place these translations onto the stops next to their Italian counterparts, thereby creating a bilingual transportation route through the city.

Vaporetto #1 stops at every station along the Grand Canal where centuries of cross-cultural exchange between Venice and the Arab world is clearly visible in the architecture along its banks. The Arabic names inscribed onto the *vaporetti* stops will put them in direct dialogue with the architecture and urban design of the surrounding buildings, thereby linking with various elements of Venice's shared heritage with the Arab world.

Forms that migrated from the Arab world are evident everywhere in Venice. It is in the architecture of places such as the Doge's Palace, Torre dell'Orologio, the campanile of the Basilica of San Pietro Castello and Ca' d'Oro, to name a few. It is apparent in the work of the architects, mosaicists and sculptors who worked on St Mark (robbed from its burial place in Alexandria by two Venetian merchants in

829). Thousands of Arab artefacts and merchandise passed through San Marco and the Rialto. The science, medicine, cartography and philosophy of the Arab world arrived in Europe through Venice. The Venetians emulated manufacturing skills of the Arab world in leather bookbinding, metalworking and textiles. Venice inherited Arab expertise in glass making such as the glass-blowing blowpipe technique invented in Palestine. Printing houses in Venice kept the cultural survival of Abu al-Walid Muhammad ibn Rushd (Averroes) and Abu 'ali al-Husayn ibn 'Addalah ibn-Sina (Avicenna) translated and alive. The first Arabic type was printed in Venice in 1514 by Gregorio de Gregorii, when he published the 'Book of Hours' entitled *Kitab Salat al Sawa'l*, probably for export to the Christian Arab communities in Syria.[1] It was also in Venice that Alessandro Paganino printed the first mechanically printed Arabic Qur'an in the world in 1537–8.

The great industry of Venice was shipbuilding, which took place in the Arsenale, the largest and busiest shipyard in the world until the end of the seventeenth century. The origin of the word *arsenale* is unknown. Some believe that it is the corruption of the Arabic *Dar-al-sina* meaning 'house of manufacture'. It was Venetian ships, which provided transportation to Palestine and dominated the transport of pilgrims to the Holy Land, thus Venice fashioned itself as a 'station' on the sacred itinerary of the pilgrimage route to Jerusalem.[2] It was also Venetian ships, which exported the building materials to repair various holy sites in Palestine such as the Dome of the Holy Sepulchre in Jerusalem. The wood sent to Palestine by Philip the Good of Burgundy to repair the roof in the Church of the Nativity in Bethlehem languished for years in the Arsenale before embarking on Venetian ships.[3] In the Church of the Nativity the image of the *Incredulity of Saint Thomas* in the north transept might have travelled to Venice in the form of an illuminated manuscript, as it corresponds exactly to the figure composition in the representation of the same event in the west vault of the central dome of San Marco.[4] Artistic exchange may have taken place in the possible presence of a Venetian mosaicist in Bethlehem in the 1160s named Zan, who is said to have worked with the indigenous Christians on their traditional mosaic work in the church.[5] In current day Akka, Venezia Square in Khan al-Franji preserves the name and some of the location and structure of the Venetian *fondaco* that once stood there Venetian noblemen and merchants went east to learn Arabic, Farsi and Turkish (all of which used Arabic script at that time). As a result of both this and trade, numerous Arabic words were absorbed into the Venetian dialect. Words that infiltrated the language include *doana, tariffa, sofa, divan, damasco, fontego, zecca, gabella, trucimano* and *caravan*. A gold ducat was a *zecchino*, taken from the Arabic word *sikka*, or 'mint'. The origin of the word *gondola* is unknown, but is said to come from the Levant.

My project seeks to transform the cityscape of Venice into a contemporary dialogue with this rich history of cross-cultural fertilisation. Arabic has an estimated more than 246 million speakers worldwide today; it is the fifth most spoken language in the world, and the official language of twenty-two countries. Yet there are never Arabic translations in any of the tourist sites and attractions, even though there are translations in a myriad of languages such as French, German, Spanish, Polish and Japanese. Addressing this rendered invisibility, my project aims to remind visitors and citizens of Venice not only of its deep and varied cultural origins, exchanges and influences, but also of possible futures of exchange.

1. M. Krek, 'The Enigma of the First Arabic Book Printed from Movable Type', *Journal of Near Eastern Studies*, vol. 38, no. 3 (1979) 203–12.
2. Deborah Howard, *Venice and the East: the Impact of the Islamic World on Venetian Architecture 1100–1500* (New Haven: Yale University Press, 1993) 190–209.
3. Ibid.
4. Ibid.
5. Lucy-Ann Hunt, 'Art and Colonialism: The Mosaics of the Church of the Nativity of Bethlehem (1169) and the Problem of "Crusader" Art', *Dumbarton Oaks Papers*, no.45 (1991) 69–85.

Emily Jacir, 'Stazione', from *Palestine c/o Venice*, ed. Salwa Mikdadi (published in conjunction with the Palestine/Venice collateral event of the 53rd Art Exhibition – La Biennale di Venezia) (Beirut: Mind the Gap, 2009) 48.

Each
language
has
different
eyes
sitting
inside
its
words

Herta Müller, 'The Space between Languages', 2011

Language can escape

from its time period and from the constraints of society.

Wu Tsang, 'In Conversation with Diana d'Arenberg', 2016

CONSTRUCTING AND BECOMING

Gloria Anzaldúa
Linguistic Terrorism//1987

[...] *Deslenguadas. Somos los del español deficiente.* We are your linguistic nightmare, your linguistic aberration, your linguistic *mestisaje*, the subject of your *burla*. Because we speak with tongues of fire we are culturally crucified. Racially, culturally and linguistically *somos huérfanos* – we speak an orphan tongue.

Chicanas who grew up speaking Chicano Spanish have internalised the belief that we speak poor Spanish. It is illegitimate, a bastard language. And because we internalise how our language has been used against us by the dominant culture, we use our language differences against each other.

Chicana feminists often skirt around each other with suspicion and hesitation. For the longest time I couldn't figure it out. Then it dawned on me. To be close to another Chicana is like looking into the mirror. We are afraid of what we'll see there. *Pena*. Shame. Low estimation of self. In childhood we are told that our language is wrong. Repeated attacks on our native tongue diminish our sense of self. The attacks continue throughout our lives.

Chicanas feel uncomfortable talking in Spanish to Latinas, afraid of their censure. Their language was not outlawed in their countries. They had a whole lifetime of being immersed in their native tongue; generations, centuries in which Spanish was a first language, taught in school, heard on radio and TV, and read in the newspaper.

If a person, Chicana or Latina, has a low estimation of my native tongue, she also has a low estimation of me. Often with *mexicanas y latinas* we'll speak English as a neutral language. Even among Chicanas we tend to speak English at parties or conferences. Yet, at the same time, we're afraid the other will think we're *agringadas* because we don't speak Chicano Spanish. We oppress each other trying to out-Chicano each other, vying to be the 'real' Chicanas, to speak like Chicanos. There is no one Chicano language just as there is no one Chicano experience. A monolingual Chicana whose first language is English or Spanish is just as much a Chicana as one who speaks several variants of Spanish. A Chicana from Michigan or Chicago or Detroit is just as much a Chicana as one from the Southwest. Chicano Spanish is as diverse linguistically as it is regionally.

By the end of this century, Spanish speakers will comprise the biggest minority group in the US, a country where students in high schools and colleges are encouraged to take French classes because French is considered more 'cultured'.

But for a language to remain alive it must be used. By the end of this century English, and not Spanish, will be the mother tongue of most Chicanos and Latinos.

So, if you want to really hurt me, talk badly about my language. Ethnic identity is twin skin to linguistic identity – I am my language. Until I can take pride in my language, I cannot take pride in myself. Until I can accept as legitimate Chicano Texas Spanish, Tex-Mex and all the other languages I speak, I cannot accept the legitimacy of myself. Until I am free to write bilingually and to switch codes without having always to translate, while I still have to speak English or Spanish when I would rather speak Spanglish, and as long as I have to accommodate the English speakers rather than having them accommodate me, my tongue will be illegitimate.

I will no longer be made to feel ashamed of existing. I will have my voice: Indian, Spanish, white. I will have my serpent's tongue – my woman's voice, my sexual voice, my poet's voice I will overcome the tradition of silence. [...]

Gloria Anzaldúa, extract from *Borderlands/La Frontera: The New Mestiza* (San Francisco: Aunt Lute Books, 1987) 58–9 [footnotes omitted].

Arjun Appadurai
Patriotism and its Futures//1993

We need to think ourselves beyond the nation. This is not to suggest that thought alone will carry us beyond the nation or that the nation is largely a thought or an imagined thing. Rather, it is to suggest that the role of intellectual practices is to identify the current crisis of the nation and in identifying it to provide part of the apparatus of recognition for post-national social forms. [...]

The Form of the Transnation
The formula of hyphenation (as in Italian-Americans, Asian-Americans, and African-Americans) is reaching the point of saturation, and the right-hand side of the hyphen can barely contain the unruliness of the left-hand side. Even as the legitimacy of nation-states in their own territorial contexts is increasingly under threat, the idea of the nation flourishes transnationally. Safe from the depredations of their home states, diasporic communities become doubly loyal to their nations of origin and thus ambivalent about their loyalties to America. The politics of ethnic identity in the United States is inseparably linked to the

global spread of originally focal national identities. For every nation-state that has exported significant numbers of its populations to the United States as refugees, tourists, or students, there is now a delocalised transnation, which retains a special ideological link to a putative place of origin but is otherwise a thoroughly diasporic collectivity. No existing conception of Americanness can contain this large variety of transnations.

In this scenario, the hyphenated American might have to be twice hyphenated (Asian-American-Japanese or Native-American-Seneca or African-American-Jamaican or Hispanic-American-Bolivian) as diasporic identities stay mobile and grow more protean. Or perhaps the sides of the hyphen will have to be reversed, and we can become a federation of diasporas: American-Italians, American-Haitians, American-Irish, American-Africans. Dual citizenships might increase if the societies from which we came remain or become more open. We might recognise that diasporic diversity actually puts loyalty to a non-territorial transnation first, while recognising that there is a special American way to connect to these global host of global identities and diasporic loyalties. It might come to be seen as a model of how to arrange one territorial locus (among others) for a cross-hatching of diasporic communities. In this regard, the American problem resembles those of other wealthy industrial democracies (such as Sweden, Germany, Holland and France), all of which face the challenge of squaring Enlightenment universalisms and diasporic pluralism. [...]

Arjun Appadurai, extracts from 'Patriotism and its Futures', *Public Culture*, vol. 5, no. 3 (Spring 1993) 411, 424–5.

Dmitry Vilensky
The Insoluble Sediment of Translation//2009

I would argue that the focus on linguistic and cultural matters and the implicit assumptions of the nation as an abstract cultural space with borders that must be crossed or 'translated' in order to intervene in the ongoing narration of the nation, obscures the importance of contemporary economic processes. In doing so it obscures the materiality that stands behind the construction of the nation as an economy, land, history, sovereignty and language – critique should not essentialise these factors but draw them into materialist scrutiny.

Is hybridity a space of subversion? We should think about this question and try to answer it. This term is attractive because of the inherent instability associated with it – hybridity seems to offer a satisfyingly unstable and ambivalent alternative to the rigid concept of the nation. For many critics, conceptualisations of the mobile, marginal, contradictory and ambiguous are important, especially after a period where a growing number of Marxist and feminist scholars have invested great intellectual efforts in order to locate and shape the potentiality of its actual resistance.

The 'third space' of hybridity and the liminal spaces these discourses describe have been offered as new sites of hope. These liminal spaces are theorised as important positions in the tactical war against dominant hegemonies. In particular, they are conceptualised as key sites of intervention in narratives of race and nation and as the crossover spaces of a progressive and liberatory transnational culture. We should be open but cautious around these problems because they could lead us towards wrong directions wherein we can easily fetishise and overestimate the potentiality and progressiveness and even radical character of hybrid identity and overlook how today's hybrid identities of migrant and global diasporas may be a marker, not of potentiality of resistance to globalisation but, instead, of more often than not instrumentalised relations which are used for the task of developing a new stability deeply embedded in the new modes of global capitalist production not of just commodities, but of culture and the redefinition of rather conservative national paradigms.

Universal and Particular – the Search for a Revolutionary Subject

In history we are all familiar with a traditional dialectical opposition between national, local, particular, singular and universal. The whole history of culture and art has been devoted to resolving these oppositions and finding a new type of subject that could harmoniously embrace these oppositions and create a new synthesis.

But I would like first to question the current concept of hybrid subject positions in relation to the universal. We must admit that the old generic forms of radical subjects – such as proletariat as represented by mostly male industrial worker, are over – and its forms of organisation through the intervention of an external body – the revolutionary party – are finally saturated and the main issue is: who is going to play these role[s] in current history... The particular power of this subject was incorporated into the universality of the language that this subjectivity developed – this was the language of Marxism and the theory of historical materialism.

It is quite clear that if we are imagining the continuation of the struggle for emancipation, we should try to find a new subjectivity that could fulfil its role in the history... and we know that recently a few attempts have been made in this direction... Let's consider how Alain Badiou poses this problem:

The question of the political process is something that is, paradoxically, a generic identity.

It's the question of finding something that is, paradoxically, a generic identity, the identity of no-identity, the identity which is beyond all identities. In the *Manuscripts of 1844*, Marx writes that the very nature of the proletariat is to be generic. It's not an identity. It's something like an identity which is non-identity; it's humanity as such. That's why for Marx the liberation of the working class is liberation of humanity as such, because the working class is something generic and not a pure identity. Probably that function of the working class is saturated. We cannot substitute a mere collection of identities for the saturated generic identity of the working class. Marx's solution is a sort of miracle: you find the group which is also the generic group. It was an extraordinary invention. The history of this Marxist invention, in its concrete political determination, was not so much the history of the generic group, of the working class as such, but rather history of the representation of this generic group in a political organisation: it was the history of the party. The crisis now is the crisis of representation, and also the crisis of the idea of the generic group.

If the idea of the working class as a generic group is saturated, you have the choice of saying that there are only identities, and that the best hope is the revolt of some particular identity. Or you can say that we have to find something much more universal, much more generic. But probably without the representative generic group.[1]

There is a great temptation to confer upon the nomad, migrant, hybrid or displaced group of people such a generic role and claim one of these, based on Badiou's suggestion, as non-identities that possess a generic character. But can they really fulfil this role? It is perhaps worth a try, but if we make such a move then we definitely have to get rid of the discourse of identities regarding these group[s]… and we have to see them as humanity as such.

The Questions of Nation, Language and Translation

Vladimir Lenin once mentioned that there is not *one* national culture – that inside any national culture we must recognise at least two cultures – the cultures of oppressed and that of the rulers. For example, there is a culture in Latvia that derives from incredibly intense workers' revolutionary tradition (remember that Lenin's personal guards were Latvian *strelki* – an extremely well-respected military force during the Russian revolution) and there is also a culture of collaboration with the Nazis – the culture of Latvian nationalists, capitalist and local fascists.

This is why I would not accept a wholesale critique of national culture in a favour of hybridisation.

We should be very careful with the issue of language because the construction of national culture is a process of different translations and is always happening within the space of national languages. One can hardly imagine a process whereby one hybrid person would translate the process of hybridisation into hybrid language – there was an attempt to artificially construct the Esperanto language that was intended to overcome the local national borders and become a universal tool of communication but this failed.

So any translation is usually understood as a linguistic production. We translate from one language into another. That's how languages develop and become mature, subtler and attain their ability not to simply reflect the world, but to shape new personal experiences which in their turn become able to transform the world. Is it possible that the new media language and broken English that we all use can become our new Esperanto? I doubt it. For many reasons we must admit the hegemonic domination of this mode of communication, but it always takes place inside different national traditions. And if these particular national traditions are understood as the local traditions of emancipation then these were and still are the most important engine of alter-globalisation.

The Search for a Universal Identity

As many may know, the Russian revolution triggered wide-ranging discussions on relations of form and national content in art. A particularly intensive debate unfolded around Jewish culture. As a gesture of opposition to the Zionist project, which was oriented around the promise of a Holy land and holy language, one the largest groupings of Jewish socialists decided to promote the Yiddish language as the real language of the Jewish poor and one of the clearest examples in Europe of a so-called Creolised language – a language that appeared quite late after a long gestation within a diasporic situation.

It is interesting to observe how, in this debate, finally a sort of universal formula was developed – one which became famous as the basis of socialist realist cultural production – 'national in form, socialist in content'. I want to propose this as a still appealing formula for a radical way of constructing a new revolutionary culture that might overcome narrow conceptualisations of identity – it does not matter if it is hybrid or national, and it claims a high degree of universalism.

Perhaps it is an old fashioned position but what is at stake today is the necessity to recover a new horizon of universality. As we see, the universal is by default a 'hybrid' construction but as a true dialectician would say, it is based on the idea of the dialectical unity between one and many when the one is split not only into two but can organise the unity of the many. This is what was at stake after October Revolution – how one could combine both the national and the socialist. Or to translate it into contemporary situation – how do we organise the exchange between marginalised local struggles and a global plane of resistance when the whole survival of the planet demands transnational solidarity actions.

I would like to finish with a paradox. I was impressed by one of Sarat Maharaj's statements – that globalisation is a monster of ultra-rapid translations. And in the art world it seems we live under the constant celebration of this speed and easy access. But too often we ignore that the most important experiences are untranslatable and I would like to suggest that this fundamental untranslatability – 'the insoluble sediment' of any operation of translation – is one of the most exciting things about the world. This quality of life and human society is somehow related to this generic possibility of the universal which cannot be fully translated into the multiplicity of local identitarian experiences. This might be the last space of hope in resistance.

1   Alain Badiou, 'The Saturated Generic Identity of the Working Class' (2006) (https://chtodelat.org/
     b8-newspapers/12-59/the-saturated-generic-identity-of-the-working-class/)

Dmitri Vilensky, 'The Insoluble Sediment of Translation or Some Notes on the Critique of Hybridisation', an edited version of the public talk at the conference organised by the Latvian Centre of Contemporary Art, Riga (April, 2009).

Gilles Deleuze and Félix Guattari
What Is a Minor Literature?//1986

[...] The problem of expression is staked out by Kafka not in an abstract and universal fashion but in relation to those literatures that are considered minor, for example, the Jewish literature of Warsaw and Prague. A minor literature doesn't come from a minor language; it is rather that which a minority constructs within a major language. But the first characteristic of minor literature in any case is that in it language is affected with a high coefficient of deterritorialisation. In this sense, Kafka marks the impasse that bars access to writing for the Jews of Prague and turns their literature into something impossible – the impossibility of not writing, the impossibility of writing in German, the impossibility of writing otherwise.[1] The impossibility of not writing because national consciousness, uncertain or oppressed, necessarily exists by means of literature ('The literary struggle has its real justification at the highest possible levels'). The impossibility of writing other than in German is for the Prague Jews the feeling of an irreducible distance from their primitive Czech territoriality. And the impossibility of writing in German is the deterritoralisation of the German population itself, an oppressive minority that speaks a language cut off from the masses, like a 'paper language' or an artificial language; this is all the more true for the Jews who are simultaneously a part of this minority and excluded from it, like 'gypsies who have stolen a German child from its crib'. In short, Prague German is a deterritorialised language, appropriate for strange and minor uses. […]

The three characteristics of minor literature are the deterritorialisation of language, the connection of the individual to a political immediacy, and the collective assemblage of enunciation. We might as well say that minor no longer designates specific literatures but the revolutionary conditions for every literature within the heart of what is called great (or established) literature. Even he who has the misfortune of being born in the country of a great literature must write in its language, just as a Czech Jew writes in German, or an Ouzbekian writes in Russian. Writing like a dog digging a hole, a rat digging its burrow. And to do that, finding his own point of underdevelopment, his own *patois,* his own third world, his own desert. […]

How many people today live in a language that is not their own? Or no longer, or not yet, even know their own and know poorly the major language that they are forced to serve? This is the problem of immigrants, and especially of their children, the problem of minorities, the problem of a minor literature, but also a problem for all of us: how to tear a minor literature away from its own language, allowing it to challenge the language and making it follow a sober revolutionary path? How to become a nomad and an immigrant and a gypsy in relation to one's own language? […]

Wagenbach insists on this point: all these marks of the poverty of a language show up in Kafka but have been taken over by a creative utilisation for the purposes of a new sobriety, a new expressivity, a new flexibility, a new intensity.[2] 'Almost every word I write jars up against the next, I hear the consonants rub leadenly against each other and the vowels sing an accompaniment like Negroes in a minstrel show.'[3] *Language stops being representative in order to now move toward its extremities or its limits.* […]

Kafka's own situation: he is one of the few Jewish writers in Prague to understand and speak Czech (and this language will have a great importance in his relationship with Milena). German plays precisely the double role of vehicular and cultural language, with Goethe always on the horizon (Kafka also knows French, Italian, and probably a bit of English). He will not learn Hebrew until later. What is complicated is Kafka's relation to Yiddish; he sees it less as a sort of linguistic territoriality for the Jews than as a nomadic movement of deterritorialisation that reworks German language. [...]

1   See letter to Brod, Kafka, *Letters*, June 1921, 289, and commentaries in Wagenbach, *Franz Kafka*, 84.

2   [Footnote 17 in source] Wagenbach, Franz Kafka, 77–88 (especially 78, 81, 88).

3   [18] Kafka, *Diaries*, 15 December 1910, 33.

Gilles Deleuze and Félix Guattari, extracts from 'What Is a Minor Literature?', in *Kafka: Toward a Minor Literature*, trans. Dana Polan (Minneapolis: University of Minnesota Press, 1986) 16–17, 18, 20–21, 23, 25–27.

Meriç Algün
Ö (The Mutual Letter)//2011

abdomen abdomen
abdominal abdominal
abort abort
abrakadabra abrakadabra
absorbent absorbent
adenin adenin
adenit adenit
adenoid adenoid
adenom adenom
adrenalin adrenalin
aerosol aerosol
agoni agoni
agorafobi agorafobi
agronomi agronomi
ah ah aha aha
aids aids
akademi akademi
akne akne akonitin akonitin
akrobat akrobat
akrobatik akrobatik
akropol akropol

aktivist aktivist
aktris aktris
aktör aktör
akupunktur akupunktur
akustik akustik
akut akut
akvamarin akvamarin
alarm alarm
albino albino
albumin albumin
aldrin aldrin [...]

Meriç Algün, extract from Ö *(The Mutual Letter)*, 2011, offset print on paper, bound in booklets, each booklet 105 x 148 mm, 40 pages, endless copies, sound, c. 2 hours, loop. Courtesy of the artist.

Meriç Algün
In Conversation with Jacob Fabricius//2013

Jacob Fabricius You were born and raised in Turkey. For the last five years you have tried to become European – or should I say become legally accepted as an EU citizen? That process and your battle with the authorities has also been the subject of artworks. What has that process been like?

Meriç Algün I come from Istanbul – a quite particular place to grow up in. Its position, being divided by the Bosporus, having land both in Europe and Asia, makes the Istanbul people almost schizophrenic in a way. When you cross the bridge to go to work, it says: 'Welcome to Europe' and then you go back home again: 'Welcome to Asia'. You can never make up your mind as to where you belong; you end up always being in an in-between state.

This relationship has become even more complex for me over the past five years with me moving to Sweden, which sometimes feels like the antipode of where I come from. The different socio-political structures and cultural differences became more visible and I became more 'in-between' than ever.

Using the battle with the authorities in my work became a way of exemplifying this complex relationship. For instance, my latest work, *Becoming European* (2012), shows the ways and days I have resided within the EU over the past five years. I exist when I am in its territories and when I am outside of its borders I disappear. And this work stopped when I became an EU citizen. [...]

Fabricius The flaws, traps and difficulties that we sometimes experience with language (as Turkish and Danish we are both non native-English speakers) and the possible mistakes that this may involve often creates charming language/ linguistic nuances. Could you describe the work *Ö (The Mutual Letter)* (2011)?

Algün The language that dominated my life after I moved to Sweden was English. In the beginning, I was very enthusiastic about learning the Swedish language and adapting to life here, but after a while not learning the language almost became like a resistance and a way of maintaining that in-between position. However, Swedish isn't foreign to me; I understand many things even though I can't really speak it and after a while I could hear that there were a lot of words that were the same in Swedish and Turkish. So I did some very primitive research – I went through the entire Swedish dictionary whilst cross checking it with the Turkish dictionary, to find the words the two languages had in common. It took four months of daily labour and I found 1,270 words in total.

Not really useful words, mostly terms adapted from French or English, but the striking thing was that they not only meant the same thing but were also spelled the same.

Jacob Fabricius, extracts from 'Meriç Algün Ringborg', *ArtReview* (January–February 2013). Available at https://artreview.com/features/jan_feb_2013_feature_meri_algn_ringborg_interview/

Wu Tsang
In Conversation with Diana d'Arenberg//2016

Diana d'Arenberg Wu Tsang, you first came to China in 2005 to reconnect with your ethnic roots – your father was born in Chongqing. It was there that you came across the historical figures of Qiu Jin and Wu Zhiying. Tell me about this?

Wu Tsang In the museum there was this amazing story about Qiu Jin and her relationship with Wu Zhiying. At this point a lot of it is speculation, but I've done a lot of research. I think what is most inspiring to me, which I didn't expect ten years ago, is this iconic figure. The writing has been healing for me, working with the poetry. It makes me think a lot about how language can escape from its time period and from the constraints of society. It can allow us to express desire or ways of being. I am trying to create a language here to communicate with others.

d'Arenberg I really felt that you had a kinship with the two women, portrayed as they were with such sensitivity. But which of the two did you most relate to, Qiu Jin or Wu Zhiyang?

Tsang I gravitated more towards Wu Zhiying, she's my doppelganger, I can really relate to her more, because Qiu Jin is such a monolithic figure. She's an official communist hero, and a Chinese martyr... I became interested as well in the pop cultural imagination, all the many ways that people have represented her in theatre and comic books. Wu Zhiyang is this interesting figure because she's not really known. She's this obscure figure that you only really encounter in scholarship through her writings. At the time Qiu Jin was persecuted and executed; she was not known at all. She was basically a convicted felon and a nameless person. Wu Zhiyang played the role of not only burying her but becoming her biographer and mourning her, at the risk of her own life and reputation. That idea of how we create narratives and history began with Wu Zhiyang's own involvement of preserving and sharing Qiu Jin's story. Everything we know about her is mediated through Wu Zhiyang's telling of the story.

I love the folklore. I don't care how much is true.

d'Arenberg You travelled to China to do research and it's also where you came across the female *Wushu* group that you then used in your film. Why not just film in China, instead of Hong Kong? How does Hong Kong inform the film for you?

Tsang When I set out to do this project ten years ago, I never set out with Hong Kong in mind. But being here now has allowed me to see China from a very different perspective. People have a relationship with their Chinese identity here, yet its also completely different. It's very hybrid in a way that is very familiar to me and the way I grew up.

We filmed most of the film on a boat on Hong Kong harbour. My thinking on that was that I really wanted to create a world that was floating between different time periods: between the past and the present, but also between Hong Kong and China because I think being in Hong Kong has been a significant way for me to reflect on Chinese identity and nationalism and come at it from a critical perspective. Also, my father's family fled China in 1949 during the Communist Revolution. The first place my family went to was Hong Kong; I think Hong Kong has always been a place for people to go. This idea of a counter narrative or counter identity or stories, Hong Kong feels really appropriate to this project. And also the diversity of voices in the film, they're different people I've encountered during the making of the project who I invited to do translations with me. Everyone is coming from the queer community perspective, and all Hong Kong based.

I read the SCMP one day and they were talking about how the Communist Party [of China] is making it illegal to distort history, and I thought, 'Huh? What?' Because that's all I think history really is; it is a distortion. I was thinking about how being in Hong Kong there is this palpable anxiety about what's going to happen to the city in relation to mainland China: anxiety about censorship and freedom of speech and a way of life. There's a sense of antagonism, a sense of urgency and questioning about what's going to happen.

d'Arenberg You mentioned that the film is moving between different worlds, and that you yourself like to work between the different worlds of film and performance. In your work, there's this theme of different worlds: the afterworld alluded to with the coffin installation; the world of contemporary Hong Kong; and Qing Dynasty China. This creates identity slippages: the idea of being able to float between one world and another, of exploring different sides of one's identity. What is the importance of identity to your films and to your work as an artist in general?

Tsang It's definitely a word that I love and hate. Mostly I am so invested in it, and having possibilities rather than closing down who we are. When I started this project, I had a narrative in mind; it was going to be a story about two women who wanted to be together at a time when it was forbidden. But what I discovered was that it wasn't a big deal at all. At the turn of the century in China there were all kinds of female relationships and they weren't even private. They just had different ways of defining intimacy and desire. In that sense the identity categories that we have now just don't apply, and I found that to be inspiring. Qiu Jin for me in a sense is a trans figure – of course there's the surface thing; she dressed in men's clothing, carried a sword and had this persona of a male figure, like a knight – but in a deeper sense she really created a way of being that didn't exist at the time. There was no rulebook and no role model. It was just her and her friends, travelling independently as women and doing things that you just didn't do. Love was just one layer of their struggle to define themselves and exist in a time when it wasn't easy to be a woman. [...]

d'Arenberg This project has been a ten-year commitment – longer than any Hollywood marriage – and it's quite a part of your life. What is it about these two women that really inspired you to do this project? Is it a desire to do justice to Qiu Jin's story, to bring into the spotlight the marginalised and neglected parts of her history?

Tsang I'm just telling the stories that are important to me. I don't consider her to be marginal because it's central to me. I'm interested in how that word [marginal] operates in relation to identity, it presumes that there is a centre. She's a vessel. This idea of the martyr or the hero, or even the love story, that's a vessel. Who doesn't love a love story? Or a tragic love story. It provides a structure, a kind of formula to say a lot of other complex things.

I think a lot of my things use performance to get at something real, not fantasy. The play-acting becomes a way in which we unconsciously reveal ourselves. That's why the aspect of the community involvement and the creation of the content which led to the script, is not so much about telling a story as about creating a portrait of the world around me. She's a vessel enabling me to do that.

I feel very sensitive and aware of the fact that anything to do with queer identity, people tend to gravitate and focus on that, but if there's one thing I hope people take away... my interest and focus is really on language and how language defines what is and what's not possible: how we are bound by it, but also how we can escape through it or from it. And also, not to claim Qiu Jin as a queer person or queer hero, but really telling a story in parallel to her story. That's the only thing I really want to try to create a conversation about.

Wu Tsang, extracts from 'In Conversation with Diana d'Arenberg', *Ocula Magazine* (April 2016). Available at https://ocula.com/magazine/conversations/wu-tsang/#!

Kate Sutton
Taus Makhacheva//2016

Flanked by the Caucasus Mountains on the highest plateau in Dagestan, the village of Tsovkra-1 has parlayed the perils of its topography into a peculiar claim to fame: that every able-bodied member of its roughly four-hundred-person population can walk a tight-rope. While locals say that this skill was first developed simply as a way to traverse the region's slopes and crevices, tightrope walking is now considered an integral part of the republic's cultural heritage.

It is no wonder, then, that the artist Taus Makhacheva chose to site her recent piece, *Tightrope*, 2015, just outside Tsovkra-1. Filmed using drone-mounted cameras, the video opens with a low-slung shot of the titular wire, which spans an abyss between twin hilltops. Stationed on one summit is a simple black metal rack full of paintings and works on paper, standing on edge in a line that ascends according to height. The opposite crest is crowned with a cube-shaped shelving system composed of overlapping squares and rectangles made from the same black metal. When viewed from the side, the structure reads like a Mondrian grid, an alien element of geometric order within the rocky terrain. Over the course of seventy-three minutes, a tightrope walker methodically transports the artworks from the first hilltop to the second, eventually sliding each picture into its allotted place within the cube.

The work is an exercise in extreme art handling – but it is also more than that. At face value, *Tightrope* functions as a primer on the cultural history of Dagestan. The pictures used in the performance were copied from the collection of the P.S. Gamzatova Dagestan Museum of Fine Arts. Ideologically rooted in multiple museum-building initiatives from the turn of the century, the institution was only officially established in the late 1950s, after prodding from the Soviet Ministry of Culture, which helped pad the collection by redistributing holdings from collections in Moscow and Tbilisi, as well as from the local museum of arts and crafts. The institution mingles paintings from Dagestan-based masters alongside a condensed canon of Soviet staples, from Ivan Aivazovsky and Isaac Levitan to Aleksandra Ekster and Aleksandr Rodchenko. A separate collection presents nineteenth- century images of the Caucasus by Russian painters, who churned out romanticized depictions of the region's rugged landscape and tumultuous history to feed on the empire's hunger for exoticism. [...]

In the 60s, as part of Khrushchev's push to promote a unified population, nationally identified pavilions were replaced by showcases of Space Race–inspired technology. This willful erasure of cultural difference particularly affected the northern Caucasus, especially Dagestan, which, with more than thirty ethnicities among its three million inhabitants and fourteen officially recognised languages, is home to the most heterogeneous population in the Russian Federation. Despite enjoying relatively more autonomy in the post-Soviet era, today Dagestan's institutions must still compete for resources within the larger federal framework, where they are rarely prioritised. If *Tightrope* underscores the precariousness of this specific cultural heritage, then On the Benefits trotted that same legacy out like so many trophies on display, props to emphasize the greater accomplishment of the empire. But as the performers' bodies register different pressures in each piece – the tight-rope walker faces the unpredictability of the elements, while the threat to the human pyramid comes from within, as the entire structure could topple should any one of its components falter – these works, too, suggest that neither local tradition nor state-sponsored spectacle is as monolithic as it may seem. [...] In doing so, [Makhacheva] stakes her own claim to shaping cultural narratives – but she positions herself as narrator, not prop.

Kate Sutton, extracts from 'Taus Makhacheva', *Artforum* (February 2016) 218–21.

Alice Becker-Ho
The Language of Those Who Know//1994

Only with the creation of a new language did the criminals of the fifteenth century effectively organise an independent and unified practice. The term *argot* (brotherhood of rogues[1]), the name they gave to themselves, became fused later on with their language.

This language is not simply discreet and defensive. It theorises what is going to be done: it already is a project. It never talks for the sake of talking. For those who can understand this language, every aspect of it carries the permanent confirmation of their vision of the world. Slang is not just another specialised jargon, nor is it a language grafted on to conventional speech. It is precisely the manifestation, as I have shown in *L'Essence du Jargon*[2], of an outlook exclusive to the so-called dangerous classes. If indeed 'we speak as we judge, and we judge as we feel' (Alfredo Niceforo, *Le Génie de l'argot*, 1912), then the dangerous classes enjoy the superiority over ordinary people of having fashioned out of nothing a speech which is artificial but not arbitrary in form and in which the meaning of words is divorced from the sound and image commonly attached to meaning by those languages in current use. This is how the so-called dangerous classes put both themselves and their language *wise* [*affranchi*[3] in French]. The language of slang is essentially the enemy's vernacular *turned upside down*, then *disguised*. When speech ceases to be the individual exercise of resolve and intelligence, it becomes the blunt instrument of a higher power. Speech represents this power and is represented by it. Anyone then speaking this language comes to identify with it; they will talk the way it does. Thus it was only when they came into contact with those dangerous classes making their way out of the European old world that most American blacks stopped speaking the enemy's language that, along with slavery itself, they had been learning. Slang is the complete opposite of a language spoken by slaves: it is therefore alien to all forms of ideology. Authorities everywhere know this only too well, and go in fear of it.

Being the *true speech of those who know because they have 'understood'*, slang is also the only language *that names and defines itself*: it goes just as well by the names of *jobelin, argot, bigorne, cant, Jenish, javanais, pidgin, sabir* [ex Spanish *saber* (to know)], or *lingua franca, ladino, langue verte*, etc.[4] It is in short the sum total of every criminal argot[5] whose terms, linked to the 'special' skills of each 'corporation', came to accordingly to enrich the body of slang in general use, by proceeding in the same frame of mind.

'Slangs all resemble one another, for slang represents a unity of thought. It merely translates the same words.'[6] To talk slang is above all to be recognised by one's own kind: in Spain the term *Germanía* conveys this fraternity very precisely; moreover the Latin for brother, *germanus*, gives us the Spanish *hermano*. [...]

At that time *argot* held sway over the steep little streets of Montmartre. You picked it up fast from the street corner ballads that could well leave the listener with a hankering for military prison life and conferred on that sombre piece of slaughterhouse equipment known as the guillotine a kind of social poetry that was very nurture to some youths... It was for having lived in just such an unreal and sensual world, however, that the poet François Villon nearly consigned his worthless body to the gibbet. (Pierre Mac Orlan, *Villes*, 1927) [...]

For their part, having had 'the devil and long habit as their teachers'[7], nobody has had to grasp quicker than outlaws the danger of a language wielded by government and underwritten by its slaves. For my own part, *argot* is the only thing that has enabled me with any assurance to hit upon not only the etymologies but also the exact meaning of certain words derived from argot which have passed into everyday language in such numbers. To achieve this, all I had to do was proceed and think like the dangerous classes: with distrust and lucidity. If, as seems to be the case, a wholesale reform of slang is currently underway, it will re-emerge naturally from the process as the language of those who know: those wholly scornful and dismissive of the sham and confusion endemic to machine language. This should not be too much of a problem given these machines' obliviousness to reality and their frequent propensity to blow circuits overloaded with contradictory data. As for the specialists whose job it is to 'process' the latter, they will finish up the 'machine's cuckolds', in the same way that the executioner was at once called the 'Widow's cuckold'.

1   *ach* denotes brother in Hebrew and *guit*, rogue in Dutch – the latter derived from the German term *gauner*, itself a borrowing from the Hebrew *ganaw* [a thief].

2   Éditions Gallimard, 1994; reprinted in Alice Becker-Ho, *The Essence of Jargon,* trans. John McHale (New York: Autonomedia, 2014).

3   ex the French verb *affranchir* [to free, liberate]. *Un(e) affranchi(e):* a wiseguy.

4   The meaning of each of these words along with their etymologies can be found in my *L'Essence du Jargon.*

5   The history of these different forms of argot, as well as the impact they have had over time, will be the subject of a forthcoming book. [The book in question is *Du Jargon, héritier en bastardie* [Whoreson Jargon], éditions Gallimard, 2002.]

6   Alice Becker-Ho, *Les Princes du Jargon,* Gallimard, 1993; reprinted in *The Princes of Jargon: A Neglected Factor at the Origins of Dangerous Class Slang,* trans. John McHale (Lewiston: Mellen, 2004).

7   [Footnote 10 in source] Cervantes, *Exemplary Stories.*

Alice Becker-Ho, an edited extract from 'The Language of Those Who Know', *Digraphe*, no. 70 (September 1994), trans. John McHale (2001). Updated by the translator, 2019.

Sisters of Perpetual Indulgence
The Polari Bible//2015

[…] *And the rib, which the Duchess Gloria had lelled from homie, made she a palone, and brought her unto the homie.*[1]

1   [Editors' note: translation: 'And the rib which God had taken from man was made into a woman and brought to the man.']

Sisters of Perpetual Indulgence, extract from *The Polari Bible* (Seventh Edition) (Manchester: Larlou Press, 2015) 14. Available at www.polaribible.org/bible/bible.pdf

Paul Baker
Polari: The Lost Language of Gay Men//2002

Well hello ducky, it's bona to vada your dolly old eek again. Order
to your mother dear. Take the lattie on wheels did you? Fantabulosa!
Oh vada that cod omee-palone in the naff goolie lally drags. Vada
her gildy ogle fakes! Get dooey veruas! I've nanti dinarly!

The above paragraph is written in Polari – put simply, a secret language mainly used by gay men and lesbians, in London and other UK cities with an established gay subculture, in the first 70 or so years of the twentieth century. That definition is a generalisation, but it serves well enough for the time being.

Polari was popularised during the late 1960s when the BBC comedy radio programme 'Round the Horne' showcased a pair of camp, out-of-work actors called Julian and Sandy. These two unapologetic, in-your-face 'queens' used a version of the language which was just sophisticated enough to allow jokes that were high in gay content to get past the censors, and just simplistic enough so that the majority of listeners would be able to understand exactly what they meant. [...]

The phenomenon of Polari is an important part of British gay social history, and for that reason alone it is worth documenting. When languages die out, a way of describing the collective experiences and world-view of a group is potentially lost for ever. Even if nobody intends to use that language again, it is worth being recorded and studied, adding to our existing knowledge of humanity and history.

All languages offer a potentially unique perspective of a particular society or subculture [...]. What garnered my interest in Polari in the first place was the fact that the Julian and Sandy tapes made me laugh. Polari was, and still can be, a way of expressing humour – comedy that was often in the face of adversity. Polari is playful, quick and clever – a constantly evolving language of fast put-downs, ironic self-parody and theatrical exaggeration. The lexicographer, Eric Partridge, once referred to Polari as a 'Cinderella among languages', but I prefer to think of it as one of the Ugly Sisters: brash, funny and with all the best lines in the show. [...]

It is worth bearing in mind an important distinction when considering Polari (or any language variety). It can be viewed as an abstract language system, defined by its linguistic items,[1] but it can also be thought of in terms of language use, or rather, the social contexts, mores and motivations for using language. This is perhaps similar to Saussure's concepts of *langue* and *parole*, where *langue* refers to the 'language habits of all speakers of a language' and parole refers to 'the individual uses and variations we observe'.[2]

[…] [Polari] is a language variety that places a high value on words concerning social and sexual identity. More than two-thirds of the nouns in Polari are concerned with people: their identities, what they are wearing, and the various parts of their bodies. Other types of noun categories are also concerned with people or social structures: names for money, terms of address, terms for relationships between people, and names for places and food. Many of the non-abstract nouns are terms for everyday items used by people: *dog and bone* (telephone); *glossies* (magazines); *polari pipe* (telephone); *rattling cove* (taxi); and *vogue* (cigarette), whereas many of the abstract nouns are concerned with language: *billingsgate* (bad language): *cackle* (talk); *Jav* (word); *lingo* (language); *polari* (gay language); or *sex/sexuality*: *catever cartzo* (venereal disease); *cherry* (virginity); *colour of his eyes* (penis size); *lamor* (kiss); *randy comedown* (desire for sex after taking drugs); *remould* (sex-change); and *wedding night* (first time two men have sex).

The proliferation of words to do with people, body parts and clothing testifies to the importance of people and their appearance in the Polari-speaker's world.

1   R. A. Hudson, *Sociolinguistics* (Cambridge: Cambridge Textbooks in Linguistics, 1980) 24, and R. Wardhaugh, *An Introduction to Sociolinguistics* (Oxford: Blackwell Textbooks in Linguistics, 1986) 22.

2   R. Wardhaugh, *Investigating Language: Central Problems in Linguistics* (Oxford: Blackwell, 1993) 19.

Paul Baker, extracts from *Polari – The Lost Language of Gay Men* (London and New York: Routledge, 2002) 1, 2, 39, 61.

Wong Bing Hao
Territory: Universe (Translexical Opacity)//2019

In their chapbook, *Glaire* (2017), artist and writer Jamie Crewe digitally scanned scenes from the 1908 French play *Une leçon à la Salpêtrière*, written by André de Lorde, using OCR (optical character recognition) and subsequently subjected the identified characters to Google Translate. The result is a haphazard, often incoherent, text peppered with illegible combinations of letters and symbols. Post-translation, the play's protagonist, Claire, a 'hysteric', is seldom indicated by her correct name. She is arbitrarily interpellated as 'Clear', 'Clmre', and a variety of other incomprehensible symbols. The translation process also confuses her gender, identifying her by all manner of gender pronouns – some known to us, others not yet. Her speech also becomes contorted and illogical. Crewe's translations ironically shore up Claire's (allegedly) schizophrenic subjectivity.

Likewise, in a sketch they did for the chapbook, Crewe 'graffitied' in crimson ink an illustration of Rachilde's *Monsieur Vénus*, another text that they have investigated thoroughly for the exhibition, 'Female Executioner', at Gasworks, London in 2017. Dripping blood-red, Crewe's textual annotations on the pained figures detail the discomfiting side effects (lumps, mood swings, general aches) of taking oestradiol, an oestrogen steroid hormone. In Crewe's illustration, text on transness seems to excrete in excess from the abjected body.

Through seemingly degenerative artistic gestures, Crewe's practice births other worlds of meaning, suggesting new languages, embodiments, and paradigms of gender to spectators and readers. Here, incoherence, gore, and unknowability signal infinite possibilities rather than failure or inaptitude.

Through deliberately unpredictable (mis)translations, Crewe sabotages determinacy and teleology. They deftly unravel the false sense of security inherent in our current linguistic and textual vocabularies, showing that they can (and should) indeed move beyond any fixed worldview or scope of intent.

At the heart of Crewe's inquiry into text and its forms is gender. In another recent text-based work, Terms (2018), shown at Tramway, Glasgow, Crewe lays out, with no uncertainty and admirable fortitude, rules and regulations for how to treat them as a trans person. 'I AM NOT A MAN', the text announces its arrival fiercely, unequivocally. As its title suggests, this work is direct, contractual, and austere in its demands for its maker's ontological autonomy and legitimacy. It is necessarily and ordinately harsh, unburdening from trans people the responsibility and risk of revelation while granting them infernal agency. In Crewe's thoughtful work, text and subjectivity, intertwined, propose alternate registers, spacetimes, and dimensions of value, vascularising their spectators' understanding and interpretations of gender.

It is not demanding to demand proper gendered pronouns. Contrary to misguided popular belief, this injunction is not just meant to enhance superficial knowledge and lexical literacy. It is a salvo toward becoming seen and identified as we are: celestial avatars, vaporous hoards, million-strong multitudes. From basal to cosmological levels, text transcends itself – its meaning, logic, and symbols. For trans and gender non-conforming people, text is a utilitarian index, a portal to echelons where we are allowed to convalesce and coalesce without disturbance. [...]

Speculatively linking a variety of writing styles and related propositions, from the intra-actions of electrons to lightning and queer kinship, theorist Karen Barad's writing performs the endless skies that gendered language offers.

She consequently shows that matter, even at its most elementary and humble molecular level, is 'not the given, the unchangeable', but rather 'creatively regenerative, an ongoing trans*/formation'.[1] Likewise, through her *Black Feminist Poethics*, Denise Ferreira da Silva closely analyses the minute details of materials used in artworks. By reading art 'in the raw', in other words, through its rudimentary matter, she unshackles and 'corrupts the fixity' of critical commentary and liberal discourses that paradoxically insist on deterministic subjectivisation.[2] Barad and da Silva hypothesise how horizons can be mined from the most miniscule, ignoble fragment.

Likewise, the artists discussed here show how a single word, (im)properly deployed and manipulated, can be that horizon for gendered life, one that exceeds its own regulation and purview.

1   [Footnote 2 in source] Karen Barad, 'Transmaterialities: Trans*/Matter/Realities and Queer Political Imaginings', *GLQ: A Journal of Lesbian and Gay Studies*, vol. 21, nos. 2–3 (June 2015) 387–422.

2   [3] Denise Ferreira da Silva, 'In the Raw', *e-flux Journal*, no. 93 (September 2018) (https://www.e-flux.com/journal/93/215795/in-the-raw/).

Wong Bing Hao, extracts from 'Territory: Universe (Translexical Opacity)', *The Contemporary Journal 1* (January 2019). Available at https://thecontemporaryjournal.org/issues/on-translations/territory-universe-translexical-opacity

Henry Dreyfuss
Symbol Sourcebook//1984

Here is a word
in Greek   δηλητηριον
in Japanese   毒
in Russian   отрава
in Hebrew   לער

[…] I could go on and write this word in every language in the world and literally fill several pages of this book. Yet in the interest of expediency, all I need do is substitute one simple drawing. The symbol means exactly the same as each one of these words: POISON. And it is equally intelligible whatever the language of the viewer – and perhaps even more so than the word itself. The viewer who can neither read nor write immediately recognises the danger this symbol so graphically conveys. […]

There are today some 5,000 languages and dialects in use throughout the world, of which perhaps a hundred may be considered of major importance in most instances, intercommunication among them ranges from difficult to impossible. One solution, of course, would be to establish an international language, and hundreds of attempts have in fact been made in the last two centuries to develop an official second language that in time could be adopted by all major countries. Esperanto, Interlingua, Ido, Volapük – all combining elements of existing languages – and Ro and Suma, both created artificially, are but six such attempts. However, among other drawbacks, they all rely, as does basic English, on the Roman alphabet. This restricts their usefulness to those countries which utilise the Roman alphabet, and these are actually a minority among nations.

If a system of symbols could be compiled that would be equally recognisable in Lagos and Lapland, perhaps the dream of a universal basic means of communication could be realised. I believe this is possible.

In no way do I propose that this system be yet another language, for it is not really a language at all. Rather it is a supplement to all languages to help create a better and faster understanding in specific areas. Symbols have already evolved to the point of universal acceptance in such areas as music, mathematics, and many branches of science. A Beethoven symphony sounds the same in Japanese as it does in the original German; a column of digits adds up identically in Polish and Spanish; and a Russian scientist easily deciphers equations discussed in an English scientific journal. [...]

In the beginning, man created the symbol – and pictures on Cave walls were sufficient for a time to express his ideas about the relatively simple processes of procuring food and shelter. It was when man began to feel a need to express abstractions – differences in degree nuances in definition, philosophical concepts – that symbols proved inflexible and inadequate. Then languages began to proliferate. It now appears that in some increasingly important areas we need an adjunct to our sophisticated speech and need to work our way back to the simple universality of an understandable, albeit limited, symbology. Symbols have multiplied to an alarming degree along much the same lines of divergence as languages. Today it is this very diversity and multiplicity of symbols in our international life that is a matter of such immediate concern. As the world grows steadily smaller, the need for easy communication becomes increasingly acute, and man has apparently come full circle – from prehistoric symbols, to sophisticated verbal communication, and now back to symbols, to help us all live together in today's Tower of Babel. [...]

Henry Dreyfuss, extracts from *Symbol Sourcebook: An Authoritative Guide to International Graphic Symbols* (New York: John Wiley & Sons, 1984) 16–21.

Xu Bing
On Book from the Ground//2012

Interviewer What do you call the language used in your *Book From The Ground*?

Xu Bing It is not a language, but a script. Spoken languages and written scripts are two separate things. [*Book from the Ground*] is a pictography suited to all spoken languages. A person of any nationality – a French reader or a British one for instance – will read [Book from the Ground] into their own language. Meanwhile, not a single pictogram in *Book from the Ground* is – in and of itself – pronounceable.

Interviewer Is it a sort of Esperanto?

Xu It is a script that transcends region. As long as the reader has experience of contemporary life, this script will be effective. It is not the same as Esperanto. Esperanto was impossible to popularise, promote and use because it was a language that required study. Every culture already has its own language, so why bother studying Esperanto? Esperanto had this utopian quality to it.

    The script in *Book from the Ground* requires no study; rather it has taken shape through widespread popular use. I have not created these symbols, but instead have collected them, symbols already in wide circulation.

Interviewer Is it a way to reconsider Babel?

Xu Yes, it is. As human horizons have expanded, people have realised that languages and scripts differ from region to region. With advances in technology, and the expansion and increasing commonality of cross-region communication, humanity has become aware of the inconvenience of [traditional] language. In our digitised age, this directly impacts the individual.

    Which is to say, the implications of Babel have been reawakened, and only today are people truly aware of what that implies.

Interviewer Your book borrows all the traditional codes of narrative. If the story is simple, you manage to infuse suspense, humour... . Knowing that your materials, icons, are short messages which include ellipses – meaning potential misunderstandings – how did you manage to be sure [of] being understood?

Xu Languages themselves are simple. And any written language leaves enough 'space' for its users to supplement additional meanings. We are amazed by the refined expressive capabilities of Chinese or English. However, this sense of 'refinement' is the consequence of long use; it has been developed over time by users [of the language] operating within and between the limits of pre-existing symbols. When we see hearing-impaired people 'conversing' excitedly on a bus, we have a hard time imagining that the hearing-impaired can achieve the level of expressiveness of 'normal' people. But just as with any other language, its effectiveness relies on its users supplementing [its range]. Icon-based languages are the same. An investigation of the potential of a given script, is not based merely on its current expressive range. Instead attention should be paid to its future space, the quality of its linguistic genetics and its ability to reproduce.

Interviewer What difficulties did you encounter?

Xu This project began 10 years ago. When it was published in 2012, people said that *Book from the Ground* could only be published in this era. And in the process we did confront many difficulties, the primary difficulty being that 10 years ago, pictographic symbols were not rich or varied, emoticons were all relatively simple.

And now, with the rapid development of digital technology and the rise of the internet, with the appearance of icon languages as a part of every kind of digital product, the work of collecting and organising [these icons] has become a seemingly endless task. If a few more years had passed before the writing of *Book from the Ground*, it would have been even easier, and it would have been able to express more, and more richly. The written language of symbols grows and changes with every day and month that passes, with new things [symbols] emerging practically by the day.

Globalisation has led to the continuing standardisation of transnational products and consumer lifestyles, and these globalised lifestyles have grown increasingly similar by the day. An 'environment of repetition' and copy culture has elevated the recognisability of all material things. And, at the same time, the development of media has led to the [rapid and widespread] transmission of these highly symbolised versions of material things, with the very real effect of 'eliminating illiteracy through visual recognition.' [...]

Xu Bing, extract from 'On Book From the Ground', in *The Book about Xu Bing's Book from the Ground*, ed. Mathieu Borysevicz , trans. Jesse Robert Coffino (North Adams and Cambridge, MA: Mass MoCA and The MIT Press, 2012). Available at www.xubing.com/en/database/interview/342

Erika Tan
Pidgin Interrupted//2002

[...] CUT SPELING

3. LinguaVision: Translation

If you're marketing internationally you need to talk the local language.

Pidgin English may be the business language, but Chinese is the most used world-wide. Think about that.

A billion Chinese consumers; one market, one language.

Specialising in international Business to Business Accounts we put together the whole ball of wax – Advertising, Marketing collaterals, Telesales, Direct Response Marketing, WWW and Internet marketing – simultaneously in the languages you need. Project dependent we use translation productivity tools – computer assisted and machine translation. We can proof language versions of most documentation on-line around the world.

Just think of the time and cost saving.

One brief - and the entire integrated approach is put on your desk.

And we're in a lot of countries too.

FONETIC

3.3 LinguaVision: Translaeshun

If you''re marketing internashunaly U need to tauk the loecal langgwej.

Pidgin English may be the biznes langgwej, but Chinese is the moest uezd werld-wied. Think about that.

A bilyon Chinese consoomers; wun market, wun langgwej.

Specialising in internashunal Biznes to Biznes Acounts we puut together the hoel ball of wax – Advertiezing, Marketing collaterals,, Telesales, Direct Respons Marketing, WWW and Internet marketing – siemultaeniusly in the langgwejes U need. Project dependent we ues translaeshun productivity tools – compueter asisted and masheen translaeshun. We can proof langgwej verzhuns of moest docuementaeshun on-lien around the werld.

Just think of the tiem and cost saeving.

Wun breef – and the entier integraeted aproech is puut on yur desk.

And we're in a lot of cuntrys too.

TRUSPEL

...LinguaVision: Translation

If you're marketing internnashunoolee yue need tue tauk thu loekool laengwej.

Pidgin Eenglish mae bee thu biznis laengwej, but Chieneez iz thu moest used werld-wied. Thheenk ubbout that.

U bilyun Chieneez consumers;; wun market,, wun laengwej.

Specialising in internnashunool Biznis tue Biznis Ukkounts wee poot tueggether thu hoel baul uv waks – Advertising, Marketing collaterals,, Telesales, Dirrekt Response Marketing, WWW and Internet marketing – simultaneously in thu laengwejez yue need. Praajekt dependent wee yuez translation productivity tuelz – kumpyyueter assisted and mussheen translation.. Wee kan proof laengwej verzhunz uv moest documentation aan-lien urround thu werld.

Just thheenk uv thu tiem and kaust saeveeng.

Wun breef – and thu enttier integrated uprroech iz poot aan yuer desk.

And we're in u laat uv kuntreez tue.

Erika Tan, extracts from 'Pidgin Interrupted: in conversation with Simon Willmoth', in *PIDGIN interrupted transmission*, ed. Simon Willmoth (London: Film and Video Umbrella, 2002) n.p.

From the catalogue for the exhibition 'PIDGIN interrupted transmission', Norwich Gallery, Norwich (November–December, 2001).

The formula
of hyphenation
(as in Italian-
Americans,
Asian-
Americans,
and African-
Americans)
is reaching the
point of saturation,
and the right-
hand side of
the hyphen can
barely contain
the unruliness
of the left-hand
side.

Arjun Appadurai, 'Patriotism and its Futures', 1993

I cannot EXPERIENCE
   your EXPERIENCE.
You cannot EXPERIENCE
    my EXPERIENCE.
We are both INVISIBLE men.
All men are INVISIBLE to
one another.

R.D. Laing, quoted in Sophie J. Williamson, 'Introduction: Between Languages'

THE UNTRANSLATABLE

James Joyce
Finnegans Wake//1939

[…] Bababadalgharaghtakamminarronnkonnbronntonnerronntuonnthunntro-
varrhounawanskawntoohoohoordenethurnuk […]

James Joyce, extract from *Finnegans Wake* (1939) (London and New York: Penguin, 1992) 2.

Sarat Maharaj
Perfidious Fidelity: The Untranslatability of the Other//1994

[…] The notion of 'untranslatability' was given a singular twist by Apartheid for its own ends. It projected the impossibility of translation, of transparency, to argue that self and other could never translate into or know each other. This sense of opacity served to underpin its doctrine of an absolute 'epistemic barrier' – grounds for institutionalising a radical sense of ethnic and cultural difference and separateness. Self and other were deemed to be locked in their own discrete, pure spaces. Recoiling from Apartheid's 'pessimistic', violating scripting and staging of the untranslatable, the drive has been to promote hybridity as its 'optimistic' flip side – as the triumph over untranslatability. How to recharge 'hybridity' so that it is prised free from this oppositional coupling? The aim is to prevent it from narrowing down into a reductive, celebratory term. To re-code it in a more circumspect key involves defining it as a concept that unceasingly plumbs the depths of the untranslatable and that is continually being shaped by that process. It is to reinscribe it with a double movement that cuts across 'optimism and pessimism, the opaque and the crystal-clear' – to activate it as a play-off between the poles. It amounts to reindexing hybridity as an unfinished, self-unthreading force, even as a concept against itself. […]

Where translation is understood as a process of 'carrying over' and simply in terms of 'transparency' it tends to encourage a superficial, if seductive, attitude to 'multicultural translation' as the immediate visibility of all elements of multicultural community to one another – even in the face of an adverse actuality that thwarts and distresses such an ideal at every turn. Dare we hold on to the ideal, however, for the value of its critical demand – a utopian horizon against which multiculturalism might be scanned, kept on its toes, and shown up for having fallen short of its own claims?

But to focus on untranslatability is not only to acknowledge from the start the impossibilities and limits of translation. It is to highlight the dimension of what gets lost in translation, what happens to be left over. Since what is gained in the translation tussle – elements of hybridity and difference – is so impressive it is easy to slip into thinking of it as an outright overcoming of the untranslatable. The concept then begins to function as the mirror image of 'purity' with no less of the latter's triumphal overtone. It takes on an all too positive, optimistic ring billed as the new international visual Esperanto – a telling hunky-dory word, Steiner reminds us, that half echoes the Spanish for hope.

What [is the] antidote for this drive towards becoming a reductive, one-dimensional term? A re-coding would need to index hybridity as a site shot through and traced with the untranslatable which serves as its supplement and prop. The upshot of this is to dramatise the incomplete, unfixed nature of the category. We begin to see hybridity not so much as a self-standing, fixed term but as an interdependent one – changing and re-changing as it interacts with the aura of the untranslatable, with the remains and leftovers of the translation exercise. These need to be accounted for and acknowledged at every turn for, to use Adorno's words, like blood stains in a fairytale they cannot be rubbed off.

But can the untranslatable be voiced at all? How to articulate the leftover inexpressibles of translation? Is it perhaps to be glimpsed in a back-to-front crazy word, an image's shimmer, the flick of a gesture, the intimacies of voice, in listening to its silences – an attentiveness that opens onto an erotics and ethics of the other beyond its untranslatability? Having kicked off its sturdy walking shoes, my English is in danger of perhaps becoming too comfortably slippered at this point.

Lothar Baumgarten's installation *Imago Mundi* for the Wall to Wall show (Serpentine, London, 1994) stages the international space – quite literally reindexing it through a look at the codes, lens, optics and manuals of representation itself. Wherever we stand, wherever we position ourselves we are not able to grasp the dispersed elements of the drifting continents. However acrobatically we twist, turn and contort ourselves to bring things into view, it only serves to make us aware of the limits and blind spots of the view and viewing.

Africa, Asia, Australia, Europe – no position permits a viewing without itself turning into the viewed. What prevails is the sense of watching as we are being watched, of someone looking over our shoulder as we look *l'autre l'ailleurs* – the other, elsewhere, everywhere and besides. The very transparency blocks off and shutters, occludes. We are unable to totalise this mapping of the world, each time something slips out of our grip. We grapple with the leftovers, the remainder of the untranslatable. [...]

1   [Footnote 2 in source] Gayatri Spivak, 'The Politics of Translation', in *Outside in the Teaching Machine* (Routledge, New York, 1993) 179–200.

Sarat Maharaj, extracts from 'Perfidious Fidelity: The Untranslatability of the Other', in *Global Visions: Towards a New Internationalism in the Visual Arts*, ed. Jean Fisher (London: Kala Press in association with Iniva, 1994) 28–35.

Stuart Hall
Modernity and Difference: a Conversation with Sarat Maharaj//2001

I regard translation as an unending process, a process without a beginning. Except in myth, there is no moment when cultures and identities emerge from nowhere, whole within themselves, perfectly self-sufficient, unrelated to anything outside of themselves and with boundaries which secure their space from outside intrusion. I do not think that either historically or conceptually we should think of cultures or identities or indeed texts in that way. Every text has a 'before-text', every identity has its pre-identities. I am not interested in the notion of translation in terms of rendering what has already been authentically and authoritatively fixed; what I want to do instead is to think of cultural practices as always involved in the process of translating.

Cultural processes do not have a pure beginning; they always begin with some irritant, some dirty or 'worldly' starting point, if I can call it that. When I say 'dirty', I mean that there is no pure moment of beginning; they are always already in flow and translation, therefore, is always from one idiom, language or ideolect into another. All languages have their own internal character, their own kind of ethos, their own space, and so it is therefore impossible to think of a perfect translation; no such thing exists. One has always to think of cultural production of any kind as a reworking, as inadequate to its foundations, as always lacking something. There is always something which is left out. There is always. mistranslation because a translation can never be a perfect rendering from one space or one language to another. It is bound to be somewhat misunderstood, as we are all always misunderstood in every dialogue we undertake. There is no moment of dialogic relationship with on other which is perfectly understood by them in exactly the way intended by us, because translation is a mediation between two already constituting worlds. There is no perfect transparency.

So the notion of a perfect translation does not help us at all. What we usually think of as polarised between copying or mimicking on the one hand and the moment of pure creativity on the other are really two moments that are mutually constituting – they do not exist in a pure form. Pure creativity draws on something which is already there; it moves from one space to another and the creative act is that movement. It is not that I have thought of something or said something or produced something which has never been produced before – it is not the romantic notion of a pure start. Nor is it the notion of a pure finish, because every translation generates another. No-one reads a translation without thinking, 'I bet that's what the original really means. I bet I could express it better.'

One has to think of meaning as constituted by an infinite, incomplete series of translations. The notion of meaning always depends, in part, on what is not said, and on what is not represented, as part of meaning's constitutive outside. This is the notion, derived essentially from Ferdinand de Saussure, that one cannot know what it is that one means unless one also implicitly affirms or states what one does not mean – that every marked term or signifier implicates its unmarked 'other'.

It is a rather sobering thought to realise that this absent presence is true of all identities. I do not know of any identity which, in establishing what it is, does not, at the very same moment, implicitly declare what it is not, what has to be left out, excluded. In that sense, identities are always constructed through power, even though we do not like to think that they are, because no identity can include everyone. What would be the point of on identity which includes everyone? We understand 'sameness' only through difference, presence through what it 'lacks'. The whole point is to define what I and other people like me belong to; consequently an identity establishes itself by virtue of what is not and cannot be said to belong. To say or establish anything – any position, any presence, any meaning – one has to attend to what is outside the field of meaning and what cannot be expressed – its constitutive outside.

[…] Difference, therefore, is not something that is opposed to identity; instead it is absolutely essential to it.

Stuart Hall, extracts from 'Modernity and Difference: a Conversation between Stuart Hall and Sarat Maharaj', in *Modernity and Difference* (London: Iniva, 2001) 36–56.

The Holy Bible
The Tower of Babel//c.950 BC/2009

1. Now the whole earth had one language and one speech.
2. And it came to pass, as they journeyed from the east, that they found a plain in the land a of Shinar, and they dwelt there.
3. Then they said to one another, 'Come, let us make bricks and bake them thoroughly.' They had brick for stone, and they had asphalt for mortar.
4. And they said, 'Come, let us build ourselves a city, and a tower a whose top is in the heavens; let us make a name for ourselves, lest we be scattered abroad over the face of the whole earth.'
5. But the Lord came down to see the city and the tower which the sons of men had built.
6. And the Lord said, 'Indeed a the people are one and they all have b one language, and this is what they begin to do; now nothing that they c propose to do will be withheld from them.'
7. 'Come, let Us go down and there confuse their language, that they may not understand one another's speech.'
8. So the Lord scattered them abroad from there over the face of all the earth, and they ceased building the city.
9. Therefore its name is called Babel, because there the Lord confused the language of all the earth; and from there the Lord scattered them abroad over the face of all the earth. [...]

'The Tower of Babel' (Genesis 11:1–9), *The Holy Bible: Containing the Old and New Testaments, New King James Version* (Nashville/Dallas/Mexico City/Rio de Janeiro/Beijing: Thomas Nelson, 2009) 8–9 [footnotes omitted].

Jacques Derrida
Des Tours de Babel//1985

'Babel': first a proper name, granted. But when we say 'Babel' today, do we know what we are naming? Do we know whom? If we consider the survival of a text that is a legacy, the narrative or the myth of the tower of Babel, it does not constitute just one figure among others. Telling at least of the inadequation of one tongue to another, of one place in the encyclopaedia to another, of language to itself and to meaning, and so forth it also tells of the need for figuration, for myth, for tropes, for twists and turns, for translation inadequate to compensate for that which multiplicity denies us. In this sense it would be the myth of the origin of myth, the metaphor of metaphor, the narrative of narrative, the translation of translation, and so on. It would not be the only structure hollowing itself out like that, but it would do so in its own way (itself almost untranslatable, like a proper name), and its idiom would have to be saved.

The 'tower of Babel' does not merely figure the irreducible multiplicity of tongues; it exhibits an incompletion, the impossibility of finishing, of totalising, of saturating, of completing something on the order of edification, architectural construction, system and architectonics. What the multiplicity of idioms actually limits is not only a 'true' translation, a transparent and adequate inter-expression, it is also a structural order, a coherence of construct. There is then (let us translate) something like an internal limit to formalisation, an incompleteness of the constructure. It would be easy and up to a certain point justified to see there the translation of a system in deconstruction.

One should never pass over in silence the question of the tongue in which the question of the tongue is raised and into which a discourse on translation is translated.

First: in what tongue was the tower of Babel constructed and deconstructed? In a tongue within which the proper name of Babel could also, by confusion, be translated by 'confusion'. The proper name Babel, as a proper name, should remain untranslatable, but, by a kind of associative confusion that a unique tongue rendered possible, one thought it translated in that very tongue, by a common noun signifying what we translate as confusion. Voltaire showed his astonishment in his *Dictionnaire philosophique*, at the Babel article:

I do not know why it is said in Genesis that Babel signifies confusion, for Ba signifies father in the Oriental tongues, and Bel signifies God; Babel signifies the city of God, the holy city. The Ancients gave this name to all their capitals. But it is incontestable that Babel means confusion, either because the architects were confounded after having raised their work up to eighty-one thousand Jewish feet, or because the tongues were then confounded; and it is obviously from that time on that the Germans no longer understand the Chinese; for it is clear, according to the scholar Bochart, that Chinese is originally the same tongue as High German.

The calm irony of Voltaire means that Babel means: it is not only a proper name, the reference of a pure signifier to a single being – and for this reason untranslatable – but a common noun related to the generality of a meaning. This common noun means, and means not only confusion, even though 'confusion' has at least two meanings, as Voltaire is aware, the confusion of tongues, but also the state of confusion in which the architects find themselves with the structure interrupted, so that a certain confusion has already begun to affect the two meanings of the word 'confusion'. The signification of 'confusion' is confused, at least double. [...]

Translation promises a kingdom to the reconciliation of languages. This promise, a properly symbolic event adjoining, coupling, marrying two languages like two parts of a greater whole, appeals to a language of the truth ('Sprache der Wahrheit'). Not to a language that is true, adequate to some exterior content, but to a true tongue, to a language whose truth would be referred only to itself. It would be a matter of truth as authenticity, truth of act or event which would belong to the original rather than to the translation, even if the original is already in a position of demand or debt. And if there were such authenticity and such force of event in what is ordinarily called a translation, it is that it would produce itself in some fashion like an original work. There would thus be an original and inaugural way of indebting oneself; that would be the place and date of what is called an original, a work. [...]

Jacques Derrida, extracts from 'Des Tours de Babel', in *Difference in Translation*, ed. and trans. Joseph F. Graham (Ithaca and London: Cornell University Press, 1985) 165–7, 200.

Barbara Cassin
Introduction to the Dictionary of Untranslatables//2014

[...] Multiplicity is to be found not only among languages but within each language. A language, as we have considered it, is not a fact of nature, an object, but an effect caught up in history and culture, and that ceaselessly invents itself – again, *energeia* rather than *ergon*. So the Dictionary's concern is constituted by languages in their works, and by the translations of these works into different languages, at different times. The networks of words and senses that we have sought to think through are networks of datable philosophical idioms, placed by specific authors in particular writings; they are unique, time-bound networks, linked to their address (exoteric or esoteric), to their level of language, to their style, to their relation to tradition (models, references, palimpsests, breaks, innovations). Every author, and the philosopher is an author, simultaneously writes in a language and creates his or her language – as Schleiermacher says of the relation between author and language: 'He is its organ and it is his' (*General Hermeneutics*). The untranslatable therefore is also a question of case by case.

Finally, there is multiplicity in the meanings of a word in a given language. As Jacques Lacan says in *L'étourdit*, 'A language is, among other possibilities, nothing but the sum of the ambiguities that its history has allowed to persist.' The Dictionary has led us to question the phenomenon of the homonym (same word, several definitions: the dog, celestial constellation and barking animal) in which homophony (bread, bred) is only an extreme case and a modern caricature. We know that since Aristotle and his analysis of the verb 'to be' that it is not so easy to distinguish between homonymy and polysemy: the sense of a word, also called 'meaning' in English, the sense of touch, *sens* in French meaning 'direction' – these represent traces of the polysemy of the Latin *sensus*, itself a translation from the Greek *nous* (flair, wit, intelligence, intention, intuition, etc.), which from our point of view is polysemic in a very different way. Variation from one language to another allows us to perceive these distortions and semantic fluxes; it permits us to register the ambiguities each language carries, their meaning, their history, their intersection with those of other languages.

In his introduction to Aeschylus' *Agamemnon*, which he considers to be 'untranslatable', Humboldt suggests that one should create a work that studies the 'synonymy of languages', and records the fact that every language expresses a concept with a difference: 'A word is so little the sign of a concept that without it the concept cannot even be born, still less be stabilised; the indeterminate action of the power of thought comes together in a word as a faint cluster of clouds gathers in a clear sky.' 'Such a synonymy of the principal languages … has never been attempted', he adds, 'although one finds fragments of it in many writers, but it would become, if it was treated with intelligence, one of the most seductive of works' (*Aeschylos Agamemnon*). This work that is among 'the most seductive' is perhaps our Dictionary. I hope it will make perceptible another way of doing philosophy, which does not think of the concept without thinking of the word, for there is no concept without a word. […]

How to Use This Work
The Dictionary of Untranslatables offers three types of entries.

1. Among the 'word-based' entries, some start from a single word in a single language, taken as 'untranslatable', revealing a given constellation in time and/or space, such as LEGGIADRIA, which initially expresses the gracefulness of women in the Italian Renaissance and evokes for us the smile of the Mona Lisa; or MIR , which in Russian means 'peace', 'the world', and 'peasant commune'.

Other of these entries present one or more networks and seek to bring out their particularities: for example, under POLITICS we consider both 'politics' and 'policy'; with STRUCTURE we proceed to a comparison with 'pattern' and Gestalt; and under SENSE we treat all the senses of 'sense', from their complex Latin thread (the unifying *sensus*, which renders the Greek *nous*, literally 'flair, intuition', but also refers to the meaning of a word or a text) to the Anglo-German tangle of *Sinn, Bedeutung*, 'sense', and 'meaning', which is complicated in French translations as *dénotation* or *référence*. The words in various languages that are listed just below the lemma for an entry make no claim to being translations, good or bad: they are the equivalents, approximations, analogues actually discussed in the article.

2. The more general, 'thematic' entries, metaentries in a fashion, examine the way in which one language or another works overall by starting with a crucial characteristic: for example, the difference between *ser* and *estar* in philosophical Spanish (see SPANISH) or *diglossia* in Russian (RUSSIAN). Some of them engage a major problem, like the order of words (WORD ORDER) or the mode of expressing time and aspect (ASPECT), which are immersed in the different languages. The longest entries are generally the result of a collaboration, and the boxes (which are signed when they are not written by the authors of the corresponding articles), represent so many beams of light brought to bear on a text, its translation, a terminology, or a tradition.

3. Finally, the unsigned 'directional' entries serve to guide readers. They point toward the relevant entries in foreign languages (WORLD and PEACE direct us to the Russian MIR , and MALAISE sends us to individual ways of designating the dysfunction of body and soul and its implications for existence, ACEDIA , DESENGAÑO , DOR , MELANCHOLY , SAUDADE , SEHNSUCHT , SORGE). They also propose a synthesis of difficulties and differences (*NOTHING, TIME*). [...]

Barbara Cassin, extracts from 'Introduction' and 'How to Use This Work', in *Dictionary of Untranslatables: A Philosophical Lexicon*, eds. Barbara Cassin, Emily Apter, Jacques Lezra and Michael Wood, trans. Michael Wood (Princeton: Princeton University Press, 2014) ix–xxi.

Jean Genet
Prisoner of Love//1986

The page that was blank to begin with is now crossed from top to bottom with tiny black characters – letters, words, commas, exclamation marks – and it's because of them the page is said to be legible. But a kind of uneasiness, a feeling close to nausea, an irresolution that stays my hand – these make me wonder: do these black marks add up to reality? The white of the paper is an artifice that's replaced the translucency of parchment and the ochre surface of clay tablets; but the ochre and the translucency and the whiteness may all possess more reality than the signs that mar them.

Was the Palestinian revolution really written on the void, an artifice superimposed on nothingness, and is the white page, and every little blank space between the words, more real than the black characters themselves? Reading between the lines is a level art; reading between the words a precipitous one. If the reality of time spent among – not with – the Palestinians resided anywhere, it would survive between all the words that claim to give an account of it. They claim to give an account of it, but in fact it buries itself, slots itself exactly into the spaces, recorded there rather than in the words that serve only to blot it out. Another way of putting it: the space between the words contains more reality than does the time it takes to read them. Perhaps it's the same as the time, dense and real, enclosed between the characters in Hebrew.

When I said the Blacks were the characters on the white page of America, that was too easy an image: the truth really lies where I can never quite know it, in a love between two Americans of different colour. [...]

Jean Genet, extract from *Prisoner of Love* (1986), trans. Barbara Bray (New York: New York Review of Books, 2003) 5.

.

Trinh T. Minh-ha
Other Than Myself/My Other Self//1998

[...] To travel can consist in operating a profoundly unsettling inversion of one's identity; I become me via an other. Depending on who is looking, the exotic is the other, or it is me. For the one who is off – and outside culture is not the one over there, whose familiar culture I am still a part of, or whose unfamiliar culture I come to learn from. I am the one making a detour with myself, having left upon my departure from over here not only a place but also one of my selves. The itinerary displaces the foundation, the background and what it incessantly unfolds is the very encounter of self with the other – other than myself and my other self.

In travelling, one is a being-for-other, but also a being-with-other. The seer is seen while s/he sees. To see and to be seen constitute the double approach of identity: the presence to oneself is at once impossible and immediate. 'I can't produce by myself the stranger's strangeness: it is born from [at least] two looks. 2'. Travelling allows one to see things differently from what they are, differently from how one has seen them, and differently from what one is. These three supplementary identities gained via alterity are in fact still (undeveloped or unrealised) gestures of the 'self' – the energy system that defines (albeit in a shifting and contingent mode) what and who each seer is. The voyage out of the (known) self and back into the (unknown) self sometimes takes the wanderer far away to a motley place where everything safe and sound seems to waver while the essence of language is placed in doubt and profoundly destabilised. Travelling can thus turn out to be a process whereby the self loses its fixed boundaries – a disturbing yet potentially empowering practice of difference. [...]

Trinh T. Minh-ha, extract from 'Other than myself/my other self', in *Travellers' Tales: Narratives of Home and Displacement*, eds. George Robertson et al. (London: Routledge, 1998) 22–3.

Alastair Reid
Lo que se pierde/What Gets Lost//1978

I keep translating *traduzco continuamente*
entre palabras words *que no son las mías*
into other words which are mine *de palabras a mis palabras.*
Y, finalmente, de quién es el texto? Who has written it?
Del escritor o del traductor writer, translator
o de los idiomas or language itself?
Somos fantasmas, nosotros traductores, que viven
entre aquel mundo y el nuestro
between that world and our own.
Pero poco a poco me ocurre

que el problema the problem no es cuestión
de lo que se pierde en traducción
is not a question
of what gets lost in translation
sino but rather *lo que se pierde*
what gets lost
entre la ocurrencia – sea de amor o de desesperación
between love or desperation –
y el hecho de que llega a existir en palabras
and its coming into words.

Para nosotros todos, amantes, habladores
as lovers or users of words
el problema es éste this is the difficulty.
Lo que se pierde what gets lost
no es lo que se pierde en traducción sino
is not what gets lost in translation, but rather
what gets lost in language itself *lo que se pierde*
en el hecho, en la lengua,
en la palabra misma.

Alastair Reid, 'Lo Que Se Pierde/What Gets Lost' (1978), in *Barefoot: The Collected Poems*, ed. Tom Pow (Cambridge: Galileo Publishers, 2018) 199-200. ©2018 by Leslie Clark. By permission of the Colchie Agency GP, New York. All rights reserved.

Parastou Forouhar
Written Room//2002

When I started painting the script of my mother tongue on the walls and floor of the exhibition rooms, this was not the result of a serious conceptual decision. It was more of an unremarkable beginning.

It was only when repeating and developing this work further, in the process of creation and especially in seeing again and again the moments when the characters of the script shifted back and forth between word and ornament, that this work revealed its questions and intellectual games to me. In the beginning, when I was asked what my characters meant, I couldn't understand the reasoning behind this question. The question didn't come up very often.

For me, the script of my native language served to show off its seductive and disorienting existence, to display its curves overtly in order to hide its meaning – perhaps losing it instead.

'Look how beautiful and seductive such a loss can appear.'

But such is the pathos anchored in the lives of immigrants, those who have migrated, with or without baggage, and who have left everything behind at the moment of escape. No matter what they were – perhaps they organised and archived their biography in lots of display cases or hidden cabinets, without everyday associations. Their memories become tangible reality only in painfully reconstructed moments.

It is only because I love the present that I try to break through and liquefy this barrier surrounding me; to let in the living everyday world with its surprises and its cumulative details. Sometimes only banality pours in, spreading quickly like weeds and at the same time making the frozen world of pathos seem attractive. It's an eternal back and forth in my head and I move in between, sometimes in the smallest of spaces.

The script characters of my native language, strung together with love, define an in-between space: they are transformed into ornaments that reveal only the memory of the words' meanings.

Applied to weightless ping-pong balls, the characters roll around on the floor, bumping against each other, but don't form sentences. In the monotonous clicking of the balls, the attempt at communication is garbled.

Their traces – so fleeting that they create fullness only for a moment – form new patterns that defy the attempt to hold on to them.

Like my memories, the balls are disruptive factors, unrelated to the everyday environment, which are briefly rationalised in my mind only at the moment of their sudden appearance.

It is a temporary world that contrasts simple poetry with the laws of reality.

Over the years, my native language has slipped away and has taken utterances away with it: the familiar words of my mother; the sound of the beautiful sentences with which my father always said goodbye to me.

A few years ago I wrote down my childhood memories for a while, in German. It was as if they were going to retreat from me and hide away in the silent, wordless world of images if I didn't write them down in the language that had become my everyday language. I read the texts just to my friend, a German friend who didn't want to correct them. She said they were too Persian to be corrected by a German.

Parastou Forouhar, 'Written Room', from the catalogue for the exhibition 'Wegziehen' (2002), Frauenmuseum, Bonn. Available at www.parastou-forouhar.de/wegziehen/. Translated by Philippa Hurd.

George Steiner
After Babel//1975

We do not speak one language, nor half a dozen, nor twenty or thirty. Four to five thousand languages are thought to be in current use. This figure is almost certainly on the low side. We have, until now, no language atlas which can claim to be anywhere near exhaustive. Furthermore, the four to five thousand living languages are themselves the remnant of a much larger number spoken in the past. Each year so-called rare languages, tongues spoken by isolated or moribund ethnic communities, become extinct. Today entire families of language survive only in the halting remembrance of aged, individual informants (who, by virtue of their singularity are difficult to cross-check) or in the limbo of tape-recordings. Almost at every moment in time, notably in the sphere of American Indian speech, some ancient and rich expression of articulate being is lapsing into irretrievable silence. One can only guess at the extent of lost languages. It seems reasonable to assert that the human species developed and made use of at least twice the number we can record today. A genuine philosophy of language and socio-psychology of verbal acts must grapple with the phenomenon and rationale of the human 'invention' and retention of anywhere between five and ten thousand distinct tongues. However difficult and generalising the detour, a study of translation ought to put forward some view of the evolutionary, psychic needs or opportunities which have made translation necessary. To speak seriously of translation one must first consider the possible meanings of Babel, their inherence in language and mind.

Even a cursory look at Meillet's standard compendium 1 or at more recent listings in progress under the direction of Professor Thomas Sebeok of Indiana University, shows a situation of utter intricacy and division. In many parts of the earth, the language-map is a mosaic each of whose stones, some of them minuscule, is entirely or partially distinct from all others in colour and texture. Despite decades of comparative philological study and taxonomy, no linguist is certain of the language atlas of the Caucasus, stretching from Bžedux in the north-west to Rut'ul and Küri in the Tatar regions of Azerbeidjan. Dido, Xwaši, and Qapuči, three languages spoken between the Andi and the Koissou rivers, have been tentatively identified and distinguished, but are scarcely known to any but native users. Arči, a language with a distinctive phonetic and morphological structure, is spoken by only one village of approximately 850 inhabitants. Oubykh, once a flourishing tongue on the shores of the Black Sea, survives today in a handful of Turkish localities near Ada Pazar. A comparable multiplicity and diversity marks the so-called Palaeosiberian. language families. Eroded by Russian during the nineteenth century, Kamtchadal, a language of undeniable resource and antiquity, survives in only eight hamlets in the maritime province of Koriak. In 1909, one old man was still conversant in the eastern branch of Kamtchadal. In 1845, a traveller came across five speakers of Kot (or Kotu). Today no living trace can be found. The history of Palaeosiberian cultures and migrations before the Russian conquest is largely obscure. But evidence of great linguistic variance and sophistication is unmistakable. With regard to nuances of action – possibility, probability, confirmation, necessity – Palaeosiberian languages possess a grammar of obvious precision. But we know little of the genesis of these tongues and of their affinities, if any, with other major linguistic groupings. [...]

Blank spaces and question marks cover immense tracts of the linguistic geography of the Amazon basin and the savannah. At latest count, ethno-linguists discriminate between 109 families, many with multiple sub-classes. But scores of Indian tongues remain unidentified or resist inclusion in any agreed category. Thus a recently discovered tongue spoken by Brazilian Indians of the Itapucuru river territory seems to be related to no previously defined set. Puelce, Guenoa, Atakama, and a dozen others are names designating languages and dialects spoken, perhaps over millions of square miles, by migrant and vanishing peoples. Their history and morphological structure are barely charted. Many will dim into oblivion before rudimentary grammars or word-lists can be salvaged. Each takes with it a storehouse of consciousness.

The language catalogue begins with Aha, an Altaic idiom spoken by Tatars, and ends with Zyriene, a Finno-Ugaritic speech in use between the Urals and the Arctic shore. It conveys an image of man as a language animal of implausible variety and waste. By comparison, the classification of different types of stars, planets, and asteroids runs to a mere handful.

What can possibly explain this crazy quilt? How are we to rationalise the fact that human beings of identical ethnic provenance, living on the same terrain, under equal climatic and ecological conditions, often organised in the same types of communal structure, sharing kinship systems and beliefs, speak entirely different languages? What sense can be read into a situation in which villages a few miles apart or valleys divided by low, long-eroded hills use tongues incomprehensible to each other and morphologically unrelated? I put the question repetitively because, for a long time, obviousness has disguised its extreme importance and difficulty.

A Darwinian scheme of gradual evolution and ramification, of adaptive variation and selective survival, may look credible. Consciously or not, many linguists seem to have worked with some such analogy. But it only masks the problem. Though many details of the actual evolutionary process remain obscure, the strength of Darwin's argument lies in the demonstrable economy and specificity of the adaptive mechanism; living forms mutate with seemingly random profusion, but their survival depends on adjustment to natural circumstance. It can be shown, over a wide range of species, that extinction does relate to a failure or inexactitude of vital response.

The language manifold offers no genuine counterpart to these visible, verifiable criteria. We have no standards (or only the most conjectural) by which to assert that any human language is intrinsically superior to any other, that it survives because it meshes more efficiently than any other with the demands of sensibility and physical existence. We have no sound basis on which to argue that extinct languages failed their speakers, that only the most comprehensive or those with the greatest wealth of grammatical means have endured. On the contrary: a number of dead languages are among the obvious splendours of human intelligence. Many a linguistic mastodon is a more finely articulated, more 'advanced' piece of life than its descendants. There appears to be no correlation, moreover, between linguistic wealth and other resources of a community. Idioms of fantasticelaboration and refinement coexist with utterly primitive, economically harsh modes of subsistence. Often, cultures seem to expend on their vocabulary and syntax acquisitive energies and ostentations entirely lacking in their material lives. Linguistic riches seem to act as a compensatory mechanism. Starving bands of Amazonian Indians may lavish on their condition more verb tenses than could Plato.

The Darwinian parallel also breaks down on the crucial point of large numbers. The multiplicity of fauna and flora does not represent randomness or waste. It is an immediate factor of the dynamics of evolutionary breeding, cross-fertilisation, and competitive selection which Darwin set out. Given the range of ecological possibilities, the multiplication of species is, quite conceivably, economical. No language is demonstrably adaptive in this sense. None is concordant with any particular geophysical environment. With the simple addition of neologisms and borrowed words, any language can be used fairly efficiently anywhere; Eskimo syntax is appropriate to the Sahara. Far from being economic and demonstrably advantageous, the immense number and variety of human idioms, together with the fact of mutual incomprehensibility, is a powerful obstacle to the material and social progress of the species. We will come back to the key question of whether or not linguistic differentiations may provide certain psychic, poetic benefits. But the many ways in which they have impeded human progress are clear to see. No conceivable gain can have accrued to the crowded; economically harried Philippine islands from their division by the Bikol, Chabokano, Ermitano, Tagalog, and Wraywaray languages (to name only the most prominent of some thirty tongues), or from the related fact that for four of these five idioms the United States Employment Service can list only one qualified translator. Numerous cultures and communities have passed out of history as linguistic 'drop-outs'. Not because their own particular speech was in any way inadequate, but because it prevented communication with the principal currents of intellectual and political force. Countless tribal societies have withered inward, isolated by language barriers even from their near neighbours. Time and again, linguistic differences and the profoundly exasperating inability of human beings to understand each other have bred hatred and reciprocal contempt. To the baffled ear, the incomprehensible parley of neighbouring peoples is gibberish or suspected insult. Linguistically atomised, large areas of Africa, India, and South America have never gathered their common energies either against foreign predators or economic stagnation. Though sometimes sharing a lingua franca, such as Swahili, their consciousness of kinship and common need has remained artificial. The deeper springs of action stay rooted in linguistic separateness. Robbed of their own language by conquerors and modem civilisation, many underdeveloped cultures have never recovered a vital identity. In short: languages have been, throughout human history, zones of silence to other men and razor-edges of division.

George Steiner, extracts from *After Babel: Aspects of Language and Translation* (Oxford and New York: Oxford University Press, 1975) 51–2, 53–6.

Susan Hiller
The Last Silent Movie//2008

The Last Silent Movie opens the unvisited, silent archives of extinct and endangered languages to create a composition of voices that are not silent. In *The Last Silent Movie*, some of these voices sing, some tell stories, some recite vocabulary lists and some of them, directly or indirectly, accuse us, the listeners, of injustice.

An old man confronts us with some truths about language. The strangeness of his voice merges with the buzzing and humming artefacts of an archaic recording mechanism. A young girl repeats words she is trying to learn in what sounds like French. Several men exuberantly chant fragments of a creation myth. Next, an elderly woman tells a story of jealousy and murder to an appreciative listener. Then a gruff voice enquires about fishing conditions... .

In an interview, I once said 'Our lives are haunted by ghosts, our own personal ghosts and the collective ghosts of our society.' These 'ghosts' are the starting points for my art practice of more than forty years, based on cultural materials.

The Last Silent Movie is a choreographed composition of voices from the forgotten archives of lost and endangered languages. In this work, we hear these voices addressing us us while a blank movie screen provides an opportunity for reflection, contemplation and empathy.

The film is accompanied by etchings that visually represent oscilloscope renderings of the unique sounds of the individual voices speaking to us.

Susan Hiller, 'The Last Silent Movie', artist's statement, 2008. Courtesy of the estate of Susan Hiller.

Kathy Acker
Against Ordinary Language//1993

I have now been bodybuilding for ten years, seriously for almost five years.

During the past few years, I have been trying to write about bodybuilding. Having failed time and time again, upon being offered the opportunity to write this essay, I made the following plan: I would attend the gym as usual. Immediately after each workout, I would describe all I had just experienced, thought and done. Such diary descriptions would provide the raw material.

After each workout, I forgot to write. Repeatedly. I... some part of me... the part of the 'I' who bodybuilds... was rejecting language, any verbal description of the processes of bodybuilding. [...]

I am in the gym every three out of four days. What happens there? What does language in that place look like?

According to cliché, athletes are stupid. Meaning: they are inarticulate. The spoken language of bodybuilders makes this cliché real. The verbal language in the gym is minimal and almost senseless, reduced to numbers and a few nouns. 'Sets', 'squats', 'reps'... the only verbs are 'do' or 'fail' adjectives and adverbs no longer exist; sentences, if they are at all, are simple.

This spoken language is kin to the 'language games' Wittgenstein proposes in his *The Brown Book*.[1]

In a gym, verbal language or language whose purpose is meaning occurs, if at all, only at the edge of its becoming lost.

But when I am in the gym, my experience is that I am immersed in a complex and rich world.

What actually takes place when I bodybuild? The crossing of the threshold from the world defined by verbal language into the gym in which the outside world is not allowed (and all of its languages) (in this sense, the gym is sacred) takes several minutes. What happens during these minutes is that I forget. Masses of swirling thought, verbalised insofar as I am conscious of them, disappear as mind or thought begins to focus. [...]

Certain bodybuilders have said that bodybuilding is a form of meditation.

What do I do when I bodybuild? I visualise and I count. I estimate weight; I count sets; I count repetitions; I count seconds between repetitions; I count time, seconds or minutes, between sets: From the beginning to the end of each workout, in order to maintain intensity, I must continually count.

For this reason, a bodybuilder's language is reduced to a minimal, even a closed, set of nouns and to numerical repetition, to one of the simplest of language games.

Let us name this language game, *the language of the body*. [...]

If ordinary language or meanings lie outside essence, what is the position of that language game which I have named *the language of the body*? For bodybuilding (a language of the body) rejects ordinary language and yet itself constitutes a language, a method for understanding and controlling the physical which in this case is also the self.

I can now directly talk about bodybuilding. (As if speech is ever direct.) The language game named the language of the body is not arbitrary. When a bodybuilder is counting, he or she is counting his or her own breath.

[Elias] Canetti speaks of the beggars of Marrakesh who possess a similar and even simpler language game: they repeat the name of God.

In ordinary language, meaning is contextual. Whereas the cry of the beggar means nothing other than what it is; in the cry of the beggar, the impossible (as the Wittgenstein of the *Tructutus* and Heidegger see it) occurs in that meaning and breath become one.

Here is the language of the body; here, perhaps, is the reason why bodybuilders experience bodybuilding as a form of meditation.

'I understood the seduction there is in a life that reduces everything to the simplest kind of repetition,' Canetti says.[2] A life in which meaning and essence no longer oppose each other. A life of meditation.

1   [Footnote 2 in source] Here and throughout the rest of this article, whenever I use the phrase 'language game', I am referring to Ludwig Wittgenstein's discussion of language games in *The Brown Book* (Wittgenstein, *The Blue and Brown Books* (New York: Harper and Row, 1960)).

2   [7] Elias Canetti, *The Voices of Marrakesh* (New York: The Seabury Press, 1978) 25.

Kathy Acker, extracts from 'Against Ordinary Language: The Language of the Body', in *The Last Sex: Feminism and Outlaw Bodies*, eds. Arthur Kroker & Marilouise Kroker (Basingstoke: Palgrave Macmillan, 1993) 20–23, 25.

Katarina Zdjelar
I Think That Here I Have Heard My Own Voice Coming to Me from Somewhere Else//2009

[...] We all enter into language with the same vocal apparatus, the same language ability. This ability holds the promise that any language can become ours. But as we grow up and learn to speak our mother tongue, our ability is shaped in specific ways and adjusts to successful communication within the particular community we inhabit. We become trained to hear and utter certain sounds, but perfecting our mastery of the proper sounds of our language (or their suitable variations) is to the detriment of other sounds that have no currency in it. No single person would therefore be able to utter the different sounds of all languages.

We are at home with our mother tongue and develop a particular loyalty to it, but while it protects us there it reveals us elsewhere. The imprint of our mother tongue stays with us when we enter a foreign language. The minute we open our mouth the motherness of our tongue makes itself apparent and undermines any efforts to become neutral, colourless or to blend in. We are marked by our accent, our grammar, syntax, rhythm, pitch, our choice of words. When I speak a language other than my mother tongue my speech falls between me speaking language and language speaking me. My effort to speak may enable me to communicate, but it also exposes me, identifying me as a member of a particular (language) community.

Speaking a foreign language is, of course, about speaking someone else's language. The foreign in language is what native speakers detect as strange about the way non-native speakers speak their language. It is an act in which both parties become aware of the attachment and loyalty that has developed through listening to and speaking a mother tongue. When we speak or hear foreign words or sounds, we speak and hear something similar to the particular word or sound, something like it but we cannot hear or speak it the same. It is exactly this similarity that makes it foreign, strange. A foreign word appears somewhat like a fake Adidas trainer presenting itself as an original 'Abidas'. The cut might be just right but maybe the texture of the material feels different, maybe there is something extra – an uncut thread, waving with each step, signalling difference. We do our best to produce foreign words or sounds, we actually utter something that, to us, may sound right but to the native speaker does not 'ring true'. It is not only that we may have difficulty articulating the foreign sounds accurately; we may not even be able to perceive them properly in the first place – the attuning of our hearing to the specific sounds of our mother tongue becoming an additional obstacle to our attempt to inhabit another language. With a simple sentence such as 'sun is shining!' we reveal a great deal about ourselves. The sentence simultaneously communicates that I am not from here. It is the 'sh' in 'shining' that will mark us, it is the misplaced 'the' that betrays us, it is exactly the modulation of 'sun' that locates us, the pitch of 'is' will always linger. We hit the wrong notes and play to a different rhythm. A foreign word appears counterfeit, never completely articulated, never completely in its proper place, but constantly hovering between an approved and denied modulation. Is this the space in which we become our counterfeit selves?

These subtleties in the language we speak can thus unite us as well as distinguish us. [...]

Clark Lunberry, an American teaching English in Japan, coined the term 'para-poetics' to describe the poetic force conveyed by the broken English of his Japanese students. Para-poetics is a use of language that accidentally or unconsciously employs words or sentences in unexpected arrangements. With the para-poetic, rules of correct language use are often violated resulting in unusual formations of grammar, word-choice, syntax, punctuation or spelling. Lunberry notes that these violations are not deliberate transgressions but an unintentional straying beyond unseen boundaries. [...]

The difference between para-poetics and broken English (in this case) is a matter of one's point of view: the first appreciates the potential of language whilst the second notices its imperfections. The tradition of using language in unconventional ways is often related to writers and artists, whose disregard for convention is intentional. However, the para-poetic writer is disinterested in creativity or displaying linguistic virtuosity of any kind. Para-poetics is produced through the speaker's lack of language. He is oblivious to the linguistic system that carries with it the force to challenge, destabilise, enrich, or create some depth in the system.

The production of a para-poetic dimension to language is not only a privilege for those learning a foreign language, but it can also manifest itself in the process of forgetting language we no longer use. We find ourselves uttering isolated words, twisting grammar, allowing for unnecessarily long gaps between words to let them find their place, but if we fail to find the right words, we produce silence.

Failings in translation yield the same results. A slip of the tongue may sanction a rebellious act.

Translation is not simply about transcribing one language into another, nor for that matter is it about trying to transfer narratives and concepts; it is also concerned with transporting the logic of one language into that of another. I have noticed during my time in the Netherlands that some non-native Dutch speakers would make their own word constructions in their new language, keeping the sound and meaning of the original Dutch word: *vliegtuig* (airplane) into *vliegtuit* (it flies out), *gasfornuis* (gas stove) into *gas voor huis* (gas for house) etc. The level of creativity, violation, straying, internalisation and appropriation of language is dependent on the speakers' fluency, of course. To be able to translate *vliegtuig* into *vliegtuit* requires at least a basic command of Dutch, just as, don't joke me substitutes are you serious? as one possible translation which appropriates the English language into the logic of Croatian. When we are not quite sure what we hear, when we don't speak the language we hear and try to translate our experience of listening into speech, we enter the sphere of a provisional and improvisational production of sounds and meanings. [...]

Katarina Zdjelar, extracts from 'I Think That Here I have Heard My Own Voice Coming to Me From Somewhere Else', in *Katarina Zdjelar: But If You Take My Voice, What Will Be Left To Me?* (The Serbian Pavilion at the 53rd Biennale di Venezia, 6 June–22 November, 2009), eds. Anke Bangma & Katarina Zdjelar (Belgrade: Publikum, 2009) 63–79 [footnotes omitted].

Dana Friis-Hansen
Joseph Grigely//1995

Joseph Grigely's work pivots around his 'invisible difference', deafness that is only revealed when he is spoken to. His art explores the basics of everyday communication, and takes the form of what he calls 'inscribed conversations'. He has explained, 'Partly because I am totally deaf, written communication is the only practical and efficient way for me to communicate with people who do not know sign language: they write to me and I talk back. As we continue to talk, the words and pages pile up.' Statistics tell that while only one in every 1000 of us is deaf there is a very strong deaf community in the United States and even a Deaf Culture, which defines itself not by any disability, but as a linguistic minority. Their sense of identity within this subculture comes primarily from their form of communication (for example, American Sign Language) which is usually gained from peers rather than parents. Grigely is certainly well connected with this world, having been a professor of English at Gallaudet University (the most important university for the Deaf in the United States) off and on since 1983. And yet his artistic focus is not on deafness at all, but on exchanges outside that community, as is series subtitle reveals, *Conversations with the Hearing*.

Grigely, who is also a critical theorist and very knowledgeable in the field of linguistics, expands upon the problems and pleasures of communication. He carefully arranges the paper conversations in ways that draw out their uniqueness as inscriptions that exist somewhere between speech and writing, without being one or the other. 'Although these words and pages are written, they do not constitute a form of drawing: they are, that is, drawings of speech, particularly the way in which they exemplify the discursive nature of speech.'

For his art he collects 'found conversation objects' and makes a kind of still life arrangement, then adds to each one a typed 'context card' in a small black frame which explains the situation and offers insights into the mechanics of the exchange. For example, alongside a scribbled explanation 'did you know they were speaking Japanese?' one reads:

> One of the more ubiquitous and frustrating problems when you can't hear is not knowing what language the people next to you are speaking. In the large cities of Europe you cannot assume that the language being spoken by the people around you is the language of the country that you are in. This is especially true in a city like Venice. Sometime I try to lip-read people to see if I can figure out what language they're speaking, but lip-reading is so inherently inadequate that it doesn't help much. A couple of times I tried asking people what language they were speaking, and they gave me a really weird look like I was dumb or something. Now I usually wait for someone to tell me what's going on. It's less complicated that way.

Often the papers are pinned to the wall alongside the framed card, but he has also created complicated environmental installations which replicate, like some *trompe l'oeil* sculpture, the site of verbal exchanges. For the Palazzo's recently refurbished 'Salla Giallo', where the silk weavings do not allow use of the walls, he has created *Lo Studio/The Study* (1995), a major installation which makes use of the fact that the room was originally a study, or in Italian *Lo Studio* – a serendipitous translinguistic reference to the site of artists' creation. Grigely was in residence for almost three weeks and used this room to meet people and to make his work, which presents in the form of both a scholar's study and an artist's studio – and an exhibition. He includes as furnishings both a modern plastic chair placed by a folding table overflowing with his working materials, and a heavy formal oak chair and table contemporary with the room, which features 'finished' works, arranged as if ready for hanging. Great care was taken with the formal visual aspects such as colour, scale, form and material. In the corners of the room are other carefully scattered traces of his artistic thinking and working process – clean writing papers, empty frames, pencils and an eraser, texts being edited, even books about language in different languages (i.e. *Lingua, test, enigma* in Italian, [*Language, Text* and *Enigma*]). Traces of the artist himself have been left – his jacket sits over the back of one chair, a tea saucer holds some plum pits while the cup holds some pencil shavings, and a vase of fresh flowers brightens the room.

While the whole series *Conversations with the Hearing* explores exchanges between Deaf and those who can hear, *Lo Studio/The Study* also addresses intercultural and intracultural exchanges, as the exhibition contains conversations with people across many nationalities and linguistic groups. After first arriving in Italy, Grigely went to spend five days with his mother's family in southern Italy – an Italian-American returning to his ancestral home. He explained 'The conversations themselves are drawn from the ordinary events that define social interaction: conversations that took place over meals, conversations that took place in the streets, conversations via fax exchanges, conversations with friends, conversations with strangers – conversations that in the end, are perfectly ordinary because they happen to all of us in such ways – yet are also unordinary by virtue of the fact that they inscribed.' Among the scraps of writing which falls somewhere between Italian and English we find this:

> I met Totò in Reggio Calabria when I was visiting my mother's family. Like me, Totò is deaf. When a mutual acquaintance introduced us, it was hard to tell who was more surprised by the coincidence – Totò or me. We sat down together on a small bench outside Signora Polimeni's grocery store, and using sign language – Totò's Italian Sign Language, and my American Sign Language – we talked, and talked, and talked. Neither language is in a strict sense mutually intelligible, but because both share a common and recent etymological origin – French Sign Language – we were still able to find enough cognate signs to have a good conversation. It felt a little strange to be situated in southern Italy and to find another deaf person who knew sign language, but in retrospect it wasn't strange at all: deafness isn't 'visible', we're not always aware there are deaf people near us, even if they're standing right beside us. I don't have any inscribed conversations from my time with Totò – neither of us, for obvious reasons, had any need to write.

Grigely's rich and complex installation is not about deafness, but rather a tribute to the human will to communicate with one another, and is full of smart and witty proof of our struggles to overcome barriers which might want to keep up apart.

Dana Friis-Hansen, 'Joseph Grigely', in *TransCulture: La Biennale di Venezia 1995* (Tokyo: Fukutake Science and Culture Foundation/The Japan Foundation, 1995) 120 [footnotes omitted].

What if things could speak

What would they tell us

Or are they speaking already
and we just don't hear them

And who is going to
translate them

Hito Steyerl, 'The Language of Things', 2006

TRANSFERENCE AND TRANSFORMATION

Hito Steyerl
The Language of Things//2006

Who does the lamp communicate with? The mountain? The fox?
– Walter Benjamin

What if things could speak? What would they tell us? Or are they speaking already and we just don't hear them? And who is going to translate them?

Ask Walter Benjamin. In fact he started asking those quite bizarre questions already in 1916 in a text called: 'On Language as Such and on the Language of Man'. Of all the weird texts by Benjamin, this is definitely the weirdest. In this text he develops the concept of a language of things. According to Benjamin this language of things is mute, it is magical and its medium is material community. Thus, we have to assume that there is a language of stones, pans and cardboard boxes. Lamps speak as if inhabited by spirits. Mountains and foxes are involved in discourse. High-rise buildings chat with each other. Paintings gossip. There exists even, if you will, besides the language communicated by telephone a language of the telephone itself.

[...] But, you may ask: what is the point of this eccentric plot? Let's pretend that the point is translation. Because obviously, the language of things has to be translated in order to become intelligible for those of us who are dumb for its silent splendour. But the idea of translation, which Benjamin has in mind, is a completely different concept of translation than the one we are used to. Because, from the most ordinary to the most sophisticated translation theories, one thing is usually taken for granted: that translation takes place between different human languages or the cultures, which are supposed to nurture them. Thus, languages are assumed to be an expression of different cultures and nations. This combination is hastily identified as the political aspect of translation and even language as such. And on this level standard translation theory is always already implicated in political practice and governmental strategies.

But Benjamin's idea of translation – at least in this text – boldly ignores this obvious and perhaps banal feature of translation. And thus, an entirely different concept of a politics of translation emerges. Instead of national languages, which are only mentioned passingly in this text, he focuses on what I would call languages of practice: the language of law, technology, art, the language of music and sculpture. And more importantly: translation doesn't take place between them, but within them. That is: between the language of things and the language of men, at the base of language itself. Thus, a few very important modifications are introduced with regard to traditional translation theory: firstly language is defined not by common origin, belonging or nation, but by common practice. Secondly, translation primarily takes place within language not between languages. And thirdly, translation addresses the relationship of human language and thing language. [...]

In this perspective translation is highly political, because it directly addresses issues of power within language formation. It concerns the relationship of humans to the world as a whole. It addresses the emergence of practice and the languages, which correspond to it. Thus, Benjamin relates translation directly to power – by looking at the form of the translation, not its content. The respective form of translation will decide, if and how the language of things with its inherent forces and energies and its productive powers is subjected to the power/knowledge schemes of human forms of government or not. It decides, whether human language creates ruling subjects and subordinate objects or whether it engages with the energies of the material world.

While this may still sound completely unpractical [...], the contrary is the case. One might even say, that most human practice is constantly engaged in this process of translation. Let me give you now one very obvious example of such a translation from the language of things into the one of humans. And that is the example of the documentary form.

The Documentary Form as Translation

A documentary image obviously translates the language of things into the language of humans. On the one hand it is closely anchored within the realm of material reality. But it also participates in the language of humans, and especially the language of judgement, which objectifies the thing in question, fixes its meaning and constructs stable categories of knowledge to understand it. It is half visual, half vocal, it is at once receptive and productive, inquisitive and explanatory, it participates in the exchange of things but also freezes the relations between them within visual and conceptual still images. Things articulate themselves within the documentary forms, but documentary forms also articulate things.

And it is also obvious, how Benjamin's politics of translation functions with regard to the documentary image. In documentary articulations, things can either be treated as objects, as evidence for human plots, or they can be subjected to the language of judgement and thus overruled. I have once referred to this condition as documentality, that is the way in which documents govern and are implicated in creating power/knowledge. Or else, the forces, which organise the relationships between them, can be channelled in view of their transformation. The documentary form can also let itself be seduced and even overwhelmed by the magic of the language of things – although we will see, that this is not necessarily a good idea. But basically, this is how the relation between *potestas* and *potentia* is articulated within the documentary form. It is the relationship of productivity vs. verification, of the asignifying vs. the signified, of material reality vs. their idealist interpretation.

But let me make one thing very clear: to engage in the language of things in the realm of the documentary form is not equivalent to using realist forms in representing them. It is not about representation at all, but about actualising whatever the things have to say in the present. And to do so is not a matter of realism, but rather of relationalism – it is a matter of presencing and thus transforming the social, historical and also material relations, which determine things. [...]

According to Benjamin, things are never just inert objects, passive items or lifeless shucks at the disposal of the documentary gaze. But they consist of tensions, forces, hidden powers, which keep being exchanged. While this opinion borders on magical thought, according to which things are invested with supernatural powers, it is also a classical materialist one. Because the commodity, too, is not understood as a simple object, but a condensation of social forces. Thus things can be interpreted as conglomerates of desires, wishes, intensities and power relations. And a thing language, which is thus charged with the energy of matter can also exceed description and become productive. It can move beyond representation and become creative in the sense of a transformation of the relations, which define it. [...]

Hito Steyerl, extracts from 'The language of things', from *under translation* (Vienna and Linz: eipcp – European Institute for Progressive Cultural Policies, 2006) (http://eipcp.net/transversal/0606/steyerl/en).

Kurt Schwitters
Letter to Raoul Hausmann//1940

[...] The language is only a medium to feel. Not to understand.
Do you understand that?
You understand?
Do you really understand?
Do you understand that there are things which you cannot understand?
You understand, it is difficult, not to understand.

Why speak a language which you shall not stand under?
Why paint a picture which you shall not read? Which you cannot understand?
You reader; you!
You shall become a feeler. [...]

Kurt Schwitters, extract from 'Personal Letter to Raoul Hausmann' (1940), in *Kurt Schwitters in Exile: The Late Work 1937–1948* (London: Marlborough Fine Art, 1981) n.p. [footnotes omitted].

Stefan Themerson
Kurt Schwitters in England//1958

[...] To us today, it may perhaps seem that the act of putting two innocent words together, the act of saying:

'Blue is the colour of thy yellow hair,' is an innocent aesthetic affair – that the act of putting together two of three innocent objects, such as a railway ticket and a flower and a bit of wood – is an innocent aesthetic affair. Well it is not so at all. Tickets belong to railway companies; flowers to gardeners; bits of wood to timer merchants. If you mix these things together you are making havoc of the classification system on which the regime is established, you are carrying away people's minds from the customary modes of thought, and people's customary modes of thought are the very foundation of Order, whether it is the Old Order or the New Order, and, therefore, if you meddle with the customary modes of thought then, whether you are Galileo or Giordano Bruno with their funny ideas about motion, or Einstein with his funny ideas about space and time, or Schönberg with his funny ideas about the black and white keys of the keyboard, or the Cubist with their funny ideas about shapes, or Dadaist or Merzists with their funny ideas about introducing 'symmetries and rhythms instead of principles' – you are, whether you want it or not, in the very bowels of political changes. Hitler knew it. And that was why Kurt Schwitters was kicked out of Germany. [...]

Stefan Themerson, extract from *Kurt Schwitters in England* (London: Gaberbocchus, 1958) 14.

Geta Brătescu
The Tree from the Neighbouring Courtyard//2009

10 May, 2002

I had decided not to write any more – for the time being. To go back to the drawing board, to resume my timid battle with objects and space. But I think that salvation – if salvation is possible – still resides in words: to stimulate them, to write, to write. The notebook, in which year after year I have written down so many thoughts, is almost full. I think of it as finished. I have moved on to this large exercise book, where I intend to flow – a river. So many, many words. The words pull other words behind them.

[...] *The pleasure of the cursive line*, of writing – I don't know whether people who haven't experienced the pleasure of writing are familiar with this state. I think that the act that produces the writing (be it textual, be it purely graphic) is necessarily commanded by the mental gesticulation, a spatial movement, an image of an abstract or figurative journey. Whatever it might be, whatever its origin might be, this mental movement produces a discharge of energy, an extraordinary pleasure. By its cerebral nature, it is a cursive movement – when it becomes syncopated, the discomfort can go as far as pain. But there is also the cursiveness of syncopes, which come one after the other like the waves of a calm sea. The calmness of the alive contains the movement; the tranquility of the alive is a certain kind of movement. A straight line on a page is the image of a movement; it is the traversal of a space. Immobility is only a certain kind of movement, since the limits of the immobile object are a movement in space, the movement that defines its spatial existence. I know that this is a chair because I have foreknowledge of the description of a chair; and every description is a movement. Silver flakes race across the sky. The sun shines on the eye that the eyelid covers from time to time. The tree is all green. My painful knees have warmed up. One hundred twenty small women set off toward the window – dozens more wait on the drawing board to take their places in the growing series. A simple, nervous line and a silhouette, like a letter written from left to right, it is alive. The cactuses lean into the light; from their thorny bellies grow buds, a multitude.

[...] When I draw I get the feeling of writing – I write an image, I write a form, I write a design. Using the letters of the alphabet I can give life to the image, to form, to the design, by describing them. The absurd cannot be perceived as a form unless it has its own logic – the logic of the absurd. Similarly the logic of the informal causes the *unformed* to exist as form. We escape this natural 'constraint' only through madness. Even if I draw with my eyes closed, the 'constraint' is operative: its necessity becomes manifest through the pronounced activity of vision – i.e. the activity of the image constituted in the mind. In the periods when I don't draw, I have to write; and vice versa. [...]

October 20, 2007
But now, with the imminent prospect of a few lines, I feel wonderful. The magic of words: the words call to each other, the way forms call to each other, whether or not they wish to repeat themselves. A black, substantial thread has bunched up in my hand, becoming Form – the other forms, the drawn ones, legitimise it. A true miracle. The creation of the world came about in the same way, little by little. The movement of the drawing, captured on the paper like a snapshot, is propagated and in this way the series of snapshots creates the conjunction of space and time; this is exactly what happens in music too. A wall of the studio, covered with drawings, sings. [...]

For me, drawing is not only a professional task; it is the discharge of *rational energy*; it might be thought that the *idea* that gives rise to *images* is prior; but the idea-image relationship is so intimate, so hard is it to discern when and how these two mental products overlap and which of them is prior, that it is better to abandon the problem. Regardless of the artist's attitude, be it realist, be it impressionist, be it conceptualist, she experiences the idea-image relationship in her own way; the same as the writer experiences the idea-word relationship. When I draw I know that I *write* using letters I myself have invented. When drawing, I *de-scribe* my imaginary world. [...]

Geta Brătescu, extracts from 'The Tree from the Neighbouring Courtyard' (2009), in *Geta Brătescu: Apparitions*, eds. Marius Babias, Magda Radu and Diana Ursan (London: Koenig Books, 2017) 181–222.

Susan Rosenberg
Trisha Brown's Notations//2012

In the years 1965 to 1976, Trisha Brown found herself investigating various ways in which the body could be said to *think*. [A] selection of documents from her private archives shows Brown doing so, working through strategies of accumulation and de-accumulation, seriality, language and numbers in dialogue with her contemporaries in visual art. [...]

In 1965, shortly after the birth of her son, Brown, unable to dance, solicited scores from her friends. Among the responses were a postcard from Earle Brown and a typed text from Walter De Maria. Brown was delighted, declaring both card and text to be self-sufficient dances. In the days and years that followed, she came to regard these unperformed scores as an inspiration for her use of texts to generate choreographic ideas, particularly for her important choreography-as-recorded and -spoken-word score *Skymap* (1969). Another echo of one of the works can be found in her choice of the deliberately mysterious title *Son of Gone Fishin'* (1980), for which she consciously drew upon the proclaimed 'purpose' of De Maria's score – 'the spreading of the vision through the storytelling of the people who saw it'. In the case of her work, Brown explained to journalists, the title was designed to make an impression on audiences that would encounter it in reviews without seeing its performance.

Visually, Brown's drawings of the early 1970s resonate with the work of contemporaries outside of dance, in part because she was constantly turning texts into images. This notebook page from 1972, for example, seems to be in dialogue with Robert Smithson's *A Heap of Language* (1966). In Brown's drawing, however, the page is treated as an analogue for the body's ability to think in language as a way of moving in space. Her visualisation of motion records her consistent fascination with gravity (the increments of 'falling'), and registers nature's motions, which she likewise explored in her body itself through dramatic incidents ('splashing') or subtle humming below the surface ('pooling'). Puns and wordplay pervade Brown's notebooks of the period, appearing on many hand-drawn and written representations devised to advertise her programmes. [...]

In some sketches, the diabolical complexity of Brown's work – and her ongoing application of Cagean time structures to generate choreography and drawing – can be seen with particular vividness. For example, her musico-choreographic score for *Figure 8* (1974), which Brown envisioned as a 'time crossing'. Rendered in the period's visual lingua franca, the drawing records the counts (one accumulating and ascending, the other diminishing and descending) that Brown devised for dancers to perform on two sides of the body. The 'crossing', pictured in the diagram as a diagonal, occurs in performance in the form of the centre-crossing of each dancer's body. The movements, pictured in the document as numbered counts, are accumulated with the right arm, and deaccumulated with the left in simple gestures: rounded arms extend to the sides of the body and rise, arcing towards the centre of the head, touched by the fingers. It is from here that, as in *Accumulation*, gesture originates. The elegance of this visual representation, and of the performance, is in contrast to the choreography's severe kinesthetic and cognitive challenges. [...]

A tribute to the persistent influence of Robert Dunn's teaching and John Cage's ideas on Brown's choreography, *Untitled (Bodyparts)* (1975) visualises indeterminacy and chance. The drawing contains instructions for scoring a dance – 'a 12-count phrase made by dropping 12 Vitamin B pills on a collection of written body parts' – and thus only documents the first step towards generating a choreography which she never made. The strange overlaps, where letters and numbers meet in the circles to obliterate one another, visualise the interpenetrating systems through which Brown marked the body with ideas – and perhaps how she experienced her body as a site where informational codes were scrambled and reinvented before their physical externalisation in dance. [...]

Choreography as Visual Art

Skymap (1969), among the works that Brown presented at the Whitney programme, pursued to its conclusion the concept of dance in the absence of performance, reflecting a convergence of ideas around the scoring of art, emanating from John Cage.[1]

Brown's calm, clinical voice instructed audiences to envision, and mentally enact, words being moved, tossed and placed on the gallery's sixth wall. [...]

In May 1971, six weeks after the Whitney program, Brown presented an investigation of choreography as defined by relationships between vision, physical memory and movement's realisation. She established dancers as the fixed points to which choreography travelled across nine rooftops, from her residence at 53 Wooster Street to Robert Rauschenberg's 381 Lafayette Street studio.[2] Brown introduced simple, 'semaphoric' gestures: the dancers were instructed to reproduce the movements they *saw*, relaying each gesture to one another; midway through the performance the last dancer switched places with the first, initiating a new movement phrase and completing the circle of gesture's travel. Reviewers compared the process to the child's game 'telephone', aptly describing choreography's timeworn model of person-to-person transmission.[3]

But *Roof Piece* transforms the choreographer into an instigator of movements that are broadcast, received, and actualised through idiosyncrasies of each dancer's vision and body.[4] Each 'transmission' of fleeting gestural material reveals the imperfect translation of perception into physical response. Space and vision interfere to alter movement's neurological, kinesthetic reception, demonstrating the indeterminate relationship governing *Roof Piece*'s choreographic concept and its performance.[5]

Designed to reveal movements as visual, cognitive and physical facts, *Roof Piece* radically democratises the artist's signature choreographic mark, introducing it as always already subject to the failure of intentionality, inherent to choreography's utterance, which 'produce[s] effects beyond [the author's] presence'.[6] A visually apparent spatial rupture separates the initial choreographic mark from its subsequent iterations.[7] This perceptible gap defines choreography as imperfectly repeated, as a 'machine that is in turn productive, and [which the choreographer's] future disappearance, in principle, will not prevent from functioning and from yielding, and yielding itself to, reading and rewriting'.[8] *Roof Piece* distinguishes the body's materialisation of movement from choreography; abstract and evanescent, gesture erodes in the work's performance, demonstrating the necessity and priority of *vision* and conscious imitation in choreography's transmission, and contesting the idea of choreography's survival as fixed forms that are memorised and repeated. Brown called *Roof Piece*'s gestures 'semaphoric': what she had in mind was the system of visual signals used by on-the-ground air-traffic controllers, a *language* for communicating visual information in alphabet-like code across large distances.

The dancers' gestures were bound by a language of movement, but it was one in which entropy reigned. [...]

With *Untitled (Locus)* (1975), associations between Brown's choreography and conceptualism in visual art reached a crescendo. Based on a visual and verbal score that Brown discussed with critics, *Locus*' choreography maps an imaginary three-dimensional cube with twenty-six numbers, each corresponding to a place held by a letter of the alphabet (with a neutral, twenty-seventh point at the centre). Brown drew, numbered and lettered the cube; then she wrote a simple biographical statement, matching each letter to its corresponding numerical digit. The choreography performs this autobiographical phrase, with each movement touching an alpha-numeric point in space. Contrasting with Merce Cunningham's vision of choreographic space as without fixed points, *Locus* travels to fixed points according to an impersonal, structural procedure. It is more complexly three-dimensional than *Man Walking Down the Side of a Building*.[9] *Locus* spatialises and makes repeatable a sequential narrative of origination, rewriting biography as a structural system of graphic/textual scoring and non-subjective iterations.[10]

Locus's tasks, moves made to touch points on the cube from 'T' to 'R' to 'I', etc., are a machine for moving through space and generating a vocabulary of gesture whose logic is grounded in that of *Accumulation*. The work's geometrical construct was technically difficult and required trained dancers to perform it. As Brown explained to her audiences, the Gestalt of the cube, its words and sentences and drawn score, elevated the significance of its geometric structure and systematic task instructions over its language of movement. Although *Locus*' drawn/written scores specify, in written descriptions, the individual movements for touching each point in space, Brown never discussed these instructions or *Locus*' vocabulary: she emphasised *Locus* as a visual construction. Consistent with her previous methods, she provided no rules for transitions between movements in performance, introducing indeterminacy into the *Locus* score and also producing unforeseen movement that Brown recognised and called *dancing*. [...]

1   [Footnote 55 in source] A further inspiration for *Skymap* was the score sent from Geneva by composer Earle Brown: on a postcard he wrote, 'This is a dance (if I say it is), Hommage [sic] to Rauschenberg's Portrait of Iris' – a message invoking Rauschenberg's 1961 homage to Marcel Duchamp, shown at Iris Clert gallery, Paris. The work was a telegram stating, 'this is a portrait of Iris Clert if I say so/Robert Rauschenberg'. Trisha Brown Archive.

2   [60] Unfolding in the real time and non-illusionistic space of the spectator's partial vision, *Roof Piece* possesses a scale that challenges the rigidly monocular perceptual experience of 'seeing dance' on the proscenium stage, an undemocratic setting that organizes viewing positions in relation to a single ideal location. *Roof Piece* responds to Cage's critique of the proscenium stage, which he said, [assumes] 'people will see it if they all look in one direction… But our experience nowadays is not so focused at one point. We live in, and are more and more aware of living in, the space around us. Current developments in theatre are changing architecture from the Renaissance notion to something else that relates to our lives.' See John Cage, Michael Kirby and Richard Schechner, 'An Interview with John Cage', *The Tulane Drama Review*, vol. 10, no. 2 (Winter 1965) 51. As Carrie Lambert-Beatty has pointed out, conditions of spatial dispersal were realised by Allan Kaprow's Happenings; see *Being Watched*, 34.

3   [61] Though Brown first presented *Roof Piece* in 1971, its documentation dates to the 1973 presentation of the work, also in SoHo. Brown wrote about *Roof Piece*'s 'semaphore like' gestures in 'Three Pieces', *TDR* 19, no. 1 (March 1975) 26.

4   [62] In an unacknowledged appropriation of *Roof Piece*'s concept, Christian Jankowski's *Rooftop Routine* (2007) substituted a commercial movement (hula hooping) for dance, an example of Trisha Brown's enduring influence on contemporary art, but also of the precariousness of choreography's artistic legacies.

5   [63] See Joseph, *Beyond the Dream Syndicate*, 78.

6   [64] Jacques Derrida, 'Signature, Event, Context', in *Margins of Philosophy*, trans. Alan Bass (Chicago: University of Chicago Press, 1985) 312.

7   [65] Ibid., 316. 'This force of rupture is due to the spacing which constitutes the written sign: the spacing which separates it from other elements of the internal contextual chain (the always open possibility of its extraction and grafting), but also from all the forms of a present referent (past or to come in the modified form of the present past or to come) that is objective or subjective. This spacing is not the simple negativity of a lack, but the emergence of the mark.'

8   [66] Ibid., 315.

9   [82] *Locus* transforms Rudolf Laban's notational mapping of the body's harmonious movement through space – his concept of the 'kinesphere' – into an indeterminate choreographic format and form.

10   [83] See Rosalind Krauss, 'Grids', *October,* no. 9 (Summer 1979) 50–64; and Eve Meltzer, 'The Dream of the Information World', *Oxford Art Journal* 29, no.1 (March 2006) 115–35.

Susan Rosenberg, extracts from 'Trisha Brown's Notebooks' and 'Trisha Brown: Choreography as Visual Art', *October*, no. 140 (Spring 2012) 3–5, 8–9, 13, 15–16, 27, 34–37, 40.

Humberto Beck
Reading and Looking: On *Life in the Folds* by Carlos Amorales//2017

One of the most striking aspects of the project *Life in the Folds* – and, in general, of Carlos Amorales' exploration of the symbolic and formal possibilities of abstract alphabets and asemic writing – is the way the multidimensional nature of language is revealed in it. In *Life in the Folds*, spoken and written language is codified by means of an abstract alphabet which functions in turn as a 'semantic score' to be decoded musically. Amorales' previous work with this alphabet – made of paper cutouts – had already highlighted his exploration of the graphic dimension of text, but now, through the integration of a new element (the music of the *ocarinas*), a new layer of exploration is added: the auditory dimension of signs.[1] The *ocarinas* literally transform each letter of the alphabet into a wind instrument. In this way, the work highlights the different facets of language: strictly textual, but also conceptual, auditory, and visual.

Life in the Folds recalls Ezra Pound's insight into the three dimensions of poetic language: the language of a poem, according to Pound, is the sound of the words, but also the images they evoke and the concepts they represent. To these three perspectives (sound, image, and concept) I would add a fourth: the strictly *graphic* facet of the poem, the *materiality* of the text, which in some sense has always existed – since writing has been writing – but which in modern poetry became manifest and conscious of itself thanks to the formal and typographical experiments of authors such as Mallarmé, Apollinaire, e. e. cummings, and, among Mexican poets, José Juan Tablada.

The auditory translation of the alphabet that takes place in *Life in the Folds* reminds us, therefore, that every unit of language – and especially a letter – is a four-dimensional object: it is image, sound, and idea, but it is also *body*, *volume*, *presence*.

The *ocarinas* remind us in a very tangible way of the process of the birth and evolution of language: the operation whereby a gesture becomes a sign, and then an object and a sound, and finally, to complete the cycle, a gesture once again. [...]

This facet of Amorales's works establishes a dialogue, it seems to me, with lettrism, the avant-garde movement created by the French–Romanian artist Isidore Isou in the 1950s. Isou had developed a practice of writing, which he called 'metagraphics' or 'hypergraphics', whereby he sought to explore the visual, specifically plastic facet of the forms of phonetic notation, in the aim of transmitting a more exact rendering of reality than that represented in traditional forms of notation, such as the alphabet. In spite of this possible dialogue, however, *Life in the Folds* illuminates something more: the reality that all language is fundamentally endowed with these multiple characteristics – the notion that every verbal sign exists simultaneously in all of these dimensions.

The discovery of the multidimensional nature of language is an intuition of the modernist aesthetic. It is explicitly present in Rimbaud's famous 'Vowels' sonnet. When we pronounce 'a' or 'e', Rimbaud seems to suggest, we are not pronouncing 'just a letter', but are mobilising a copious series of phonetic, visual, symbolic, and intellectual sensations and evocations. Valéry put it in a different way: 'A letter is literature.' If we pay enough attention to what is happening on each one of the planes of language, and to their interaction, every time a group of letters is combined to form a word, a phrase, a dialogue, a text, the effect can be overwhelming, exuberant, uncontainable. The invitation to fix one's attention on these different planes and their interaction, *dramatising* them, is a fundamental part of the viewer's experience of *Life in the Folds.*

In Amorales' works, this staging of the dimensions of languages is also connected with an exploration of that uncertain, liquid, unstable frontier between the fields of abstraction and figuration. This exploration also touches on the question of the fluidity between text and image, which is exemplified in the ways we connect as spectators/readers with typography itself. Is it necessary to recall that even the letters of our alphabet were once, in their remote origins, ideograms? Or that, if a typographically trained eye gives free rein to the imagination behind it, it is possible to recover something of that primitive hieroglyphic character, as in the case nowadays of emojis and emoticons? Typography is text and image: exposing oneself to the signs of the alphabet is at once *reading* and *looking*. To look at letters (reading them), to read letters (looking at them) is to decipher in them, as Henri Michaux would have it, 'interior gestures', abstract figures which – like the objects and the landscapes themselves – become concrete, only to turn abstract again. [...]

The shifts between image and writing, between abstraction and figuration, place at the heart of the matter the question of readability, especially in one of its forms: that 'esoteric' dimension of writing – as Leo Strauss called it – related to the search for modes of expression distinct from 'direct' language, designed to avoid a danger, escape persecution, or transmit a deeper truth in coded form. We can intuit that this process of codification is never, in itself, neutral or transparent. Every detour in expression, every 'lateral' way of saying something, always necessarily adds a new layer of meaning: it is never limited to reproducing, in another code, the original message, but involves a transformation of that message. It says *something more*, something new. That 'something' tends to be *language itself*. [...]

In the folds of every accumulation of signs, of every text, there is concealed a double message that discloses something previously unknown to us. The musical and abstract letters of Amorales' alphabet are like the surviving fragments of a primordial figure, the pieces left over from a fable of origins: a handful of fragmentary signs in which we can sometimes read language, or our own story.

1   [Ed. note. The *ocarina* is an ancient wind musical instrument, a type of vessel flute.]

Humberto Beck, extracts from 'Reading and Looking: On *Life in the Folds*' in *Carlos Amorales: La Vida En Los Pliegues / Life in the Folds,* ed. Isaac Olvera (Mexico City/ Barcelona: Instituto Nacional de Bellas Artes/Coordinación Nacional de Artes Visuales/RM Verlag, 2017) 65–72.

Rick Poynor
Typotranslation//2000

Richard Hamilton's typographic translation of Marcel Duchamp's handwritten notes for *The Bride Stripped Bare by Her Bachelors, Even*, published in 1960, is one of the strangest, most audacious typographic documents ever created by a visual artist. Duchamp gave full support and encouragement to Hamilton's careful endeavour, revising the translation from French to English three times. It was an undertaking of deep significance for both men. For Hamilton, the forensic insight he gained into the thinking of one of the twentieth century's most enigmatic artists was to have a decisive impact on his paintings of the period, such as *Hommage à Chrysler Corp.* And for Duchamp? Hamilton heard later that the artist who embraced the 'beauty of indifference' carried the slim *Green Book* with him everywhere. He didn't read it or even look at it, but placed it by his bedside, like a *Gideon Bible* found in a hotel room. [...]

The Great Decipherer
The first task, once [Alexina] Teeny Duchamp (Marcel's widow, then still alive) had given the project her blessing, was to make a new translation of the notes. Hamilton has always played down his contribution in this respect, describing himself as 'monolingual'. Yet, as the art historian Sarat Maharaj has shown, despite Hamilton's protestations of ignorance, his letters to Duchamp in the late 1950s reveal a dogged determination to arrive at exact English equivalents of the French. Duchamp called him '*mon grand déchiffreur*' (my great decipherer). 'With guesses, hunches, and

hints,' writes Maharaj, 'he sought to strike the right note regarding the text's larger drift.' *The Green Box* translation is best viewed as a three-way discussion between Hamilton, American art historian George Heard Hamilton and Duchamp.

The White Box notes were translated, with similar, painstaking care, by Hamilton, Jackie Matisse, daughter of Teeny Duchamp, and Ecke Bonk, author of *Marcel Duchamp: The Portable Museum*. [...]

A New Typographic Isomorph

Bonk worked with Hamilton on the *White Box* typotranslation, though Hamilton, an early convert to digital technology, retained control of the master file. Previous attempts to edit and streamline Duchamp's jottings into tight, linear, regularised typographic form always seemed to compromise and betray the free play of thought in the original notes, sketches and diagrams. Duchamp evidently understood this when he chose to publish them in facsimile form. As with the *Green Book*, Hamilton's aim with à l'infinitif was to create a new typographic and graphic 'isomorph' of the original. 'What the manuscript demands', he writes, 'is a transcription that retains the original's graphic complexity... Variations in typeface, tone and colour can simulate changes in the writing medium; preserving the deletions and insertions reveals the development of ideas – even erratic spacing and punctuation can contribute to our understanding of the flow of thought.'

To convey this graphic complexity, Hamilton and Bonk employ no fewer than seventeen fonts – Akzidenz Grotesk, Baskerville, Bembo, Bodoni, Caslon, Charlemagne, Clarendon, Copperplate, Gothic, Garamond, Helvetica, News Gothic, Perpetua, Plantin, Sabon, Symbol, Times New Roman and Walbaum – though they avoid using italic because it is too close to script. The widely letter-spaced, super-elastic typography, with continuous modulations of type size, type style, ink colour, indentation, line-spacing and line width, gives their pages a typographic character that has few obvious precedents. It's as though a science textbook has been put into type by an intoxicated typographer with a strange sense of humour and unusual aesthetic flair.

Yet the eccentricities of form are always grounded in the need to transliterate the original with the utmost faithfulness and lucidity. [...]

Rick Poynor, extracts from 'Typotranslation', *Eye*, vol. 10, no. 38 (2000). Available at www.eyemagazine.com/feature/article/typotranslation

Jennifer Tee
In Conversation with Sophie J. Williamson//2019

Sophie J. Williamson Your work is full of so many different cultural references and influences, magpielike. How do you find shared languages and synergies between them?

Jennifer Tee A good example is *Ether Plane~Material Plane*, made for Manifesta 11. I was interested in the way different cultures created belief systems, rituals and artefacts for the transition between life and death. I brought together ethnographic ritual objects from collections in Zurich, each of which dealt with this transitional state, death, and the presence of the body and the soul. Photographed as collages along with my own ceramic works, they created a visual dialogue between different cultures, locations and time periods, connecting these worlds and belief systems. Of course, they were all already inherently connected: they each shared a political history that placed them in collections in the city. They shared a physical history as well, as I mostly used artefacts from clay that endured the process of firing; I borrowed terracotta figures from the Nok, a mysterious and ancient civilisation from West-Africa, and a female burial urn from Colombia, which was believed to sprout new life. And they each shared a social connection, in the exchanges between myself and the dealers, curators and private collectors who had lent them. The worlds and stories behind each ritual object crossed paths in the making of the work.

Williamson Many of the materials you use have very specific local histories or meanings. For example, in *Let It Come Down* you use the Rembrandt tulip petals and the South Sumatran ship weaving designs. Does it matter if their relevance is lost in translation depending on the culture in which the work is shown?

Tee My process of making is very much guided by material. I recently finished a public commission for Amsterdam's Central Station, mural made from 100,000 dried tulip petals. The image resembles the large weavings of ship cloths from the south of Sumatra; usually depicting a ship, they suggest the idea of human souls in motion to the afterlife. Both tulips and ship cloths have a personal significance to me: my father travelled by sea to the Netherlands from Indonesia with his family in the 1950's, and my maternal grandfather and great-grandfather were tulip bulb exporters. For this commission, I worked with many tulip growers – I got to know everything about tulips, their origins, the colours, the industry.

Meanwhile I was also researching the purpose and cultural meaning of the Sumatran ship cloths the island had a long trade history with Indians, Chinese, Javanese, Arabs, Portuguese and the Dutch. Traces of these exchanges became part of the motifs in the textiles, becoming a sort of collective memory.

I wanted to explore the different themes and meanings within these textiles, and this resulted in a series of tulip petal collages. For the collage, *Let It Come Down* (the title for which is borrowed from *Macbeth*), I used black tulip petals and Rembrandt petals, these to me translated best this feeling that I wanted to capture of falling matter, collapsing structures. I'm not too worried about the relevance getting lost. Many of my works are informed by more than one source of reference, as is the case in *Let it Come Down*. The patterns of falling black tulip petals referenced different things for me: on the one hand I was thinking of 'black rain', which refers to the nuclear dust after the nuclear bombings in Japan, but I was also thinking of the similarities between the Navajo diamond pattern weavings and the wave pattern in the South Sumatran ship cloths. The loom-woven patterns are common to many different cultural traditions, so the works are likely to evoke different references for other people. I like to work visually, so I would rather not rely on an explanation of the work through a text, I hope the work gives enough to be interpreted by the viewer.

Williamson I was also thinking of the specific colour dyes that you use in the yarns for your textile works. These have specific meanings, but these will vary in different cultures – or eras. Why is colour important to you?

Tee I am from a culturally mixed background, my father is an ethnic Chinese from Indonesia and my mother is half English and half Dutch. Because of this I had always noticed cultural differences to understand my social surroundings. When I started art school, this led me to an interest in artists who combined art and life experience, for example Helio Oiticica and Joseph Beuys. Both artists use materials with a certain (personal) meaning as part of their work. Vibrant colour is not very common in European contemporary art; when I was in art school, I felt like colourful work was assumed to be shallow. When I discovered these two artists, I came to understand the meaningful potential of materials: Beuys' felt or beeswax or the vibrant pigments of Oiticica's *Box-Bolides*. Both were very interested in transformation and the alchemy of one thing turning into another, and both sought to activate colour as a therapeutic strategy, for Beuys his own personal healing and for Oiticica as a means to heal society.

I have described my knitted floor pieces as 'resist shapes' in the *Let It Come Down* exhibition at Camden Arts Centre. They are sculptures but also places, island or zones within the exhibition space, on which a performance can take place or on which you can recline and meditate on a hand-dyed knitted rug. I choose a turmeric colour yarn for one of the works, as turmeric is associated with healing properties; it has been used in Asia for thousands of years and is a major part of Ayurveda and traditional Chinese medicines. It's also a spice that is commonly use for dying, for example for the ochre yellows in the Sumatran ship cloths. It is well researched that the colour of our surroundings influences us unconsciously, so it was important to me that I was aware of the different cultural readings and implications of the colours I used in these spaces.

Williamson You've spoken to me before about 'in-betweenness' or transience. For example, the crystal appears regularly in your work, a form that is between a solid and liquid, or the idea of the soul in limbo. Why does this in-between, unstable or transformative space interest you?

Tee The knitted floor pieces are geometrical shapes derived from crystalline forms and structures. Additionally, crystals usually form formations and so the lay out with the floor pieces can also be seen as a model for an infinite space. The floor pieces also hover between sculpture and stage, their arrangement forming both a negative and positive space, simultaneously taking up the room's volume and cutting into it. For me these vibrant floor pieces create a conduit space for the mind and body to connect.

I have been working with the idea of *the soul in limbo* since 2004. I came across this line 'I am the soul in limbo' as a statement by Nadja, the central character in the surrealist novel of the same title by André Breton. The sentence made me realise all the different ways you can feel in *limbo* – mentally and physically. Whilst researching the African artefacts that I borrowed for the Manifesta11 work, I discovered that in many African belief systems it's common to travel between different realms. Future, past and dream states can shift, and the black and white patterns you find in some of the African objects symbolise these different realms. Through trance or other forms of ritual it is believed possible to transcend to different planes of being, translating between different realities, for example Candomblé, an Afro-Brazilian religious tradition practised in Brazil. I've also been interested in the description of outer-bodily experiences and occupation of the body by other identities as frightfully described in Paul Schrebers Memoirs of *My Nervous Illness*. For me, 'the soul in limbo' became a way to address the fluidity of identity, the fractured moments of which reality is made of and as a place of resistance: personal, spiritual, physical or political.

Williamson Languages seem central to your work. By this I mean languages of colour, shape and materials. Then you further employ the languages of different art forms to transfer or transform these once again, for example through poetry, literature or dance. What is it in this flux or somersaulting that you are drawn to?

Tee In the past I have been working around the idea of the 'event'. For me the event is a zone of transition, where people, objects and the surroundings are connected in something I've called a 'situationistic border': between a world in calling and a present reality.

In Lévi-Strauss' memoir, *Tristes-Tropiques,* he describes the paradoxical status of the anthropologist as the observer while nevertheless maintaining the need to engage as a human. For me, exhibiting throughout the world – Mongolia, Brazil, Korea, China, Australia and so on – also made me very conscious about the effects of travel on the mind, and our connection to the world and to others. That's why I often want to work with local materials, like clay from the yellow mountains, or bamboo, or cacao fruits, but also with people with whom I develop language-based performances. I've also worked with actors and dancers in Brazil around common local words but whose meaning is somewhat untranslatable. For example, the word *saudades* means a deep emotional state of nostalgic or profound melancholic longing for an absent thing or person that one loves. Body language, tone, speech and rhythm is ingrained in each culture, for example in Brazil the rhythm of Bosa Nova music and dance seems tangibly inherited from generation to generation: with time outsiders can learn this, but it seems to come so naturally to locals. For the Gwanju Biennial, I was introduced to a Korean art form in which singing is connected to objects and movement, like fan dancing and ghost dancing. I am drawn to the different cultural complexities of the spirit and of communication with them: how a medium is sensitive to other worlds. I became interested in combining choreography with objects and breathing: the sound of breathing, or a pause in breathing during singing or moving. I also worked with Mongolian throat singers, I was very interested in how the throat singing connects to the body and the lyrics to the landscape and history of Mongolians as a nomadic people. In the performances that I make, I combine these different kinds of languages that I encounter with my own, it's sort of sound poetry.

Williamson I was wondering about your collaboration with dancers and choreography, Miri Lee. This seems to me to be a form of translation or interpretation; translating the visual and the tactile into movement. What is the collaborative process? How does it influence the work?

Tee After my experience in Korea, I was inspired to continue working with movement in relation to objects. When I was invited by Witte de With to show in Shanghai, I wanted to work again with language, but unlike my experience of the Brazilian Bossa nova or Mongolian throat singing, where I could grasp the implied emotion without understanding the language, I couldn't do this with Mandarin. Instead, I was drawn to Chinese characters: how they derive from a pictorial image, as well as having in mind the motion of creating calligraphy characters. I made a group of 12 vessels with clay from the Yellow Mountains and I worked with 5 female dancers and a choreographer from Shanghai, creating a choreography on 5 knitted floor pieces based on the titles I gave to the vessels and the Chinese characters they translated to. The characters became the choreography, as well as the Chinese idea that the vessel is as much about the empty space as about the vessel.

I met Miri Lee in 2010, she's a Korean dancer who came to Amsterdam to study improvisation. Her movements are very fluid, but also very influenced by her studies in Korea, in which the breathing and moments of stillness are followed by a set of intense movements. Her movements are very low to the ground, very different I felt from European dance, which is much more vertical. This language of low movements, connected really well to my work and floor pieces.

Jennifer Tee, 'In Conversation with Sophie J. Williamson', a new interview conducted for this book, 2019.

Stephen Willats
Universal Meaning//1979

One of the basic assumptions that underlies transmissional communication networks is that the meaning of language can be universal. In art practice such an assumption is reinforced by the idea that an artwork as object can be successfully transferred from place to place. Of course, though an artwork's universality may be proclaimed, everyone knows its actual performance is bound by context, especially so when the artist de-constructs and then re-constructs reality. Here reality has been taken by the artist to be uniquely his own experience, and by encoding it into a symbolic state, it can be relayed to the audience via their engagement with his artwork.

Stephen Willats, 'Universal Meaning' (1979), in *Society Through Art* (The Hague: Haags Centrum voor Aktuele Kunst, 1990). Available at http://stephenwillats.com/texts/art-institution-and-artist-rely-audience-acquiring/

Nicholas Bourriaud
The Radicant//2010

[...] What emerges from [the] proliferation of nomadic and expeditionary projects in contemporary art is an insistence on displacement. Faced with rigid and ossified representations of knowledge, artists activate that knowledge by constructing cognitive mechanisms that generate gaps and prompt them to distance themselves from established fields and disciplines, setting knowledge in motion. Globalisation offers a complex image of the world, fragmented by particularisms and political borders even as it forms a single economic zone. Today's artists travel this expanse and insert the forms they produce into networks or lines; in works that generate knowledge effects today, the space of contemporary life appears as a four-dimensional expanse in which time is one of the coordinates of space. [...]

'Aboriginals, it was true, could not imagine territory as a block of land hemmed in by frontiers: but rather as an interlocking network of "lines" or "ways through." "All our words for country", he said, "are the same as words for *line*."'[1] This is how the writer Bruce Chatwin introduces his description of the 'walkabouts' of the Australian aborigines, a practice whose adoption by the West might cause a true topographical revolution, The walkabout is a ritual journey in which the aborigines walk in the footsteps of their ancestors and 'sing the country' as they travel through it. Each strophe recapitulates the creation of the world, since the ancestors created and named all things by singing. 'What the whites used to call the "Walkabout"', Chatwin writes, 'was, in practice, a kind of bush-telegraph-cum-stock-exchange, spreading messages between peoples who never saw each other, who might be unaware of the other's existence'. [2] It is hard not to see the vision of space revealed in the walkabout as a wonderful metaphor for the contemporary art exhibition and as the prototype of the journey-form. Topography, used so much by contemporary artists, defines a pictorial site that is geared to the viewer's real movements in everyday life. Walking constitutes a text in itself, which the artwork translates into the language of topology. [3]

Even though it expresses a path, the journey-form puts linearity in crisis by injecting time into space and space into time. [...]

If time today has been spatialised, then the heavy presence of the journey and of nomadism in contemporary art is linked to our relationship with history: the universe is a territory the entire dimensions of which can be travelled – the temporal as well as the spatial. Today, contemporary artists enact their relations with the history of art under the sign of travel, by using nomadic forms or adopting vocabularies that come from the interest in 'elsewhere'. The past is always present; one need only make up one's mind to go there. [...]

Thus, radicant artists construct their paths in history as well as geography. Modernist radicality (which sought to return to the origin in order to efface the past of tradition and rebuild it on new foundations) is succeeded by a radicant subjectivity, which might be defined as a new modality for representing the world: as a fragmentary space that blends the virtual and the real, in which time represents another dimension of space. This unification, however, is the spitting image of the ultimate objective of global capitalism: translated into economic terms, it is a question of a vast common market, a free-trade zone unsegmented by any border. For time and history, like borders, are producers of distinctions, factors of division, disruptive elements that the logic of globalisation tends to weaken by diluting them in the smooth and unobstructed space of free trade. What is the only solution available to artists that does not involve contributing to the project of global cultural 'sweetening'? It is that which consists in the activation of space by time and time by space, in the symbolic reconstruction of fault lines, divisions, fences, and paths in the very place where the fluidified space of merchandise is established. In short working on alternative maps of the contemporary world and processes of filtration. [...]

Simon Starling, an archaeologist of the relations between nature and the world of modernism, is one of those artists who thematise the traceability of things, who analyse the social and economic components of our environment. Thus, for *Rescued Rhododendrons* (1999), he transported seven rhododendron plants from the north of Scotland to the south of Spain in a Swedish car (a Volvo), thus reconstructing the migration of this plant, which was introduced by a Swedish botanist in 1763, in reverse. For *Flaga*, 1972-2000 (2002), Starling drove a Fiat 126 – manufactured in 1974 – the distance of 1,290 kilometres that separates Turin, the automaker's headquarters, from the Polish city of Cieszyn, where some of that model's parts were manufactured at the time. Once back in Turin, Starling removed the car's engine, painted its body white and red – the colours of the Polish flag – and hung it on the wall, an object 'informed' by the journey that it made. Having balsa wood shipped from Ecuador and using it to build a model of a French airplane in Australia, transporting a Spanish cactus to Frankfurt, Starling models exports and exchanges, mapping modes of production by executing drawings within reality itself. In praise of metamorphosis, of permanent transformation: he takes apart a shed and turns it into a boat, aboard which he then goes sailing on the Rhine (*Shedboatshed* [*Mobile Architecture No.2*], 2005); travelling around a Spanish desert on a moped whose engine leaks water, he uses the latter to produce a watercolour of a cactus (*Tabernas Desert Run*, 2004). [...] But what today's artists above all retain from psychoanalysis is a knowledge of connections: how do things link up? What happens when one passes from one system to another, when a sign appears in a variety of assumed forms? Unlike the regime of transformation of energy described by psychoanalysis, translation has its own laws and norms. And even more clearly, it brings distinct and autonomous realities face to face and organises their displacement.

[…] Thus, one might define contemporary art in terms of a criterion of translatability, that is, according to the nature of the contents it transcodes, the manner in which it viatorises them and inserts them into a signifying chain. […]

Transformations, Translations, Transcodings

Since the 1980s, the planet has been dancing to the tune of the universal trend toward digitisation. Images, texts, and sounds are passing from an analogue state to a digital one, which allows them to be read by new generations of machines and subjected to novel types of processing. This development is not without repercussions for contemporary art. On the one hand, this is because it affects the sources and materials artists use; on the other, because it ceaselessly creates obsolescence (where does one go to find a VCR to play an old VHS videocassette? and what about those old vinyl records?); but also because digitisation is gradually destroying the old disciplinary divisions that held sway in the realm of technical equipment: on a computer today, one can listen to music, watch a movie, read a text, or look at reproductions of artworks. Its the end of the division of labour among household appliances; cultural post-Fordism for the family.

A single system of codes – the binary language of computing – now makes it possible to pass from a sound to a graphic representation and to manipulate images in a thousand different ways. Images are now defined by their density, by the quantity of atoms they contain.

How many pixels (picture elements)? Such is the new condition of the reading and transmission of images, centred on the capabilities of the computer, which today forms the basis of a new formal grammar developed by a new generation of artists. Artists, however, who do not necessarily utilise digital tools – for such tools are in any case part of the fabric of our manner of conceptualising, representing, processing and transmitting information.

Since it first took hold in the 1980s, home computing has gradually spread to all modes of thought and production. At the moment, however, its most innovative artistic applications stem from artists whose practice is quite distant from digital art of any kind – no doubt while waiting for something better to come along. But this is an area in which the computer as object is of very little importance compared to the new forms it generates, foremost among them [is] the mental operation at the very heart of the digital: transcoding. This passage from one code to another establishes, in contemporary artworks, a novel vision of space-time that undermines the notions of origin and originality: digitisation weakens the presence of the source, since every generation of an image is merely one moment in a chain without beginning or end. One can only reencode what was already encoded to begin with, and every act of encoding dissolves the authenticity of the object in the very formula of its duplication. The work of Kelley Walker may be regarded as emblematic of this practice of transferring, of keeping signs in intermediate formats that permit their propagation, like those microbial agents stored at ultra-low temperatures to maintain their virulence. These signs without origins or stable identities represent the base materials of form in the radicant era. Instead of producing an object, the artist works to develop a ribbon of significations, to propagate a wavelength, to modulate the conceptual frequency on which his propositions will be deciphered by an audience. Thus, an idea can pass from solid to supple, from subject matter to concept, from material work to a multiplicity of extensions and declensions. The art of the transfer one transports data or signs from one point to another, and this act is more expressive of our era than any other, Transformation, transcoding, passage, and formed displacement are the figures of this contemporary transferism.

To cite a few examples, when Pierre Huyghe transcribes his journey to Antarctica, he does so first in the form of an exhibition, then in that of a film, and then in that of an opera on ice. Liam Gillick transforms the story of a protest campaign by workers at a Volvo factory in Sweden into a series of minimal sculptural sequences – as if an abstract film had been subtitled by striking workers (*A Short Text on the Possibility of Creating an Economy of Equivalence*, 2005). Saâdane Afif uses André Cadere's sculptures from the 1970s as a kind of colour-coding system, which he then transforms into guitar chords played by automatons (*Power Chords*, 2005). He also produced musical equivalents of his own works in the form of poems commissioned from writers, which he then set to music (*Lyrics*, 2005). In a video presented at the Whitney Biennial in 2006, Jordan Wolfson translates Charlie Chaplin's speech in *The Great Dictator* into sign language. Jonathan Monk engages in literal acts of translation when he takes a conceptual work by Robert Barry and translates its English-language content first into one language, then another, then that into a third, and so on until the original meaning is completely lost in a final, incomprehensible English sentence (*Translation Piece*, 2002). In Peter Coffin's work, a sound becomes an integral factor in the growth of a green plant; a thought becomes a winding thread that materialises in neon, evoking certain works by Keith Sonnier; modernist artworks become elements of a shadow theatre; and a compilation of pieces of music becomes the tensor that will alter the configuration of a brain. Loris Greaud records an encephalogram of the moment in which he mentally elaborates one of his exhibitions, thus producing a diagram that will be translated into luminous impacts intended for a series of lamps that will blink on and off at the exhibition. A logic of connections: in these works, every element used is valued for its ability to modify the form of another. One could cite countless examples of these *transformat* practices, all of which attest to the fact that the invention of modes of passage from one regime of expression to another is indeed a major concern for the art of the 2000s. [...]

Translated Forms

The transfer: a practice of displacement, which highlights as such the passage of signs from one format to another. Speaking of the collective project *Ann Lee*, which involved the participation of a dozen artists, Philippe Parreno insists on the notion of passage: 'For me, it's a simple act of exhibition: the passage of a sign from hand to hand. *Ann Lee* was a flag without a cause (the cause was invented as it passed from hand to hand).'[4] As it happens, the medium used for this project was neither video nor any other specific discipline, but a character. A fictional character, the rights to which were acquired from a Japanese studio by Parreno and Pierre Huyghe, and which each artist – from Pierre Joseph and Doug Aitken to Dominique Gonzalez-Foerster and Richard Philips – was free to stage and interpret as he or she chose. The project *Ann Lee* thus made use of a system of formal translations based on a renewal of the idea of the medium, or rather on its original meaning as an 'intermediary between the world of the living and that of ghosts.' According to Walter Benjamin, a translation above all permits the original to survive, but it also entails its death. From the translation, there is no path leading back to the original text. Ann Lee, a Manga character, ultimately died a legal death at the end of her artistic use; thus, she only existed in and through her passage from one format to another, through the intervention of artists who brought her to 'life.' [...]

For his part, Barthélémy Toguo connects his giant watercolours, African motifs, and cardboard boxes to the economic flows linking Africa to multinational corporations. Kim Soo-Ja, a Korean artist, develops a vision inspired by the Tao in exhibitions that combine Minimal art with ancestral motifs, while Surasi Kusolwong constructs formal processes in which products of Thai folk and popular culture find themselves informed and deformed by Minimal and Conceptual art. Navin Rawanchaikul places the aesthetic of the Indian movie poster and Hollywood science fiction in the service of a narrative epic that stages the role of art and its definition in the style of Conceptual art. All these practices have in common a focus on translation: elements belonging to a local visual or philosophical culture are transferred from a traditional universe in which they were strictly codified and fixed to one in which they are set in motion and placed beneath the gaze of a critical reading.

1   [Footnote 93 in source] Bruce Chatwin, *Songlines* (New York: Penguin, 1987) 56.

2   [94] Ibid., 56–7.

3   [95] Doug Aitken, 'A Thousand Words: Doug Aitken Talks About Electric Earth (Interview by Saul Antoni)', *Artforum*, vol. 38, no. 9 (May 2000) 160.

4   [110] Philippe Parreno, 'Ann Lee: Vie et Mort d'un Signe. Entretien Avec Frédéric Chapon', *Frog*, no.3 (Spring/Summer 2006).

Nicolas Bourriaud, extracts from *The Radicant* (New York: Lukas & Sternberg, 2010) 112–4, 121–2, 124–5, 126–7, 131–6, 138–40.

Barbara Casavecchia
Pratchaya Phinthong//2011

[...] Another work by Phinthong on show in Basel, *An Average Thai Berry Picker's Income* (2010) 2,513 Swedish krona (about £240), framed and presented in an orderly grid of notes and coins – is part of the project 'give more than you take', developed by the artist during 2010 and 2011 at the Centre d'art contemporain in Brétigny and the Galleria d'Arte Moderna e Contemporanea in Bergamo. Instead of participating in a residency he had been granted in Paris, Phinthong (who graduated in 2004 from Frankfurt's Städelschule, where he studied under Tobias Rehberger) decided to travel to northern Sweden and join a group of seasonal Thai workers hired to pick berries and paid in accordance with the amount of fruit collected. He sent a daily text message to curator Pierre Bal-Blanc in Brétigny informing him of the number of kilos he had collected and asking him 'to organise a collection of useless objects, waste, recycling or leftover items' in the exhibition space each day to match the weight of berries he had picked. After two months, this had accumulated to 549 kilos. Phinthong was paid 8,000 Swedish krona, but after deductions for petrol and food, he was left with only 2,513 krona.

While he was away, Phinthong didn't leave any instructions about how to install and display the objects. When the exhibition travelled to Bergamo, curator Alessandro Rabottini was afforded the same freedom as Bal-Blanc. As a result, the 'translation' of the work into different visual and formal currencies produced two dissimilar equivalents: in Paris the accumulation was cool, bulky and hard-edged, while in Bergamo the use of fresh earth from an area of the museum still under construction, and the transcription of the initial email exchange in handwriting along the walls, gave the piece a softer, narrative edge. Both curators were forced to draw from their own 'aesthetic capital' and assume the less comfortable role of artistic producers vis-à-vis their audience. Phinthong's use of money as a conceptual tool to produce art work echoes Lawrence Weiner's famous *Declaration of Intent* (1968):

1. The artist may construct the piece.
2. The piece may be fabricated.
3. The piece need not be built. Each being equal and consistent with the intent of the artist the decision as to condition rests with the receiver upon the occasion of receivership.

But Phinthong's approach also calls attention to the wider (dare one say) existential issues involved. Another of his pieces consists of two identical copies of Scottish philosopher John Macquarrie's book *Existentialism* (1976): one was partly eaten by termites, which Phinthong replicated in the other edition, down to every hole and ripped corner. Indeed, even in the art world, the labour involved sometimes can be reduced to the choice between – as the title of the work suggests – *my brain or my stomach* (2008).

Barbara Casavecchia, extract from 'In Focus: Pratchaya Phinthong', *frieze* (November 2011). Available at https://frieze.com/article/focus-pratchaya-phinthong

Walid Raad
Section 139: The Atlas Group (1989–2004)//2014

In 2005 the Sfeir-Semler Gallery opened in Beirut, in an industrial quarter called Karantina.

Some of you already know that Karantina was the site of a brutal massacre of civilians in 1976. I am not going to talk about this here.

The Sfeir-Semler Gallery opened on the fourth floor of a large former warehouse. It is an 800-square-meter space, with clean four-meter-high, sixty-centimeter-thick white walls, smooth concrete floors, and diffuse northern lighting all around. It is the white cube of white cubes. We have never had a space this beautiful in Beirut. Some of us have been waiting for a space like this for forty years.

The name of the person who opened the gallery is Andrée Sfeir. Andrée also owns a gallery in Hamburg that I work with. And when she opened the new space in Beirut, Andrée began asking me about the possibility of exhibiting my project called *The Atlas Group (1989–2004)* in the Beirut gallery.

I should say that *The Atlas Group (1989–2004)* is a project I worked on for fifteen years. It is a project about the wars in Lebanon, but it is also a project I have never shown in Lebanon. For some reason, I could never do it. I always feared that something would happen to the works. It's not that I thought it would be censored or anything like that. I just felt that the works would somehow be affected, though I could not say exactly how.

In 2005 I refused Andrée's persistent offers to show this work in Beirut. And I tried to explain my feelings to her, without much success.

In 2006 she asked me again. I refused again.

In 2007 she asked me again. I refused again.

In 2008 she asked me again. But this time, I agreed. I don't know why. I just agreed to do it.

I proceeded to print and frame my photographs, to produce the sculptures and videos, to design the exhibition space, to print all the wall texts. And I sent these to the gallery in Beirut.

Three weeks later I went to the gallery to see my mounted display, and this is what I confronted. I found myself facing the reduction in scale of every single one of my artworks to 1/100th of their original size. Each and every artwork I had done now appeared to me as a miniature object.

At first, and given my psychological history, I thought my mind was playing tricks on me. I was convinced that I was in the midst of a psychotic episode.

So I called Hassan. Hassan is an installer in the gallery. I asked him to stand with me in front of this "situation" and to describe to me what he saw.

Hassan arrived, and immediately he began to marvel at the detail of the small-scale reproductions, which proved to me that the works also appeared to Hassan at 1/100th of their original size. But I also know from my own reading in psychology that, in the history of psychiatry, no two people have ever experienced the exact same psychotic episode at the same time. And I doubted that this situation was a historical exception. I then became convinced that I was not in fact in the midst of a psychotic episode but that my assistant, my framer, and my printer were behind all of this. I became convinced that, without telling me, they had decided to make everything small. They produced all my works at 1/100th of their size as some kind of practical joke. Or better yet, as some kind of gift, because they know how fond I am of all things miniaturised.

A couple of hours later, when my assistant, my framer, and my printer arrived, they were all struck by the technical aspects of the miniaturisation. They assured me that they had nothing to do with this. In fact, they felt that the joke was on them. They also felt betrayed by the fact that I went behind their backs and chose to work with another team on this piece, as if they were not up to the technical challenge. One of them even said to me spitefully: your works look better small anyhow, when one cannot see them well.

Hearing this, I immediately realised that I had no other choice. I was forced to face the fact that, in 2008, in Beirut, all my artworks shrank.

So I decided that I needed to build a new white cube better suited to the new dimensions of my works. And that is exactly what I did.

Walid Raad, 'Section 139: The Atlas Group (1989–2004)', *e-flux Journal*, no. 51 (January 2014) (https://www.e-flux.com/journal/51/59947/section-139-the-atlas-group-1989-2004/).

Basel Abbas and Ruanne Abou-Rahme
And Yet My Mask is Powerful//2016

First the air is blue and then
it is bluer and then green and then
black I am blacking out and yet
my mask is powerful
It pumps my blood with power*

The clearing. We find ourselves in the wreck once again and then again. A perpetual crisis leaves us suspended at ground zero. The potential to radically re-imagine the world, so palpable only a blink of an eye ago, now tastes bitter in our mouths.

Neolithic masks, taken from the West Bank and surrounding areas, stored in private collections are hacked and 3D-printed. The oldest known masks, dating 9,000 years, mutate from fossil to living matter. Copies circulate in Palestine, eerily akin to a black ski mask. A group of youths wear them at the site of a destroyed Palestinian village in Israel. Becoming other, becoming anonymous, in this accidental moment of ritual and myth. Initiating a series of trips to possess, and almost be possessed by, these strangely living sites of erasure and wreckage. Only now, returning to the site of destruction as the very site from which to cast a new projection that evokes the potential of an unrealised time, not bound by the here and now of colonial time.

And yet my mask is powerful confronts the apocalyptic imaginary and violence that dominates our contemporary moment, a vision that seems to clog up even the pores in our bodies. Taking Adrienne Rich's poem 'Diving into the Wreck' as the beginnings of a script, the work asks what happens to people/place/things/ materials when a living fabric is destroyed. How in the face of such violence can we then begin to retrieve and reconstitute living matter from the wreck itself. The project uses the trips taken by young Palestinians to sites of destroyed villages inside Israel, as an avatar for re-thinking the site of wreckage. In these returns the site of wreckage becomes the very material from which to trace the faint contours of another possible time.

Something strange happens in these returns. The destroyed sites emerge not just as places of ruin or trauma, but appear full of an unmediated vitality. The young people making these trips treat the site as a living fabric. They reactivate the disused spaces, camp out on site, eat, sing, dance.

Because of the possibility of these very returns, more times than not the site is hidden in one way or another, often cordoned off by barbed wire and signs that forbid entry. These acts of enclosure attempt to freeze and fossilise the sites, to transform them into a dead space of archaeological interest rather than living sites that can be reinhabited. Whose buildings, land and vegetation can be almost too easily rehabilitated back into the present tense. At many of these sites, people return to use the Churches and Mosques, though later they may find them closed off in the name of 'restoration'. What is implicit is that once the sites are 'restored' they will become archeological sites, the spaces can no longer be used - they enter the dead time of history rather than the living time of the present. And yet these policies don't seem to be successful. People continue to return creating openings in the wires wide enough for bodies to pass through, into another possible present.

But even more, something in the very tissue of the site itself is undeniably living. It permeates from the soil into the stone and back into every bit of vegetation. There is a swarm of non-human life forces here, from the insects to the wild thorns, to the pomegranate trees that are inscribed with the living memory and story of the site. And it is here in the living archive of the vegetation itself that the site lives and breathes. Often one can not find the destroyed village. It has been obscured by pines planted in the wake of the destruction, planted sometimes to obscure the remains. And yet the signs of the old vegetation lead you to the remains. Often it could be the sign of cactus, or the smell of wild fennel, the trails of wild asparagus, or a lone pomegranate tree. There is a strange sort of magic in being led by plants and trees back to these sites. These non-human forms of life resist the erasure of these sites as much if not more than the young people returning to them. Every Spring they bloom again as if by magic, insisting on the living in a site that has been declared dead, in a space that was meant to be forgotten.

In its intersections between performativity and ritual, body and artefact, thingness and virtuality, *And yet my mask is powerful* begins to splice together a counter-mythology to the dominant mythologies of the present. A counter-mythology that holds on to our imaginative space as the last terrain to be occupied. The layers of images, text, sound and things perform and activate various forms of returns, flash-forwards and déja vu unfolding in this gesture a dense story of erasures and reappearances, dispossession and resistance, the archaic resonating in the contemporary.

*extract from Adrienne Rich, 'Diving into the Wreck', 1973

Basel Abbas and Ruanne Abou-Rahme, 'And Yet My Mask is Powerful (2016–2018) [footnotes omitted]. Earlier version available at www.carrollfletcher.com/exhibitions/57/overview/

And those aspiring changemakers could communicate with each other like never before. […] a new traffic of words and information appeared, flowing for the first time in centuries from both South to North

and North to South. A new equality had arrived between the disenfranchised youth of the world.

Omar Robert Hamilton, 'Moments of Clarity', 2016

SPEAKING GLOBALLY

Karl Marx and Friedrich Engels
The Manifesto of the Communist Party//1848

The bourgeoisie has through its exploitation of the world market given a cosmopolitan character to production and consumption in every country. To the great chagrin of Reactionists, it has drawn from under the feet of industry the national ground on which it stood. All old-established national industries have been destroyed or are daily being destroyed. They are dislodged by new industries, whose introduction becomes a life and death question for all civilised nations, by industries that no longer work up indigenous raw material, but raw material drawn from the remotest zones; industries whose products are consumed, not only at home, but in every quarter of the globe. In place of the old wants, satisfied by the production of the country, we find new wants, requiring for their satisfaction the products of distant lands and climes. In place of the old local and national seclusion and self-sufficiency, we have intercourse in every direction, universal inter-dependence of nations. And as in material, so also in intellectual production. The intellectual creations of individual nations become common property. National one-sidedness and narrow-mindedness become more and more impossible, and from the numerous national and local literatures, there arises a world literature.

Karl Marx and Friedrich Engels, *Manifesto of the Communist Party* (1848) (New York: International Publishers, 1998) 12–13.

S.S. Prawer
Karl Marx and World Literature//1978

[...] The articles that Marx published in the *Neue Rheinische Zeitung* appeared – like all other articles in that journal – without their author's name. This was a matter of principle [...] What mattered were the causes the journal fought for – the success of the German revolution, a war of liberation against Russia, self-determination for Italians, Hungarians, Poles, and the advance of the proletariat throughout the world. it wanted to be a thorn in the flesh of reactionary authorities, not 'a mere collection of literary contributions'.

The very first article, however, which later research has traced unequivocally to Marx himself, demonstrates how important a part literary quotation, allusion, adaptation, and parody was once again destined to play in his polemics.

[...] There are quotations also from Heine's 'Ritter Olaf', 'Der Tannhauser, 'Our Navy' (*Unsere Marine*), 'Georg Herwegh', 'Anno 1829', 'The Changeling' (*Der Wechselbalg*), Atta Troll, and 'Kahldorfon the Nobility' (*Kahldorf über den Adel*). Quotations from Burger's 'Lenore' and from a play by Ferdinand Raimund appear in the *Neue Rheinische Zeitung* in contexts similar to those in which Heine had used them. There are constant references to, and quotations from, the literature of the past: Homer, Virgil, the Bible, the Arabian Nights, Shakespeare, Moliere, Beaumarchais, Goethe, and Schiller; minor works like Arnold Kortum's eighteenth-century mock epic *The Adventures of Hieronymus Jobs* (*Die Jobsiade*) are not neglected; and we find an allusion to Cooper's *The Last of the Mohicans*, a snatch from Matthias Claudius's 'Rheinweinlied', as well as repeated references to Freiligrath's translation of Robert Burns' 'For a' that and a' that'. [...]

Many of Marx's literary and mythological allusions are parodistic. Thus a Prussian state-solicitor appears as Aphrodite, the Prussian militia as Theseus, the *Neue Rheinische Zeitung* itself as Ariadne, Prince William of Prussia as Aeneas, the minister in charge of the Prussian police forces as 'the faithful Eckart of constitutional liberty', and so on. Biblical references in particular are often introduced into deliberately incongruous contexts – as when German patriots are ironically enjoined to behave, in face of antiquated and tyrannous customs, like Moses before the burning bush. [...]

Sometimes Marx heightens or varies a well-known quotation, one which most of his readers would know sufficiently well to hold against his variation: as when he says, in face of the Prussian counter-revolution, that not 'something' but everything is rotten in this 'state of Denmark'. It is striking to notice how frequently a quotation from one of the authors Marx most admired – Shakespeare, Goethe, Heine – will form the climax of one of those carefully constructed yet impassioned periods which are so characteristic a feature of his journalistic prose. He needed the words of great writers to confirm and sanction his own.

S.S. Prawer, extracts from *Karl Marx and World Literature* (Oxford: Oxford University Press, 1978) 152–3, 156–7, 158.

Hito Steyerl
Can the Subaltern Speak German?//2002

[...] The debate on cultural globalisation also often involves so-called postcolonial theory. What does this encompass? According to Ruth Frankenbert and Lata Mani, postcolonialism refers to a specific 'conjuncture' of social force fields and a type of political positioning in relation to local conditions.[1] Geopolitical power gradients strongly influence these social relations. They influence the emergence of certain subjectivities – and thus also the production of art and the formation of the aesthetic and cognitive categories of its perception.[...]

> Although there are important differences between migrant, forced and guest workers, and these cannot be treated equally or uniformly at all, it is worth looking for lines of connection. This makes it possible to reveal differences as well as what they have in common, which enable statements about structures that have a lasting effect, as well as discourses and practices across different eras. [...] When we look at the initial foundation of postcolonial migration in the Federal Republic of [Germany], then we immediately recognise a number of historical, discursive and functional parallels between so-called migrant, alien and guest workers, which indicate continued racist colonialist practices [2] [...]

Those who are 'silent about colonial presences', according to Ha, should not even begin to speak of phenomena such as 'hybridity' or postcolonialism. Postcoloniality, according to Ha, is namely 'not primarily a chronological epochal term marking the period after formal political independence from western colonial powers, but rather a politically motivated category of analysis of the historical, political, cultural and discursive aspects of the colonial discourse that is not yet closed'.[3]

According to this reading, postcoloniality comprises 'a site of political positioning. This site is woven into the memory and the legacy of a colonial past and its present formation and effectivity.'[4]

The differences between the various local conjunctures of postcoloniality must therefore be investigated in a locally specific analysis. This investigation also enables the development of analytical instruments, which take into consideration the local historical and political background of phenomena of ethnicising, gendering and class-specific positioning that are specific to globalisation. Here, the analysis of postcolonial, feminist, and anti-racist critique means paying attention to the geographical and political context, in which this critique is produced and through which it is formed.

This also applies most of all to a critical consideration of the artistic and theoretical language of forms, which has repeatedly been named in conjunction with postcolonial critique as its privileged medium, specifically so-called hybrid mixed forms. As Umut Erel stresses, the possibilities of the hybridity discourse are not only subject to analytical and strategic limitations.[5] Hierarchies of different cultural hybrids and genres also emerge within the framework of a global, western-dominated capitalism that is nourished by local differences. The effect of these hierarchies is that primarily Anglo-American forms of hybridity are privileged over others and interpreted as universal and solely valid examples of cultural mixtures. In conjunction with the conditions of utilisation in the global cultural industry, they are objectified, exoticised, sexualised, and thus de-politicised. In this hierarchisation of cultural hybrid forms, a ranking prevails, which privileges the products of economically and militarily dominant countries such as England or the USA – but which rejects cultural productions from the global south as being archaic, backwards and thus inferior. The hierarchies of the international distribution of labour translate directly into culturally racist hierarchies in the aesthetic field. Different languages of form must first be recontextualised, in order for these reductionist readings to be interpreted as the effects of discursive power relations in the context of global capitalist forms of utilisation.

In comparison, an analysis of various artistic and theoretical languages of form in postcolonial conjunctures that are just as diverse demonstrates the global interdependence of different forms of articulation all over the world.[6] In contrast to cultural studies one-sidedly oriented to the cultural production of the north, Ella Shohat and Robert Stam argue for an analysis of the effects of global inequality on cultural and theoretical articulations worldwide, oriented to the world-system theory.[7] In contrast to Eurocentric constraints, they favour an investigation of 'multi-temporal heterogeneities', in other words the analysis of simultaneous, mutually superimposed space-temporalities, which influence the production of social texts. This approach is based on the assumption that structural overdevelopment and underdevelopment not only influence one another in the area of economics, but also affect artistic articulations.

This becomes particularly evident if not only postcolonial contexts in the global northwest are investigated, but if these are also placed in relation to worldwide feminist articulations. Postcolonial contexts in Eastern Europe thus differ not only in their formal articulations, but also in the multiple logics of domination manifested in them.

What must be taken into consideration in categorising different cultural and theoretical productions in different postcolonial contexts, are therefore the locally specific conditions of their production. The postcolonial cultural hybrid forms of the north are also entangled in global capitalism's ways of production and thus reproduce existing power gradients in the context of the international distribution of labour. Social inequality is coded as cultural difference or even deficiency and thus made invisible. This constant reproduction of culturalised inequality forms the law of the 'unequal development' of global capitalism. The Eurocentric hierarchisations of various postcolonial contexts thus reproduce culture-racist mechanisms of exclusion, which for their part represent a fundamental structural element of global capitalist forms of utilisation and/or exploitation.

In reference to the contextualisation of various postcolonial articulations in conjunction with their global interdependence, the question - rephrased from a saying by Gayatri Spivak – must be raised, 'what sort of coding has produced this text?'.[8] Spivak's interest focuses on the specific power relations that enable an individual to describe and explain herself or himself within a certain logic.

In reference to the transfer of postcolonial approaches to the context, in this sense we must not only ask with Spivak's words: Can the subaltern speak?, or even: Can the subaltern speak German? Instead the question must be: But even if he or she has been talking on for centuries – why didn't anybody listen?

1   Ruth Frankenberg & Lata Mani, 'Crosscurrents, Crosstalk: Race, "Postcoloniality" and the Politics of Location', in *Cultural Studies* vol. 7 no. 2, 292–310 (1993) 292. Kien Nghi Ha, *Postkoloniale Migration, Rassismus und die Frage der Hybridität* (u.v.M, 2002).

2   Kien Nghi Ha, *Postkoloniale Migration, Rassismus und die Frage der Hybridität* (u.v.M, 2002).

3   Kien Nghi Ha, *Ethnizität und Migration* (Opladen, 1999).

4   (Gutiérrez Rodriguez, 2000) [full reference not provided in original].

5   Umut Erel, 'Grenzüberschreitungen und kulturelle Mischformen als antirassistischer Widerstand?', in eds. Cathy Gelbin, Kader Konuk and Peggy Piesche, *Aufbrüche. Kulturelle Produktionen von Migrantinnen, Schwarzen und jüdischen Frauen in Deutschland* (Königstein, 1999).

6   Ella Shohat & Robert Stam, 'Narrativizing Visual Culture – Towards a Polycentric Aesthetics', in ed. Nicholas Mizoeff, *The Visual Culture Reader* (London and New York: Routledge, 2000).

7   Immanuel Wallerstein, *The Modern World-System, I: Capitalist Agriculture and the Origins of European World-Economy in the Sixteenth Century* (New York and London, 1974).

8   Gayatri Chakravorty Spivak, 'Can the Subaltern Speak?', in eds. C. Nelson & L. Grossberg, *Marxism and the Interpretation of Culture* (Chicago: University of Illinois, 1988).

Hito Steyerl, extracts from 'Can the Subaltern speak German? Postcolonial Critique', trans. Aileen Derieg, from *under translation* (Vienna and Linz: eipcp – European Institute for Progressive Cultural Policies, 2002) (http://translate.eipcp.net/strands/03/steyerl-strands01en/print).

Shahidul Alam
In Conversation with Naeem Mohaiemen//2006

[...] *Naeem Mohaiemen* In the 1980s, you left London to move back to Dhaka and start Drik. In your writing, you've talked about the need to locate media work outside the dominant narrative spaces. Both you and your partner, anthropologist Rahnuma Ahmed, also consciously made a decision to conduct all your work in the Bengali language, Bangla, even in the difficult case of transliterated email.

Shahidul Alam I returned to Bangladesh, where I was always going to be. The biggest need was to change the way majority-world countries were portrayed. I was working with a London-based studio, and the only pictures they ever seemed to be interested in were pictures of disaster or poverty. So being based in Dhaka was a fairly automatic decision.

My partner Rahnuma and I were involved in the anti-military junta agitations at that time, so I began documenting that movement. It was a much more 'lived' experience than I had felt before. The move towards speaking Bangla and the introduction of new media were, in combination, a mechanism aimed at reducing the digital divide. Without international lines, faxes, or money to make expensive calls, we needed to find other ways to communicate. So setting up Bangladesh's first email network was an obvious choice.

The introduction of written Bangla in Roman text dramatically changed the demographics of participants in our internet network, which brought home the centrality of the vernacular, even in urban, literate circles. Since then we've brought out several books and a photography magazine in Bangla. Later we developed a Bangla font that could be used on the net, which we used in the online magazine I was publishing, so we could reverse the information flow.

Mohaiemen [...] This brings to mind all the differences in privilege, access, interests, methodology and networks that are created when artists migrate. Bangladesh has a different trajectory from the exile dynamics in locales like Lebanon, Iran or Sri Lanka, but at times we've had equally volatile eruptions, especially the turbulent Seventies with coups, counter-coups, and dirty wars. Those in exile or in diasporic conditions may choose to locate in 'the belly of the beast', to challenge from inside. But for this to work, diaspora cultural producers need a theoretical and practical framework for exchanges between those who 'stayed' and those who 'left'.

Alam Leaving aside my overseas education, I was conscious of the fact that I was highly privileged in Bangladesh, by the fact that I had the opportunity to study and did not have to worry about tomorrow's meal. We had all used the resources of this country for our education, but wealthier countries were reaping the benefits of that training. Through us, Bangladesh was effectively subsidising the West.

If enabling social change is measured, it is in Bangladesh that one can get the maximum returns for one's efforts. This works at a personal and emotional level, and also if you evaluate how we can change our lives. But there are obvious risks of working in Bangladesh, particularly for journalists for whom this is said to be the most dangerous country after Iraq [according to the Committee to Protect Journalists]. [...] Being overseas allows one to work with greater impunity and substantially lower risk. Technological benefits, as well as greater mobility, and the ability to [this] network gives advantages that working here does not. Travelling on a Bangladeshi passport also makes a lot of my international work quite difficult (I was off-loaded from flights twice after 9/11). I see clearly different roles for those who work within and those outside. Moral judgement and self-righteousness shouldn't enter either sphere. [...]

Mohaiemen Drik has always maintained the difficult position of not being dependent on donor money but surviving instead through your own commercial assignments. You also have an honourable commitment to internal wage equity, so that your salary is only slightly higher than the entry-level employee. But some of the photographers you train eventually leave to take higherpaying jobs with NGOs and foreign donor agencies. What are your thoughts about this dynamic?

Alam Being financially independent is essential for the credibility of a media organisation. But we do take on contractual work, some of which is derived from grants. From a donor perspective, 'partnership' can be simply a pretty word to use, and consultants and machinery continue to be tied to sources of funds. So donors assume a subservience in any partnership they enter into. The USIS [United States Information Service] reminded us that they would never work with us since we opposed Clinton's visit to Bangladesh. Similarly, the British Council reminded us that Bangla-right's [banglarights.net] opposition to the invasion of Iraq would jeopardise future projects. They would never demonstrate such arrogance in their own countries (and have learned never to try it again with Drik). We know that we are black-listed by many donor organisations and will never get work from them, but we take that as an indicator of our success.

Our salary structure does cause problems, and things like our equal bonus policy is not always welcomed by those in higher ranks, and yes, we do lose people to NGOs and donor agencies, which is not a bad thing. What disappoints me is when bright energetic youngsters with spark get head-hunted by the donors and turned into well-paid clerks who do the donkey-work for their western counterparts. [...]

Naeem Mohaiemen, extracts from 'A Conversation with Shahidul Alam', *Bidoun: Arts and Culture from the Middle East* (Autumn 2006). Available at https://bidoun.org/articles/shahidul-alam-and-naeem-mohaiemen

Suzana Milevska
Is Balkan Art History Global?//2007

[...] The issue of translation in art history is in a way related to the issue of historicity and backwardness.[1] If Western art history is taken, as it usually is, as a point of reference, then it comes as no surprise that the question of translation produces the effect of lag and backwardness. The sooner the translation of a certain book is published, the more widely it can spread in the academic world. However, it is important to underline here that the translation of art history books from one language to another is, more than any other kind of translation an issue of cultural translation. The translation of an art historical text is a question not of names, facts, or dates, but of geographic settings.

Academics from remote countries that are not a part of the Western scholarly world often complain because they do not have to the latest books written in English and published by renowned university professors in the West. I find that one of the greatest obstacles to the globalisation of art history is the focus on only one direction of translation. I would argue that cultural translation, unlike linguistic translation, is only possible if it goes in reciprocal directions and that art history is not an exception of this rule. [...]

In 1980, I witnessed a dramatic event at the Art History Department in Skopje (then Yugoslavia, today Macedonia). I was a second-year student and I was invited to attend a press conference held by our professors (today most of them are retired). The immediate reason for the conference was a journalist's attack that had been published in a local newspaper by an ex-student of art history from the same department. He had written a severe critique, claiming basically that the professors were lazy, and that they had not produced any relevant articles or books. One of the professors who had been asked to deal with the 'hot potato' led the press conference; he brought into the room a great pile of books, magazines, abstracts and other materials that were to prove that the newspaper article was simply a mean and naïve attempt at revenge for some disagreements between the student and his ex-professors. The number of papers was really amazing, and at first I thought the department was astonishingly productive.

What struck me then, and stays with me even now as I think back to this episode, is that not one single book on display in that pile that was an attempt to summarise Western and Eastern European art in the span of a single volume. Not a single book or essay discussed anything but Macedonian art, regardless of the period (ancient, medieval, or contemporary). All the texts on display were nationally oriented historical overviews of certain medieval monuments, monographs on contemporary artists or on Macedonian art in general, or textbooks that were solely devoted to Western European artists. There was not a single translation of any article or a book by an internationally renowned art historian. Moreover, there was not a single translation of a book by any of my professors into another language, not even into the neighbouring languages – into any of the twenty Balkan languages. This episode took place twenty-five years ago. Many things have changed since then, except the last.

Art history changes. It slowly opens up toward other disciplines and toward nonlinear temporalisation. It lends itself to different methodologies that go beyond the comparison between Western and non-Western art. […]

If questions of historicity and translation become clearer in the light of cultural and postcolonial studies, and if those studies have helped art history to clarify its own objectives, then the educational system should follow, and attempt to create new and more flexible models of teaching that can elevate art history to a global level.

1   [Footnote 38 in source] Maria Todorova formulated the Balkans as determined by the issues of backwardness, 'sense of lag and lack': Maria Todorova, 'The Trap of Backwardness: Modernity, Temporality, and the Study of Eastern European-Nationalism', *Slavic Review* 64, no.1 (Spring 2005) 140–64, especially 145. In her article, Todorova focused on the issue of backwardness as a dominant trope in east European historiography, especially within the discourse of nationalism until the end of the twentieth century

Suzana Milevska, extracts from 'Is Balkan Art History Global?', in *Is Art History Global?*, ed. James Elkins (New York and London: Routledge, 2007) 218–19, 220–221, 222.

Mladen Stilinović
Footwriting//1984

The subject of my work is the language of politics, i.e. its reflection in everyday life. These works are not just made up. I would like to paint. I paint, but the painting betrays me. I write, but the written word betrays me. The pictures and words become not-my-pictures, not-my-words, and this is what I want to achieve with my work not-my- painting. If the language (the colour, the image, etc.) is possessed by ideology, I too want to become the owner of such a language. I want to think it with consequences. This is neither criticism nor ambiguity. What is imposed to me is imposed as a question, as an experience, as a consequence. If colors, words and materials have several meanings, which is the one that is imposed, what does it mean and does it mean anything – or is it just idle run a delusion? The question is how to manipulate that which manipulates you, so obviously, so shamelessly, but I am not innocent either – there is no art without consequences.

Mladen Stilinović, 'Footwriting', trans. Maja Šoljan, in *Mladen Stilinović, Instalacije / Installations* (Zagreb:Studio Galerije suvremene umjetnosti, 1984) n.p. Available at https://mladenstilinovic.com/works/5-2/

Luis Camnitzer
ALPHABETIZATION: Hegemonic Language and Arbitrary Order//2009

[...] The word literacy tries to accommodate many more issues than it has room for. There is the literacy of children entering adult society, the problem of functional illiteracy among adults, and the access from one language to another. What is common to all of these is that the language chosen to define literacy acquires a status of hegemony. Functionality then is to be achieved within what can be defined as a hegemonic language. Badly implemented literacy education can displace other existing functional codes, both in terms of orality and in what would then be 'non-hegemonic' languages. Sometimes this non-hegemonic language is just a communication code (from a baby's cry onward); sometimes it is a dialect or vernacular, sometimes a foreign language (in which there might be full illiteracy or just an inability to read the new, hegemonic language).

In the introduction to *The Making of Literate Societies*, David Olson and Nancy Torrance point out that when a new written code (language) forcefully enters a culture that has a pre-existing code (written or oral), this immediately generates illiteracy.[1] While the old code is devalued, the new one will not be fully acquired. Literacy therefore is simultaneously a tool of disempowerment and empowerment, one that creates a much richer and fragile situation than pedagogical methodologies manage to fully address. Literacy is presumed to allow us entrance into modern society and ensure survival, and the emphasis of teaching is on this aspect. This explains the interest of the state in offering compulsory and free primary schooling in a majority of countries. If the purpose were to empower and promote creative freedom, not only would different education systems be used, but everybody would also have access to free education up through a terminal degree.

Only later, after state interests are absorbed (or a critical distance is developed against them), may language become an instrument for freedom. Individual interests may only be satisfied once the expressive level is reached. Already in 1492 Antonio de Nebrija observed in his book about Castilian grammar: 'Language was always a partner of the Empire.'[2] Nebrija was very positive about this: the hegemonic language reduces the other languages to a secondary role or attempts to eliminate them. Spain eliminated Nahuatl in Mexico as well as another estimated 400 indigenous languages in Latin America. And when 'first languages' disappear, so does the knowledge that initially demanded and generated those languages.[3] In certain ways the same happens with the de-infantilisation of children's drawings, the loss of naïveté (or its stylistic freezing) in naïve art, or with the translation of tribal art into airport trinkets. In both the pre-literate stage and the other-literate stage the original codes used for communication are neglected, devalued, or condemned, rather than built upon. For some forms of education, colonisation may therefore be more than just metaphor. Insofar as the new code becomes the standard, class differences become sharper and new separations are created thanks to the profits brought about by the assimilation to the new code and protocols.[4]

The concept of 'multiliteracies' which emerged during the 1990s tried to address many of these issues.[5] Recognising that there is no valid 'canonic English' and responding to ideas prompted by globalisation, multiculturalism, and the changes in capitalism, 'The New London Group' developed a platform to change literacy pedagogies to both reflect and promote social change. Among the group's more radical goals is the redefinition of the teacher as a 'designer of teaching processes and environments,' and the extension of the notion of literacy from language to the broader concept of 'semiotic activities,' in which organised meaning is analysed in non-verbal activities like play. Looking for a language to encompass and help organise these more general activities, a differentiation emerged between language, dialect, and voice. Language here has the hegemonic role, while dialect may preserve some of the original codes reserved for vernacular communication, and voice gives power to the expression of the individual.

These distinctions also seem to apply to art, although with a difference in the respective emphases. In literacy, language – hegemonic language – is the medium to be mastered. In art, the hegemonic language is the reference against which one may deviate a little to show originality. In literacy and art, dialect or vernacular tends to be looked down upon. In art, clearly, it is the voice or personal expression that eventually is extolled by the market, as long it operates within the hegemonic language.

Voice/Personal Spelling

Typically, when discussing illiteracy, people make the assumption that the illiterate subject is 'ignorant' because he or she doesn't know how to translate oral code into a visual sign system. Accordingly, teaching someone how to do that is considered instruction, and the measure of success is the degree to which the product is free from deviations from the canon. Spelling rules, for example, are absolute; deviations are not only unlawful, but also seen as a badge of ignorance. Free play with spelling, made in the interests of expression, are only tolerated at a more advanced stage of education for those who qualify for the more rarified creative literature.

While there is a traditional neglect of voice and dialect in literacy, it is slowly being accepted that there should be a respect for the vernacular basis, and that there is a need to raise awareness and suggest an eventual contact with meanings.[6] Some educators even favor the development of personal forms of spelling (an opening for the 'voice') preceding the learning of the canonic one, so as to facilitate the contact of the written code with experienced reality.[7] Controversial at the early stages of literacy, the later use of vernacular misspellings and non-hegemonic wording can enhance both expression and communication. A prime example is Junot Diaz's *The Brief Wondrous Life of Oscar Wao* (2007), in which the vernacular Spanglish is so strong that the English and Spanish versions of the book become very similar.

The Placement of Order/The Arbitrary Order

Teaching coding and decoding solely as craft seriously impoverishes communication. [...]

This sequence, which is based on common sense, is not sufficient to eradicate authoritarianism in education. Authoritarianism is so deeply rooted in formal education that even 'progressive' reform committed to more 'permissive' pedagogy fails to tackle the key issues of who controls existing systems of order and their protocols, as well as the limits placed by them on thought and imagination.

Putting everything together, it would seem reasonable to start the learner on a quest to establish his or her own need for communication by exploring questions such as: What should be communicated, why, and in what system of order is that need located? Does it originate in the self, and, as a primary goal, seek its satisfaction? Is it of social use (to give pleasure, issue a warning, or provide enlightenment)? To whom is it communicated? What form of code does the idea to be communicated assume? What code should be used or created to translate the original idea? How will that code accommodate the message one has in mind? How will that communication be understood and be most persuasive?

It is ironic that these questions, in this sequence, would put teacher, illiterate student, artist, and fellow citizen all in the same position. By dispensing with hierarchies and pursuing the search, creation, and challenge of orders within which needs can be identified and decided upon, incentives for communication become the basis for constant learning and articulation. While this will not necessarily make everybody creative, at least it won't prevent the learner from being creative.

1   [Footnote 6 in source] David R. Olson & Nancy Torrance (eds.), *The Making of Literate Societies* (Oxford: Blackwell Publishers Ltd, 2001) 6.

2   [7] Fernando Báez, *A Universal History of the Destruction of Books* (New York: Atlas & Co., 2008) 126. In a petition to Queen Isabel, Nebrija wrote: 'Soon Your Majesty will have placed her yoke upon many barbarians who speak outlandish tongues. By this, your victory, these people shall stand in a new need; the need for the laws the victor owes to the vanquished, and the need for the language we shall bring with us' (cited in Illich and Sanders, 68–9).

3   [8] See K. David Harrison, *When Languages Die: The Extinction of the World's Languages and the Erosion of Human Knowledge* (New York: Oxford University Press, 2007).

4   [9] After the independence of Uganda, Milton Obote analysed the adoption of English as the official language, aware that there was no alternative: 'The Ugandan National Assembly should be a place where Uganda problems are discussed by those best able to discuss them, and in our situation it would appear that those best able to discuss our problems are those who speak English. This is a reasoning that cannot be defended anywhere; there is no alternative at the present moment.' Kwesi K. Prah, 'The Challenge of African Development', in *The Making of Literate Societies*, op. cit., 130–31.

5   [10] See The New London Group, 'A Pedagogy of Multiliteracies: Designing Social Futures', *Harvard Educational Review*, vol. 66, no. 1 (Spring 1996).

6   [11] *The Making of Literate Societies*, op. cit., 10.

7   [12] Utz Maas in 'Literacy in Germany', opposes this view, pointing out that written linguistic rules are too different for this first form of codification to be useful in the second. In *The Making of Literate Societies*, op. cit., 94–5.

Luis Camnitzer, extracts from 'ALPHABETIZATION, Part II: Hegemonic Language and Arbitrary Order', *e-flux Journal*, no. 10 (November 2009) (https://www.e-flux.com/journal/10/61355/alphabetization-part-ii-hegemonic-language-and-arbitrary-order/).

Alix Rule and David Levine
International Art English//2012

The internationalised art world relies on a unique language. Its purest articulation is found in the digital press release. This language has everything to do with English, but it is emphatically not English. It is largely an export of the Anglophone world and can thank the global dominance of English for its current reach. But what really matters for this language – what ultimately makes it a language – is the pointed distance from English that it has always cultivated. […]

Hypothesis

IAE [International Art English], like all languages, has a community of users that it both sorts and unifies. That community is the art world, by which we mean the network of people who collaborate professionally to make the objects and nonobjects that go public as contemporary art: not just artists and curators, but gallery owners and directors, bloggers, magazine editors and writers, publicists, collectors, advisers, interns, art-history professors, and so on. 'Art world' is of course a disputed term, but the common alternative – 'art industry' – doesn't reflect the reality of IAE. If IAE were simply the set of expressions required to address a professional subject matter, we would hardly be justified in calling it a language. IAE would be at best a technical vocabulary, a sort of specialised English no different than the language a car mechanic uses when he discusses harmonic balancers or popper valves. But by referring to an obscure car part, a mechanic probably isn't interpellating you as a member of a common world – as a fellow citizen, or as the case may be, a fellow traveller. He isn't identifying you as someone who does or does not get it.

When the art world talks about its transformations over recent decades, it talks about the spread of biennials. Those who have tried to account for contemporary art's peculiar nonlocal language tend to see it as the Esperanto of this fantastically mobile and glamorous world, as a rational consensus arrived at for the sake of better coordination. But that is not quite right. Of course, if you're curating an exhibition that brings art made in twenty countries to Dakar or

Sharjah, it's helpful for the artists, interns, gallerists, and publicists to be communicating in a common language. But convenience can't account for IAE. Our guess is that people all over the world have adopted this language because the distributive capacities of the Internet now allow them to believe – or to hope – that their writing will reach an international audience. We can reasonably assume that most communication about art today still involves people who share a first language: artists and fabricators, local journalists and readers. But when an art student in Skopje announces her thesis show, chances are she'll email out the invite in IAE. Because, *hey – you never know*. [...]

To appreciate this impulse and understand its implications, we need only consider e-flux, the art world's flagship digital institution. When it comes to communication about contemporary art, e-flux is the most powerful instrument and its metonym. [...] One can presume – or at very least imagine – that everyone in the art world reads it. [...]

Vocabulary

The language we use for writing about art is oddly pornographic: we know it when we see it. No one would deny its distinctiveness. Yet efforts to define it inevitably produce squeamishness, as if describing the object too precisely might reveal one's particular, perhaps peculiar, investments in it. Let us now break that unspoken rule and describe the linguistic features of IAE in some detail. IAE has a distinctive lexicon: *aporia, radically, space, proposition, biopolitical, tension, transversal, autonomy*. An artist's work inevitably interrogates, questions, encodes, transforms, subverts, imbricates, displaces – though often it doesn't do these things so much as it serves to, functions to, or seems to (or might seem to) do these things. IAE rebukes English for its lack of nouns: *Visual* becomes *visuality*, *global* becomes *globality*, *potential* becomes *potentiality*, *experience* becomes... *experiencability*. [...]

Genealogy

If e-flux is the crucible of today's IAE, the journal *October* is a viable candidate for the language's point of origin. In its pages, an American tradition of formalist art criticism associated with Clement Greenberg collided with continental philosophy. [...] In search of more rigorous interpretive criteria, *October's* editors translated and introduced to an English-speaking audience many French poststructuralist texts. The shift in criticism represented by *October* had an enormous impact on the interpretation and evaluation of art and also changed the way writing about art *sounded*. [...] [Its] emulators mimicked both the deliberate and unintentional features of the journal's writing, without discriminating between the two. Krauss and her colleagues aspired to a kind of analytic precision in their use of words, but at several degrees' remove those same words are used like everyday language: anarchically, expressively. [...] At the same time, the progeny of *October* elevated accidents of translation to the level of linguistic norms. IAE channels theoretical influences more or less aesthetically, sedimented in a style that combines their inflections and formulations freely and continually incorporates new ones. [...]

Implosion

[...] The collective project of IAE has become actively global. Acts of linguistic mimicry and one-upmanship now ricochet across the Web. (Usage of the word *speculative* spiked unaccountably in 2009; 2011 saw a sudden rage for *rupture*; *transversal* now seems poised to have its best year ever.) Their perpetrators have fewer means of recognising one another's intentions than ever. We hypothesise that the speed at which analytic terms are transformed into expressive, promotional tokens has increased.

As a language spreads, dialects inevitably emerge. The IAE of the French press release is almost too perfect: it is written, we can only imagine, by French interns imitating American interns imitating American academics imitating French academics. [...]

Alix Rule and David Levine, edited extracts from 'International Art English', *Triple Canopy*, no.16 (July 2012) (http://canopycanopycanopy.com/16/international_art_english) [footnotes omitted].

Martha Rosler
English and All That//2013

[...] I was prompted to write the present article by a request to participate in a public conversation addressing Alix Rule and David Levine's article 'International Art English', published in *Triple Canopy*. While I reserve the right to consider the original article as an elaborate joke, one hardly needs to be reminded that jokes are often a cover for hostility, and the more elaborate the joke, the more powerful the hostility may be. [...]

The universe of consumption provides a host of areas in which specialised language has great appeal. Nothing shows the power of 'expertise' more than organised sports, and men (primarily), young and old, learn to parse not only the precise rules but also the quantified actions and technical descriptions of sports, with their recollections of military formations. For the more pacific-minded, there is the language of film and television production, recently augmented by computer-derived jargons.

Migration of restricted discourses signifying expert engagement, however, requires more than a mastery of linguistic tropes; to avoid sounding ridiculous, one must learn when, where, and whether to deploy the terminology. Imitation, by cliché the sincerest form of flattery, may produce tortured language that unintentionally exposes ones's shortcomings. People aiming to sound learned or informed are often not very good at their highfalutin borrowings. [...]

Descriptive terms and phrases are the coin of the realm for copywriters, especially at demotic levels. Sniffing after the trail of press-release copy in the search for a diagnosis of a perceived art-world malady seems to misconstrue what a press release is and what it is designed to do or to be. It hardly needs to be said that a press release is a long-form piece of advertising copy, with embedded keywords.

Our diagnosticians note but may not quite understand that global English is a necessarily simplified language, most useful communicating simple ideas and instructions. [...]

After guiding us through the putative sources of the international linguistic code as used in generally non-professionally written press releases for small art venues, the article under discussion here finally reveals to us that the reductive use of this residual vocabulary of Continental theory is so *literally* uninformative that it amounts to an inadvertent poetry of sorts. But ornamental language always strives for a poetics; [...] the language is meant not so much as a validation but as a way of signalling the elevated niche in the particular universe of discourse in which the writer hopes to position the work in question. [...]

High-end venues, of course, do not need to pile on the descriptors; they don't have to try so hard [...] a rich clientele is not swayed by linguistic bling.

If someone wants to complain that the art market has so distorted the art world that all we have left in the wake of the death of critical engagement is the cannibalisation of theory into a string of faux freshwater pearls, it would be better, I should think, to put together an article exploring that subject. This would be preferable to basing a critique on a statistical model, or worse, to comparing the sales pitches of hapless, underpaid, non-native English speakers to pornography. [...] I idly speculate that the article's authors wish us to find lurking under debased copy its users' inferior taste because their writing flows from an inauthentic borrowed source.

Martha Rosler, extracts from 'English and All That', *e-flux Journal*, no. 45 (May 2013) (https://www.e-flux.com/journal/45/60103/english-and-all-that/).

Camille Henrot
Taxonomy and Power. Inventing Words vs. Inventing a Language//2016

Neologism is often one of the symptoms of the quest for authority. Each of these theories invents its own vocabulary and the reader has to create new lexicons for herself in order to approach them without misunderstanding. The philosopher is a *logothete*, and it is by this that he gains esteem and authority approaching that of a god – for what is greater than the creation of a new word?

But the abstraction and specialisation of philosophic language is an obstacle to the ethical, scientific, and political implications of the speculative materialist project, as it solidifies the authority of the knowledge of 'non-knowledge' and cements its impermeability to other disciplines. It is not new words we need in order to decentre the human, but a new language – one that is porous and capable of embracing different fields of study.

A new materialism would need to exit the incestuous circle of the academy that reinforces traditional Western figures of authority and to begin engaging in a generous dialogue with Eastern philosophies such as Buddhism, Taoism, Hinduism, and Shintoism, some of which have already posed the question of conscious matter and contemplated the mathematics of infinite possibilities.

> Non-being and being, having the same source, are distinct only in name. Call this source the obscure.
> – Lao-Tzu, *Tao Te Ching*

Camille Henrot, extract from 'Taxonomy and Power. Inventing Words vs. Inventing a Language', *October*, no. 155 (Winter 2016) 55.

Brian Droitcour
Societies of Out of Control: Language & Technology in Ryan Trecartin's Movies//2014

What we take to be graphics, sounds, and motion in our screen world is merely a thin skin under which resides miles and miles of language. Occasionally [...] the skin is punctured and, like getting a glimpse under the

hood, we see that our digital world – our images, our film and video, our sound, our words, our information – is powered by language. And all this binary information – music, video, photographs – is comprised of language, miles and miles of alphanumeric code. If you need evidence of this, think of when you've mistakenly received a .jpg attachment in an e-mail that has been rendered not as image but as code that seems to go on forever. It's all words (though perhaps not in any order that we can understand): The basic material that has propelled writing since its stabilised form is now what all media is created from as well.
– Kenneth Goldsmith[1]

When critics write about the video artist Ryan Trecartin's movies, they tend to talk about his editing, his forking and unfinished narratives, and the way their disconnections conjure the feeling of always being connected. The critics who write about Trecartin's movies tend to be art critics, and that is why they tend to write a visual analysis with a dash of social commentary, or vice versa. The dialogue gets disregarded, or it is quoted piecemeal; it is often described as 'gibberish' or 'nonsense', or assumed to be improvised. But in the seven movies of Trecartin's *Any Ever* sequence (2007-2010), and the ones that came before it, the dialogue is crafted. Trecartin began making these movies by writing scripts for them. And so his dialogue is not nonsense – or if it is, then it's nonsense in the way that the *zaum* of Russian Futurism is beyonsense. It's language so densely packed with meaning that it's impossible to apprehend on a superficial encounter. It's language that can be slowly picked apart, because it was so carefully created. When Trecartin writes a script he builds a house of language, just as his frequent collaborator, Lizzie Fitch, builds the sets for the movies, and in the editing room the movie is built from shots. The parts of the work that happen later in the process of making the movie – the camerawork, the makeup, the costumes – are prefigured in the way Trecartin works with words.

[…] One bit of wordplay that recurs in his work – sometimes in the words of the scripts, but more often in the way characters and scenarios are constructed – is a confusion of the *corporate* and the *corporeal*.

'Corporations are people,' as Mitt Romney once said. The corporation is a social technique by which a group of people acts together as one, in order to make money, to make things happen, to create changes and disturbances in a society and in the social world. How does the corporation do it? How does the corporation unite so many bodies to achieve its ends? It does it with branding, with corporate culture, with human resource management – all techniques for controlling behaviours, actions, and bodies. Language is the environment for this – and in the process language becomes a tool as well, a tool of human resource management, of corporate culture, of branding. Corporations are people but their bodies are huge and grotesque. Its avatars – the real people – have stunted bodies. Their impulses and affects are subjugated to the fluid discourses of a brand identity; they speak the stilted business tongue of PowerPoint slides and memos. We live in the time of corporate personhood – when corporate bodies and perlocutionary corporate speech make the models of how a person should be. [...]

Trecartin exploits the coincidence of homophony to elide the difference between an ontological position and a physical one. Just as the corporation's abstraction of the body is returned partially to the concrete, identity sits somewhere between a state of mind and a location of body. Mexico Korea, meanwhile, is neither an aquarium nor in one, which highlights language's status as the medium for inventing the very problems of positioning it's tasked with confronting.

Trecartin's flamboyant use of the patterns of chat and ads and other types of clichés in the dialogue isn't a direct form of copying, but a concentration of a normal condition of language use. A speaker is obliged to use words that come from outside her – and can be understood by others – while making them her own at the moment of the utterance, in order to make it seem like the utterance comes from inside her. And *K-CorealNC.K (section a)* dramatizes that condition in dialogue. And the script dramatises it in punctuation. Punctuation was invented to represent the pauses and pitches of speech. Long after it moved beyond this purpose to become a set of standards for clarifying the meaning of written language, punctuation marks were remixed as emoticons when writing began to take on the phatic functions of speech. Trecartin's unruly use of punctuation draws on all stages of its history. When, in the script's first lines, Mexico Korea says 'Yaw,,,,,' the comma does more than make a pause. It's a winking eye torn from a smiling face, repeated until it becomes a nervous tic. Colons join, parentheses cut, and in the designation of Global Korea's role – before the dialogue even starts – those marks are staggered to herald *K-CorealNC.K (section a)* as a drama of belonging and difference, of where the self stands with regards to others.

Incorporation is a technique of smoothing difference to produce inclusion and growth. Incorporation is the realization of a dream of a body that can be bigger, more powerful, more durable than a human body – better than the gross animal vessel our spirits carry around. But with the new spirit of capitalism the corporation aspires to be flexible, mutable, and fluid, unlike the old kind of company – the generations-old family business – with its rigid mimicry of aristocracy and sturdily pious Protestant values. In a time when corporations are people, the incorporated body is more like a real one – or, at least, the model it sets for how a person should be is gross. The corporate body (or its avatar) lives in a state of precarity, much like the real body is vulnerable to disease and mortality. It leaks, strains, and bulges. It screams at the world and it can't make sense of itself. […]

Bodies don't move much in Trecartin's videos yet the videos are characterised by a feeling of constant movement. What makes the movement is editing. Movement is reserved for speech and for technology; bodies move thanks to these things.

Bodies are moved by language. Like language, the houses of Trecartin's movies aren't sites; they are environments and tools for situating people. 'Neoliberal subjectivity' is a popular shorthand among critics for expressing the way that bodies behave (are handled) because of (by) capital now. The new spirit of capitalism is about subdividing the individual into nameable affinities (Facebook likes, dating profile stats) or competencies (the school assessment report, the HR office review), in order to incorporate bodies as other, more usable substances. Networked social being and bureaucratic procedure reify personal attributes and redefine subjecthood as situational and mobile – but the mobility is a characteristic of the attributes and the tools and technologies that move them, rather than of the bodies they came from. […]

The world of Trecartin's movies is a carnival. It shows everything as it could otherwise be. If a tool can be used to make something it can be used to break something. If a technique is applied to achieve an end it can be applied wrongly, to fail. If telecom technologies enable communication they can also be used to disrupt it. Every ideology opens itself to misinterpretation, abuse, and defiance by any individual. Where there are societies of control there are societies of out of control. Trecartin knows this and feels this. He likes to play with language and knows how any word that means one thing can be misheard, misread, misused, and made to mean something else. The properties of tools, techniques, technologies, and ideologies discussed in the previous paragraph are properties shared by language. And in language where there's a right syntax and there's a wrong syntax; grammar begets mistakes. Language is the medium of incorporation, or transformation of any other kind. Language provides the environment in which one substance can be understood as another one – as well as the tools for reinforcing the transformation, and normalising it.

[…] We dwell, as ever, in the house of language, but there's an addition to this house that we spend more and more time in, made of an alien machine language, where the use of natural human language is objectified and instrumentalised in highly specific ways. Trecartin is an artist of the social glitch: tools of language that are designed to be opened in a particular format – in the super-body of the corporation, or the super-body of the network – get opened by individual bodies. The misapplication of the tools of language gives a sideways glance at their utility. They appear as nonsense but they speak about the logic of the medium that they operate in – the medium that operates everything. The medium's omnipotence reveals itself and it reveals itself in its failures.

1   Kenneth Goldsmith, *Uncreative Writing* (New York: Columbia University Press, 2011).

Brian Droitcour, extracts from 'Societies of Out of Control: Language & Technology in Ryan Trecartin's Movies', in *You Are Here – Art After the Internet*, ed. Omar Kholeif (Manchester/Exeter: Cornerhouse/SPACE, 2014) 45–55.

Michael Hardt and Antonio Negri
Refrains of the 'Internationale'//2000

Internationalism was the will of an active mass subject that recognised that the nation-states were key agents of capitalist exploitation and that the multitude was continually drafted to fight their senseless wars – in short, that the nation-state was a political form whose contradictions could not be subsumed and sublimated but only destroyed. International solidarity was really a project for the destruction of the nation-state and the construction of a new global community. […].

The practice of proletarian internationalism was expressed most clearly in the international cycles of struggles. In this framework the (national) general strike and insurrection against the (nation-) state were only really conceivable as elements of communication among struggles and processes of liberation on the internationalist terrain. From Berlin to Moscow, from Paris to New Delhi, from Algiers to Hanoi, from Shanghai to Jakarta, from Havana to New York, struggles resonated with one another throughout the nineteenth and twentieth centuries. A cycle was constructed as news of a revolt was communicated and applied in each new context, just as in an earlier era merchant ships carried the news of slave revolt from island to island around the Caribbean, igniting a stubborn string of fires that could not be quenched. For a cycle to form, the recipients of the news must be able to 'translate' the events into their own language, recognise the struggles as their own, and thus add a link to the chain. In some cases this 'translation' is rather elaborate: how Chinese intellectuals at the turn of the twentieth century, for example, could hear of the anticolonial struggles in the Philippines and Cuba and translate them into the terms of their own revolutionary projects. In other cases it is much more direct: how the factory council movement in Turin, Italy, was immediately inspired by the news of the Bolshevik victory in Russia. Rather than thinking of the struggles as relating to one another like links in a chain, it might be better to conceive of them as communicating like a virus that modulates its form to find in each context an adequate host. [...]

We must admit, in fact, that even when trying to individuate the real novelty of these situations, we are hampered by the nagging impression that these struggles are always already old, outdated, and anachronistic. The struggles at Tiananmen Square spoke a language of democracy that seemed long out of fashion; the guitars, head-bands, tents, and slogans all looked like a weak echo of Berkeley in the 1960s. The Los Angeles riots, too, seemed like an aftershock of the earthquake of racial conflicts that shook the United States in the 1960s. The strikes in Paris and Seoul seemed to take us back to the era of the mass factory worker, as if they were the last gasp of a dying working class. All these struggles, which pose really new elements, appear from the beginning to be already old and outdated – precisely because they cannot communicate, because their languages cannot be translated. The struggles do not communicate despite their being hypermediatised, on television, the Internet, and every other imaginable medium. Once again we are confronted by the paradox of incommunicability.

We can certainly recognise real obstacles that block the communication of struggles. One such obstacle is the absence of a recognition of a common enemy against which the struggles are directed. Beijing, Los Angeles, Nablus, Chiapas, Paris, Seoul: the situations all seem utterly particular, but in fact they all directly attack the global order of Empire and seek a real alternative. Clarifying the nature of the common enemy is thus an essential political task. A second obstacle, which is really corollary to the first, is that there is no common language of struggles that could 'translate' the particular language of each into a cosmopolitan language. Struggles in other parts of the world and even our own struggles seem to be written in an incomprehensible foreign language. This too points toward an important political task: to construct a new common language that facilitates communication, as the languages of anti-imperialism and proletarian internationalism did for the struggles of a previous era. Perhaps this needs to be a new type of communication that functions not on the basis of resemblances but on the basis of differences: a communication of singularities. [...]

Michael Hardt and Antonio Negri, extracts from *Empire* (Harvard: Harvard College, 2000) 50–51, 56–7 [footnotes omitted].

Naoki Sakai
Translation and the Schematism of Bordering//2009

[...] So let me explain why I find the figure, image or identity of the West increasingly bothersome today. At the same time, it is also my belief that the overdetermined nature of the West serves us as an entry point to the general problems confronting us: national humanism, the global advancement of commodification, the colonial formation of the modern international world, and persistent but constantly mutating racism. On the one hand, the historical analysis of the West will provide us with a new chronology of modernity in which the transformation of capitalism was accompanied by the ethnicisation and nationalisation of population; on the other, it will help us understand the changing production of minorities. In short, an analysis of the West is indispensable to our understanding of racism.[...]

Just like the racial notion of whiteness, the West does not cohere as a concept in empirical knowledge. The unity of the West is far from being unitarily determinable on empirical grounds. The West, therefore, is a mythical construct, which achieves powerful effects on us as it gathers varying and contradicting properties around itself. Yet it is important not to forget that what we believe we apprehend by this mytheme is increasingly ambiguous and incongruous: its immoderately overdetermined nature can no longer be shrouded. This does not mean that the West has ceased to be a reality whose putative objectivity is globally accepted. And our sense of the world is still directed by this historical construct. This is why the West must be understood, first of all, as a my theme which regulates our imagination concerning how to hierarchically configure peoples and institutions on the world map and also which functions only as one term of the binary opposition of the West and the Rest. [...]

In this essay, I aim to liberate the possibility of translation from the curse bestowed on it by the view of translation organised around the image of communication: the communication of a written text from one language to another. Translation is not a task limited to the written word, but a concept which grants us the possibility of examining social action in general anew, something which offers us an invaluable gateway by which to enter an inquiry into sociality itself. Nevertheless, the traditional view of translation has elided this potent sociality that suffuses it, through its collaboration with the substantialisation of 'national' and 'ethnic' languages. It goes without saying that the argument regarding translation that I offer here tries carefully to avoid lapsing into another systematic dichotomy of the differentiability (known as phonocentrism) of the written and the spoken. But this is not all. By 'text' I do not mean the traditional view of the text which limits it to documents or books, nor do I adopt here the widely-disseminated dichotomy between the practical task of oral interpretation *(tsuyaku)* and the translation *(honyaku)* of scriptures, philosophy, and literature in written form. I simply do not accept the distinction between interpretation and translation precisely because I want to examine the operation of metaphor, which suffuses the situation of translation, while simultaneously historicising the traditional view of translation.

In studying translation, we must pay close attention not only to how trope operates, but also to how it malfunctions. In other words, in order to devise shifts in the discussion of translation, we not only need a transformation of the basic concepts, but also a recomposition of the tropes and figurations that we employ. Today the very presumption that a language has its inside and outside must be scrutinised, and we must call into question the regime of translation according to which one language is represented as external to and exclusive from another language spatially. I have referred to this regime of translation, in which translation is represented through the strict distinction between the interior and exterior of a language, as the 'homolingual address'. In my view, we must historicise the stigma of this regime of translation while at the same time, turning ourselves towards thinking of translation as a 'heterolingual address.' The 'homolingual address' derives its legitimacy from the vision of the modern international world as a juxtaposition of state sovereignties as well as the reciprocal recognition among nation-states. Of course, the international world and the nation-state offer mutual reinforcement and form a system of complicity. [...]

Naoki Sakai, extracts from 'Translation and the Schematism of Bordering', a draft paper presented at 'Translating society: A Commentator's Conference', University of Konstanz (29–31 October, 2009) (http://www.translating-society.de/conference/papers/2/).

Homi K. Bhabha
How Newness Enters the World//1994

The non-synchronous temporality of global and national cultures opens up a cultural space – a third space – where the negotiation of incommensurable differences creates a tension peculiar to borderline existences. [...]

Such assignations of social differences – where difference is neither One nor the Other but something else besides, in-between – find their agency in a form of the 'future' where the past is not originary, where the present is not simply transitory. It is, if I may stretch a point, an interstitial future, that emerges in-between the claims of the past and the needs of the present.[1]

The present of the world, that appears through the breakdown of temporality, signifies a historical intermediacy, familiar to the psychoanalytic concept of *Nachträglichkeit* (deferred action): 'a transferential function, whereby the past dissolves in the present, so that the future becomes (once again) an open question, instead of being specified by the fixity of the past.'[2] The iterative 'time' of the future as a becoming 'once again open', makes available to marginalised or minority identities a mode of performative agency that Judith Butler has elaborated for the representation of lesbian sexuality: 'a specificity [. . .] to be established, not outside or beyond that reinscription or reiteration, but in the very modality and effects of that reinscription.'[3] [...]

As the West gazes into the broken mirror of its new global unconscious – 'the extraordinary demographic displacements of mass migrant workers and of global tourists [...] to a degree unparalleled in world history'[4] – Jameson attempts, in a suggestive move, to turn the schizophrenic social imaginary of the postmodern subject into a crisis in the collective ontology of the group faced with the sheer 'number' of demographic pluralism. The perceptual (and cognitive) anxiety[5] that accompanies the loss of 'infrastructural' mapping becomes exacerbated in the postmodern city, where both Raymond Williams' 'knowable community' and Benedict Anderson's 'imagined community' have been altered by mass migration and settlement. Migrant communities are representative of a much wider trend towards the minoritisation of national societies. For Jameson this process is part of a historical irony: 'the transitional nature of the new global economy has not yet allowed its classes to form in any stable way, let alone to acquire a genuine class-consciousness'.[6] [...]

What does the narrative construction of minority discourses entail for the everyday existence of the Western metropolis? [...]

My theoretical description of blasphemy as a transgressive act of cultural translation, is borne out by Yunus Samad's reading of blasphemy in the context of the real event of the fatwah.[7] It is the medium Rushdie uses to reinterpret the Koran that constitutes the crime. In the Muslim world, Samad argues, poetry is the traditional medium of censure. By casting his revisionary narrative in the form of the novel – largely unknown to traditional Islamic literature – Rushdie violates the poetic licence granted to critics of the Islamic establishment. In Samad's words, 'Salman Rushdie's real crime, in the eyes of the clerics, was that he touched on early Islamic history in a critical, imaginative and irreverent fashion but with deep historical insight.' It could be argued, I think, that far from simply misinterpreting the Koran, Rushdie's sin lies in opening up a space of discursive contestation that places the authority of the Koran within a perspective of historical and cultural relativism. It is not that the 'content' of the Koran is directly disputed; rather, by revealing other enunciatory positions and possibilities within the framework of Koranic reading, Rushdie performs the subversion of its authenticity through the act of cultural translation – he relocates the Koran's 'intentionality' by repeating and reinscribing it in the locale of the novel of postwar cultural migrations and diasporas.

The transposition of the life of Mohamed into the melodramatic theatricality of a popular Bombay movie, *The Message,*results in a hybridised form – the 'theological'[8]– targeted to Western immigrant audiences. Blasphemy, here, is the slippage in-between the intended moral fable and its displacement into the dark, symptomatic figurations of the 'dreamwork' of cinematic fantasy. In the racist psychodrama staged around Chamcha, the Satanic goatman, 'blasphemy' stands for the phobic projections that fuel great social fears, cross frontiers, evade the normal controls, and roam loose about the city turning difference into demonism. The social fantasm of racism, driven by rumour, becomes politically credible and strategically negotiable: 'priests became involved, adding another unstable element – the linkage between the term black and the sin blasphemy – to the mix.'[9] As the unstable element – the interstice – enables the linkage black/ blasphemy, so it reveals, once more, that the 'present' of translation may not be a smooth transition, a consensual continuity, but the configuration of the disjunctive rewriting of the transcultural, migrant experience.

If hybridity is heresy, then to blaspheme is to dream. To dream not of the past or present, nor the continuous present; it is not the nostalgic dream of tradition, nor the Utopian dream of modern progress; it is the dream of translation as 'survival' as Derrida translates the 'time' of Benjamin's concept of the afterlife of translation, as *sur-vivre*, the act of living on borderlines. Rushdie translates this into the migrant's dream of survival: an initiatory interstices; an empowering condition of hybridity; an emergence that turns 'return' into reinscription or redescription; an iteration that is not belated, but ironic and insurgent. For the migrant's survival depends, as Rushdie put it, on discovering 'how newness enters the world'. The focus is on making the linkages through the unstable elements of literature and life – the dangerous tryst with the 'untranslatable' – rather than arriving at ready-made names.

The 'newness' of migrant or minority discourse has to be discovered in *medias res*: a newness that is not part of the 'progressivist' division between past and present, or the archaic and the modern; nor is it a 'newness' that can be contained in the mimesis of 'original and copy'. In both these cases, the image of the new is iconic rather than enunciatory; in both instances, temporal difference is represented as epistemological or mimetic distance from an original source. […]

Unlike Derrida and de Man, I am less interested in the metonymic fragmentation of the 'original'. I am more engaged with the 'foreign' element that reveals the interstitial; insists in the textile superfluity of folds and wrinkles; and becomes the 'unstable element of linkage', the indeterminate temporality of the in-between, that has to be engaged in creating the conditions through which 'newness comes into the world'. The foreign element 'destroys the original's structures of reference and sense communication as well'[10] not simply by negating it but by negotiating the disjunction in which successive cultural temporalities are 'preserved in the work of history and *at the same time* cancelled. […]

1   [Footnote 12 in source] J. Forrester, 'Dead on Time', in *The Seductions of Psychoanalysis: Freud, Lacan and Derrida* (Cambridge: Cambridge University Press, 1990) 206.

2   [13] J. Butler, 'Decking out: performing identities', in *Inside/Out, Lesbian Theories, Gay Theories*, ed. Diana Fuss (New York: Routledge, 1991) 17.

3   [14] For an argument that might be taken to counter this claim see F. Jameson, 'Modernism and imperialism', in Terry Eagleton; Seamus Deane; Fredric Jameson; Edward W Said, *Nationalism, Colonialism and Literature* (Minneapolis: Minnesota University Press, 1990), 53.

4   Fredric Jameson, *Postmodernism, or, The Cultural Logic of Late Capitalism* (Durham, NC: Duke University Press, 1991) 363.

5   [15] Although Jameson insists that anxiety and alienation form no part of postmodern phenomenology, I would argue that the appeal to affects of disjunction, disorientation and doubling, particularly in the context of 'emergent' knowledges and practices cannot be envisaged without fear and trembling. I have also argued above, all too briefly, for anxiety as a pedagogical address – a theme that I will be extending in the book I am currently working on, *The Measure of Dwelling*.

6   *Postmodernism,* op. cit., 348.

7   [24] Cf. Y. Samad, 'Book burning and race relations: political mobilisation of Bradford Muslims', *New Community*, vol. 18, no. 4.

8   [25] Salman Rushdie, *The Satanic Verses* (London: Viking, 1988) 272.

9   [26] Ibid., 288.

10   [27] See R. Gasché's brilliant essay on Benjamin's theory of language, 'The Saturnine Vision and the Question of Difference: Reflections on Walter Benjamin's Theory of Language', *Studies in 20th Century Literature*, vol. II, no. 1 (Fall 1986).

Homi K. Bhabha, extracts from 'How Newness Enters the World: Postmodern space, postcolonial times, and the trials of cultural translation' (1994), in *The Location of Culture* (New York and London: Routledge, 2004) 312, 313, 316, 319, 323–5, 325–6, 327, 335.

Judith Butler
Competing Universalities//2000

[…] The struggle to think hegemony anew is not quite possible, however, without inhabiting precisely that line where the norms of legitimacy, increasingly adjudicated by state apparatuses of various kinds, break down, where liminal social existence emerges in the condition of suspended ontology. Those who should ideally be included within any operation of the universal find themselves not only outside its terms but as the very outside without which the universal could not be formulated, living as the trace, the spectral remainder, which does not have a home in the forward march of the universal. This is not even to live as the particular, for the particular is, at least, constituted within the field of the political. It is to live as the unspeakable and the unspoken for, those who form the blurred human background of something called 'the population'. To make a claim on one's own behalf assumes that one speaks the language in which the claim can be made, and speaks it in such a way that the claim can be heard. This differential among languages, as Gayatri Chakravorty Spivak has argued, is the condition of power that governs the global field of language.[1] Who occupies that line between the speakable and the unspeakable, facilitating a translation there that is not the simple augmentation of the power of the dominant? There is nowhere else to stand, but there is no 'ground' there, only a reminder to keep as one's point of reference the dispossessed and the unspeakable, and to move with caution as one tries to make use of power and discourse in ways that do not renaturalise the political vernacular of the state and its status as the primary instrument of legitimating effects. Another universality emerges from the trace that only borders on political legibility: the subject who has not been given the prerogative to be a subject, whose modus vivendi is an imposed catachresis. If the spectrally human is to enter into the hegemonic reformulation of universality, a language between languages will have to be found. This will be no metalanguage, nor will it be the condition from which all languages hail. It will be the labour of transaction and translation which belongs to no single site, but is the movement between languages, and has its final destination in this movement itself. Indeed, the task will be not to assimilate the unspeakable into the domain of speakability in order to house it there, within the existing norms of dominance, but to shatter the confidence of dominance, to show how equivocal its claims to universality are, and, from that equivocation, track the break-up of its regime, an opening towards alternative versions of universality that are wrought from the work of translation itself. Such an opening will not only relieve the state of its privileged status as the primary medium through which the universal is articulated, but re-establish as the conditions of articulation itself the human trace that formalism has left behind, the left that is Left.

1   [Footnote 17 in source] Gayatri Chakravorty Spivak, 'Can the Subaltern Speak?', in *Marxism and the Interpretation of Culture*, ed. Cary Nelson & Lawrence Grossberg (Urbana: University of Illinois Press, 1988).

Judith Butler, extract from 'Competing Universalities', in *Contingency, Hegemony, Universality: Contemporary Dialogues on the Left*, eds. Judith Butler, Ernesto Laclau and Slavoj Zizek (London and New York: Verso, 2000) 178–9.

Omar Robert Hamilton
Occupy: Moments of Clarity//2016

[…] The spectacle, as it was, needed no reinterpretation, needed no middleman; it was undeniable.

We live in a time without imagination. In a global moment without possibility. We live in the end times, at the peak, the pinnacle, preparing for the fall. We live on the brink of annihilation. We live beyond our means. We live without direction. And so those months of 2011 somehow felt inevitable, as young people amassed around the world, fighting for their public spaces, for their rights, for their futures, from Wisconsin to San'a. There is no question that change was needed, and so change had arrived.

And those aspiring changemakers could communicate with each other like never before. Skype calls, YouTube videos, Twitter streams, Indymedias, email threads, bilingual pamphlets, solidarity posters – a new traffic of words and information appeared, flowing for the first time in centuries from both South to North and North to South. A new equality had arrived between the disenfranchised youth of the world. […]

Omar Robert Hamilton, extract from 'Moments of Clarity', *Dossier*, no. 23 (October 2016) 152.

Biographical Notes

Basel Abbas & Ruanne Abou-Rahme are artists working together across sound, image, text, installation and performance practices.

Kathy Acker (1947–1997) was an American experimental feminist writer.

Moradewun Adejunmobi is professor in African American and African Studies at the University of California, Davis.

Shahidul Alam is a Bangladeshi photojournalist, teacher and social activist.

Meriç Algün is a Turkish artist based in Stockholm.

Gloria Anzaldúa (1942–2004) was an American scholar of Chicana cultural theory, queer and feminist theory.

Arjun Appadurai is an Indian-American anthropologist and globalisation theorist.

Hannah Arendt (1906–1975) was a German-born American philosopher and political theorist.

José María Arguedas (1911–1969) was a Peruvian novelist, poet and anthropologist, writing in both Spanish and the indigenous Quechua language.

Barby Asante is an artist, curator, educator and occassional DJ based in London.

Amanda Baggs, also known as Mel Baggs, is an American disabled writer and artist whose work addresses her own disabilities, and social responses to disability.

Paul Baker is professor in Linguistics at University of Lancaster.

James Baldwin (1924–1987) was an American novelist, playwright and activist.

Paolo Bartoloni is Established Professor of Italian Studies at the National University of Ireland, Galway.

Humberto Beck is professor at El Colegio de México, and founder of Horizontal, a cultural and media project based in Mexico City.

Alice Becker-Ho is a French writer and poet, and collaborator with and partner of Guy Debord.

Walter Benjamin (1892–1940) was a German-Jewish critical theorist and writer associated with the Frankfurt School.

Homi K. Bhabha is the Anne F. Rothenberg Professor of English and American Literature and Language, and Director of the Mahindra Humanities Center, at Harvard University.

Sujata Bhatt is an Indian-born poet based in Germany.

Nicolas Bourriaud is a writer and curator, and director of Montpellier Contemporain, France.

Geta Brătescu (1926–1940) was a Romanian artist, whose multidisciplinary practice explored themes of identity and gender.

Susan Buck-Morss is professor in Politial Science at The Graduate Center, CUNY, New York.

Judith Butler is the Maxine Elliot Professor in the Department of Comparative Literature and the Program of Critical Theory at the University of California, Berkeley, and Hannah Arendt Chair at the European Graduate School.

Luis Camnitzer is a German-born Uruguayan artist and academic based in the United States.

Barbara Casavecchia is a writer, curator and teacher at Accademia di Brera, Milan.

Barbara Cassin is French philologist and philosopher, and emeritus director of research at the Centre national de la recherche scientifique, Paris.

Gayatri Chakravorty Spivak is University Professor, and founding member of the Institute for Comparative Literature and Society, at Columbia University, New York.

Diana d'Arenberg is a writer based in Hong Kong and Berlin.

Jesse Darling is an artist based in London and Berlin.

Gilles Deleuze (1925–1995) was a French philosopher and writer on cinema, literature and art.

Jacques Derrida (1930–2004) was a French philosopher and critical theorist.

Henry Dreyfuss (1904–1972) was an American industrial designer.

Brian Droitcour is a writer, translator and curator based in New York.

Friedrich Engels (1820–1895) was a German philosopher and social scientist.

Okwui Enwezor (1963–2019) was a Nigerian curator and writer.

Jacob Fabricius is artistic director of the Kunsthal Aarhus, Denmark.

Frantz Fanon (1925–1961) was a French West Indian psychiatrist and philosopher.

Jean Fisher (1942–2016) was a British art critic and writer.

Parastou Forouhar is an Iranian artist based in Frankfurt.

Dana Friis-Hansen is director of the Grand Rapids Art Museum, Michigan.

Jean Genet (1910–1986) was a French novelist, playwright, poet and political activist.

Félix Guattari (1930–1992) was a French psychotherapist and philosopher.

Theresa Hak Kyung Cha (1951–1982) was a Korean-born American artist and novelist.

Stuart Hall (1932–2014) was a Jamaican-born British Marxist sociologist, cultural theorist and political activist.

Omar Robert Hamilton is a British-Egyptian writer and filmmaker.

Michael Hardt is an American political philosopher and literary theorist.

Camille Henrot is a French artist based in New York.

Susan Hiller (1940–2019) was an American-born multimedia artist based in London.

bell hooks is an American author, feminist and social activist.

Immigrant Movement (IM) International was an 'artist-initiated socio-political movement' launched by Tania Bruguera in 2011 in Corona, Queens, New York.

Emily Jacir is a Palestinian artist and filmmaker.

James Joyce (1882–1941) was an Irish novelist, poet and literary critic, and key figure of the Modernist movement.

Helen Keller (1880–1968) was a deaf-blind American author and political activist, most notably for those with disabilities.

Irena Klepfisz is a Polish-born American writer and translator, and activist for feminist, lesbian and secular Jewish communities.

David Levine is an artist and writer, and Professor of the Practice of Performance, Theater and Media at Harvard University.

Sarah Maharaj is Professor of Visual Art and Knowledge Systems at Malmö Art Academy, Lund University, Sweden.

Karl Marx (1818–1883) was a German socialist philosopher and social scientist.

Suzana Milevska is a Macedonian art historian, theorist and curator.

Naeem Mohaiemen is a British-born Bangladeshi artist and filmmaker.

Stephen Morton is professor of English at the University of Southampton, UK.

Gerardo Mosquera is an independent curator, critic and writer based in Havana.

Herta Müller is a Romanian-born German writer, and winner of the 2009 Nobel Prize for Literature.

Antonio Negri is an Italian Marxist sociologist and political philosopher.

Shirin Neshat is an Iranian artist based in New York.

Christian Nyampeta is a Rwandan-born Dutch artist based in London.

Hélio Oiticica (1937–1980) was a Brazilian artist and leader of the Neo-Concrete movement.

Rick Poynor is a writer and critic specialising in graphic design and typography, and is Professor of Design and Visual Culture at the University of Reading, UK.

S.S. Prawer (1925–2012) was Taylor Emeritus Professor of German Language and Literature at the University of Oxford.

Walid Raad, also known as The Atlas Group, is a Lebanese-born artist based in New York, where he is Associate Professor of Art in The Cooper Union.

Alastair Reid (1926–2014) was a Scottish poet, translator and scholar of South American literature.

Adrienne Rich (1929–2012) was an American poet, essayist and feminist.

Philip Rizk is a German-born filmmaker and journalist based in Cairo.

Susan Rosenberg is writer and art historian based in New York.

Martha Rosler is an American artist based in Brooklyn.

Alix Rule is a social scientist and postdoctoral fellow at New York University.

Naoki Sakai is Godwin Smith Professor of Asian Studies at Cornell University.

Kurt Schwitters (1887–1948) was a German artist associated with a number of twentieth-century avant-garde art movements, and is best known for his *Merz Pictures* collages.

Yinka Shonibare CBE is a British-Nigerian artist based in London.

Sisters of Perpetual Indulgence of the Order of Perpetual Indulgence are a worldwide order of queer people of all sexualities.

Slavs and Tatars is an art collective based in Berlin.

George Steiner is French-born American literary critic, essayist and philosopher.

Hito Steyerl is a German artist and filmmaker, and professor of New Media Art at the University of the Arts, Berlin.

Mladen Stilinović (1947–2016) was a Croatian conceptual artist based in Zagreb.

Kate Sutton is a writer and international editor at *Artforum*, based in Zagreb.

Erika Tan is Singapore-born artist and teacher based in London.

Jennifer Tee is a Dutch artist based in Amsterdam.

Stefan Themerson (1910–1988) was a Polish-born artist and publisher based in London.

Trinh T. Minh-ha is a Vietnamese filmmaker and writer, and professor in Rhetoric and Gender & Women's Studies at the University of California, Berkeley.

Wu Tsang is an American artist and filmmaker based in Los Angeles.

Lawrence Venuti is an American translator, translation theorist and historian, and professor in English at Temple University, Philadelphia.

Miyó Vestrini (1938–1991) was a Venezualan poet, journalist and scriptwriter.

Dmitry Vilensky is an artist and founding member of the collective Chto Delat?/What is to be done? based in St Petersburg.

Danh Vō is a Vietnamese-born Danish artist based in Berlin and Mexico City.

Stephen Willats is a British artist based in London.

Wong Bing Hao is an independent curator and writer based in Singapore.

Xu Bing is a Chinese artist based in Beijing.

Katarina Zdjelar is a Serbian artist based in Rotterdam.

Bibliography

Adler, Phoebe, Howells, Tom and Kotsopoulos, Nikolaos, eds., *Contemporary Art in Latin America* (London: Black Dog, 2010)

Anzaldúa, Gloria, *Borderlands/La Frontera: The New Mestiza* (San Francisco: Aunt Lute Books, 1987)

Apter, Emily, Cassin, Barbara, Lezra, Jacques and Wood, Michael, eds., *Dictionary of Untranslatables: A Philosophical Lexicon*, trans. Michael Wood (Princeton: Princeton University Press, 2014)

Arguedas, José, *Los Ríos Profundos* (Barcelona: Linkgua ediciones, 2013)

Baker, Mona, ed., *Translating Dissent: Voices from and with the Egyptian Revolution* (Abingdon and New York: Routledge, 2016)

Bartoloni, Paolo, *On the Cultures of Exile, Translation, and Writing* (West Lafayette, IN: Purdue University Press, 2008)

Basualdo, Carlos, ed., *Tropicália: A Revolution in Brazilian Culture 1967–1972* (São Paolo: Cosac Naify, 2005)

Becker-Ho, Alice, *The Essence of Jargon: Gypsy Argot & the Dangerous Classes*, trans. John McHale (New York: Autonomedia, 2014)

Benjamin, Walter, *Walter Benjamin Selected Writings Vol.1, 1913-1926, eds.* Marcus Bullock & Michael W. Jennings, trans. Harry Zohn et al (Cambridge: The Belknap Press of Harvard University Press, 2004)

bell hooks, *Teaching to Transgress: Education as the Practice of Freedom* (New York: Routledge, 1994)

Bhabha, Homi K., *The Location of Culture* (New York and London: Routledge, 2004)

Bhatt, Sujata, *Point No Point: Selected Poems* (Manchester: Carcanet, 2012)

Bird, Jon, Curtis, Barry, Mash, Melinda, Robertson, George, Putnam, Tim and Tickner, Lisa, eds., *Travellers' Tales: Narratives of Home and Displacement,* (London: Routledge, 1998)

Bourriaud, Nicolas, *The Radicant* (New York: Lukas & Sternberg, 2010)

Butler, Judith, Laclau, Ernesto and Zizek, Slavoj, *Contingency, Hegemony, Universality: Contemporary Dialogues on the Left* (London and New York: Verso, 2000)

Critchley, Simon & Kataoka, Mami, *Laughing in a Foreign Language* (London: Hayward, 2008)

Deleuze, Gilles & Guattari, Félix, *Kafka: Toward a Minor Literature,* trans. Dana Polan (Minneapolis: University of Minnesota Press, 1986)

Diawara, Manthia, Guldemond, Jaap, Mackert, Gabriele, van Kooij, Barbera and Shonibare, Yinka, *Yinka Shonibare: Double Dutch* (Rotterdam/Vienna: NAi Publishers/Museum Boijmans Van Beuningen/ Kunsthalle Wien, 2004)

Elkins, James, ed., *Is Art History Global?* (New York and London: Routledge, 2007)

Engels, Friedrich & Marx, Karl, *Manifesto of the Communist Party* (1848) (New York: International Publishers, 1998)

Fanon, Frantz, *Black Skin White Masks* (London: Pluto Press, 2008)

Fisher, Jean, ed., *Global Visions: Towards a New Internationalism in the Visual Arts* (London: Kala Press in association with Iniva, 1994)

Fisher, Jean, Gevers, Ine, Haraway, Donna, Ingold, Tim and Kamphof, Ike, *Yes Naturally: How Art Saves the World ed. Laura Mudde* (Rotterdam: nai010 uitgevers, 2013)

Genet, Jean, *Prisoner of Love* (1986) (New York: New York Review of Books, 2003)

Graham, Joseph F., ed., *Difference in Translation* (Ithaca and London: Cornell University Press, 1985)

Grossman, Edith, *Why Translation Matters* (New Haven: Yale University Press, 2011)

Hall, Stuart & Maharaj, Sarat, *Modernity and Difference* (London: Iniva, 2001)

Hall, Stuart, *Representation: Cultural Representations and Signifying Practices* (London/New Delhi/ Thousand Oaks: Sage Publications, 1997)

Hardt, Michael & Negri, Antonio, *Empire* (Harvard: Harvard College, 2000)

Hlavajova, Maria & Sheikh, Simon, eds. *Former West Art and the Contemporary After 1989* (Cambridge, MA: The MIT Press, 2017)

IRWIN, ed., *East Art Map: Contemporary Art and Eastern Europe* (London: Afterall/University of the Arts, 2006)

Joyce, James, *Finnegans Wake* (London and New York: Penguin, 1992)

Kaye-Kantrowitz, Melanie & Klepfisz, Irena, eds., *The Tribe of Dina: A Jewish Women's Anthology* (Montpelier, VT: Sinister Wisdom Books, 1986)

Keller, Helen, *The World I Live In* (New York: The Century Co., 1910)

Khatib, Lina, *Image Politics in the Middle East: The Role of the Visual in Political Struggle* (London: I.B. Tauris, 2012).

Kholeif, Omar, ed., *You Are Here – Art After the Internet* (Manchester and Exeter: Cornerhouse and SPACE, 2014)

Laing, R.D., *The Politics of Experience and the Bird of Paradise* (Harmondsworth: Penguin, 1967)

Lecercle, Jean-Jacques. *Philosophy Through the Looking-Glass: Language, Nonsense and Desire* (London: Hutchinson, 1985)

Lichtenfels, Peter & Rouse, John, eds., *Performance, Politics and Activism* (Basingstoke and New York: Palgrave Macmillan, 2013)

Osborne, Peter, *Anywhere or Not at All: The Philosophy of Contemporary Art* (London and New York: Verso, 2013)

Prawer, S.S., *Karl Marx and World Literature* (Oxford: Oxford University Press, 1978)

Rich, Adrienne, *The Will to Change: Poems 1968-1970* (New York: W.W. Norton, 1971)

Robinson, Marc, ed., *Altogether Elsewhere: Writers on Exile* (London: Faber & Faber, 1994)

Rothkopf, Scott R., ed., *Glenn Ligon America* (New York: Whitney Museum of American Art, 2011)

Sakai, Naoki, *Translation and Subjectivity: On 'Japan' and Cultural Nationalism* (Minneapolis: University of Minnesota Press, 1997)

Spivak, Gayatri Chakravorty, *Outside in the Teaching Machine* (New York: Routledge, 1993)

Steiner, George, *After Babel: Aspects of Language and Translation* (Oxford and New York: Oxford University Press, 1975)

Venuti, Lawrence, *The Translator's Invisibility: A History of Translation* (London and New York: Routledge, 1995)

Vestrini, Miyó, *Grenade in Mouth: Some Poems of Miyó Vestrini,* eds. Elisa Maggi & Faride Mereb, trans. Anne Boyer & Cassandra Gillig (Chicago: Kenning Editions, 2019)

Index

ACKNOWLEDGEMENTS

Editor's acknowledgements

The editor would like to thank: Bisagra (Lima), Michaela Crimmin, Gasworks (London), Mako Ishizuka, Jenni Lomax, Jonathan Ruffer Foundation, Mason Leaver-Yap, Paula López Zambrano, Sam Ryan, Marcus Verhagen, Martin Waldmeier, Hannah Rose Whittle.

Publisher's acknowledgements

Whitechapel Gallery is grateful to all those who gave their generous permission to reproduce the listed material. Every effort has been made to secure all permissions and we apologise for any inadvertent errors or omissions. If notified, we will endeavour to correct these at the earliest opportunity. We would like to express our thanks to all who contributed to the making of this volume, especially: Basel Abbas & Ruanne Abou-Rahme, Moradweun Adejunmobi, Meriç Algün, Arjun Appadurai, Barby Asante, Paolo Bartoloni, Anne Boyer, Susan Buck-Morss, Gayatri Chakravorty Spivak, Jesse Darling, Brian Droitcour, Jacob Fabricius, Parastou Forouhar, Dana Friis-Hansen, Philippa Hurd, Emily Jacir, Irena Klepfisz, David Levine, Sarat Maharaj, John McHale, Suzana Milevska, Naeem Mohaiemen, Stephen Morton, Christian Nyampeta, Rick Poynor, Walid Raad, Jasia Reichardt, Martha Rosler, Alix Rule, Naoki Sakai, Julia Sherwood, Yinka Shonibare, Slavs and Tatars, Hito Steyerl, Branka Stipančić, Kate Sutton, Erika Tan, Jennifer Tee, Lawrence Venuti, Matias Viegener, Dmitry Vilensky, Katarina Zdjelar.

We also gratefully acknowledge the cooperation of *Asymptote Journal*, *Artforum*, Carcanet, DACS, Galerie Isabella Bortolozzi, Gladstone Gallery, the Estate of Susan Hiller and Tim Dixon at Matt's Gallery, Kenning Editions, Marian Goodman Gallery, Paula Cooper Gallery, Thomas Colchie Agency and the Estate of Alastair Reid, *Triple Canopy*, Verso, the Estate of Miyó Vestrini, W.W. Norton.

Whitechapel Gallery

whitechapelgallery.org

Whitechapel Gallery is supported by

Supported using public funding by

**ARTS COUNCIL
ENGLAND**